AF454109

المعرفة الاسلامية

Al Ghazali
A Study in
Islamic Epistemology

Mustafa Abu Sway

Qadeem Press

www.qadeempress.com

Find our titles on your favourite online bookstore using the keyword 'Qadeem Press'

This work has been selected by scholars as culturally important. This book has been reproduced from the original artefact and remains as true to the original work as possible. You may see the original copyright references, library stamps, and other notations in the work. As a reproduction of an artefact, this work may contain missing or blurred pages, poor pictures, errant marks, etc. Scholars believe, and we concur, that this work is important enough to be preserved, reproduced, and made available to the public. We appreciate the support of the preservation process and thank you for being an important part of keeping this knowledge alive and relevant.

CONTENTS

INTRODUCTION

The basic issue that this book will be concerned with is the genetic development of Al-Ghazzāliyy's epistemology. It is my contention that his epistemology evolved through various stages. Both his life and writings reflect this development. As a student, he began his academic life with an interest in traditional Islamic studies such as jurisprudence (*fiqh*) and fundamentals of jurisprudence (*uṣūl al-fiqh*). After he assumed his first teaching position at the Nizamiyyah school of Baghdad he became a methodological skeptic, a situation which prompted him to study all schools of thought available at the time in search for peremptory knowledge (*'ilm yaqīnī*). From skepticism he moved to Sufism (Islamic mysticism), and finally there are indications that he ended up studying the traditions (*Ḥadīth*) of prophet Muḥammad, which led many to claim that he shifted to the methodology of the traditionalists (*Ahl al-Ḥadīth*) and that he abandoned Sufism. It is the aim of this study to trace Al-Ghazzāliyy's quest for knowledge throughout his life.

This study will take into consideration the historical circumstances and the social context in which Al-Ghazzāliyy flourished. It is my conviction that these circumstances influenced his personal and thus his intellectual life as well.

PREVIOUS STUDIES

There are numerous previous studies of Al-Ghazzāliyy. However, most of these studies dealt with subjects such as Sufism, ethics and jurisprudence. While a very few of these studies dealt with Al-Ghazzāliyy's epistemology, none of them could be considered comprehensive: no studies so far have used all of his books to determine his epistemology. And certainly, these studies did not show the genetic development that took place in his thought.

One of the studies that dealt with Al-Ghazzāliyy's notion of knowledge (ma'rifah) is Jabre's *La Notion De La "Ma'rifa" Chez Al-Ghazāli*. Although he discussed the relationship of ethics to the notion of ma'rifah, his approach remains philological.[1] This philological method was also used by Hava-Lazarous Yafeh primarily to determine the authenticity of Al-Ghazzāliyy's works.[2]

Another study that discussed Al-Ghazzāliyy's theory of knowledge is Dunya's *Al-Haqīqah Fī Nazar Al-Ghazālī*.[3] This study was limited in its sources and depended heavily on *Mi'rāj Al-Quds*, a book that was attributed to Al-Ghazzaliyy but remains unconfirmed because non of the medieval Muslim historiographers listed this book, nor there are cross-references in Al-Ghazzāliyy's confirmed books.

I have undertaken the task of studying all of Al-Ghazzāliyy's works in order to trace the development in his epistemology. The basic working list can be found in Badawi's *Mu'allafāt Al-Ghazālī*, numbers 1–72.[5] The criteria for choosing these books are based on any of the two following conditions: the first is that there should be cross-references in Al-Ghazzāliyy's works, as it was his habit to mention books that he wrote, or those he was going to write, and the second is that it has to be mentioned by medieval historiographers such as in Ibn Al-Subkiyy's *Tabaqāt al-Shāfi'iyyah al-Kubrā*. This book is a biography of the jurists who belong to the Shāfi'iyy's school of jurisprudence; Al-

---

1 Farid Jabre, *La Notion De La "Ma'rifa" Chez Al-Ghazali* (Beyrouth: Editions des Letters Orientales, 1958).

2 Hava-Lazarous Yafeh, *Studies in Al-Ghazali* (Jerusalem: The Magnus Press – Hebrew University, 1975).

3 Sulaiman Dunya, *Al-Haqīqah fi Nazar Al-Ghazali* (Cairo: Dar Al-Ma'arif Bi-Misr, 1965).

4 'Abdur-Rahman Badawi, *Mu'allafat Al-Ghazzaliyy*, 2nd ed. (Kuwait: Wikalat al-Matbu'at, 1977) p. 244.

5 Badawi, *Mu'allafat*, pp. 1–238.

Ghazzāliyy was one of them.[6] While I have considered secondary sources, I mostly relied upon Arabic texts of Al-Ghazzāliyy's works. This was to avoid the possibility of distortions in translation.

The first chapter covers the life of Al-Ghazzāliyy. There the primary interest is to present the sociopolitical context which explains his intellectual movement. The political scene at the time and the role he played in shaping it is covered. His relationship with the existing schools of thought, and his position regarding major events are also discussed. In addition, his formal education and academic career and the events related to them are investigated.

The next five chapters survey the books that were written during the corresponding stages of the five periods in Al-Ghazzāliyy's life according to Maurice Bouyges' division[7] which I have adopted. The first of these stages begins with his life as a student; the second covers the first period of public teaching at the Nizamiyyah of Baghdad; the third deals with his years of seclusion and withdrawal from public teaching at the Nizamiyyah of Nishapur, and the fifth reflects the last stage in Al-Ghazzāliyy's life after his second withdrawal from public teaching.

Thus, in the second chapter I study the works that were written when Al-Ghazzāliyy was a student during the years 465-478 A.H./1072-1085 C.E. I begin by outlining his sources of knowledge in order to define his epistemology during this period, a process which will be repeated in each of the following chapters in an attempt to trace the development in his epistemology.

The third chapter covers Al-Ghazzāliyy's works during his first period of public teaching at the Nizamiyyah of Baghdad which extended from 478 A.H./1085 C.E. till 488 A.H./1095 C.E. In this chapter I discuss his systematic inquiry in quest of true knowledge. In addition, his encounter with the different schools of thought including the philosophers will be investigated. Finally, I explore the influence of Sufism on his epistemology and how it led to his withdrawal from public life.

6   Taj Ad-Din Al-Subkiyy, *Tabaqat al-Shafi'iyyah al-Kubra* (Cairo: 'Isa al-Babi al-Halabi & Co., 1964).
7   Badawi, *Mu'allafat*, pp. xv–xvii.

The fourth chapter covers the works written during his years of seclusion from 488 A.H./1095 C.E. till 499 A.H./1106 C.E. In this chapter I shall discuss the influence of Sufism on his epistemology. Of especial importance is his introduction of a faculty higher than reason (*malakah fawqa al-'aql*) as a source of knowledge. I shall define the nature of the relationship between this new faculty and prophecy.

The fifth chapter deals with the books that were written during the second period of public teaching at the Nizamiy-yah of Nishapur (499–503 A.H./1106–1110 C.E.).

The sixth chapter discusses the last stage in Al-Ghaz-zāliyy's life (505 A.H./1111 C.E.). This chapter questions the claim that he abandoned Sufism for the method of the traditionalists.

Dr. Mustafa Abu-Sway

Chapter ONE

THE LIFE OF AL-GHAZZĀLIYY[1]

In this chapter I shall present a sketch of Al-Ghazzāliyy's life (450–505 A.H.[2] 1058–1111 C.E.) as an aid to understanding the complexities and the controversies that surround this great Muslim thinker. Not only his writings (e.g., Al-Ghazzāliyy's books on knowledge) but also his life is a direct manifestation of his spiritual and intellectual development. This is especially true when the person is a Sufi (*Sufiyy*)[3], a muslim mystic, whose everyday life reflects the conditions he endures to acquire higher level of understanding.

In this sketch I begin with the historical conditions

---

1   In Arabic grammer, every attributed name (*Al-Nasab*) should have a stressed *Ya'* suffixed. For more details see 'Abd Al-Ghaniyy Al-Duqr, *Lexicon of Arabic Grammer*, (*Mu'jam Qawa'id al-Lughah al-Arabiyyah*) (Damascus: Dar al-Qalam, 1986) p. 496. In quotations and bibliographic citations I have used Al-Ghazzāliyy's name in its original form (e.g. Algazel.). For further discussion of his name see page 15.

2   A.H. = After Hijrah (the migration of prophet Muhammad from Mecca to Medina in 622 C.E. (Christian Era or Common Era). It was the second Caliph, 'Umar al-Khattab, who used this event to mark first year (which is lunar) of the Islamic calendar. I have chosen to use the A.H. dating because it provides a sense of time that places the topic under discussion in its proper "Islamic context".

3   The word "Sufi" is derived from Arabic *suf* (wool). Dressing wool, among the Sufis, became a symbol of detachment from wordly pleasures and affairs. For further discussion of "Sufism", see Ibn Taymiyyah, *Al-Furqan Bayn Awliya' Al-Rahman wa 'Awliya' Al-Shaytan* (Beirut: Al-Maktab al-Islamiyy, 1981) p. 42. In addition, there were those who maintained that the word "Sufi" is derived from Greek "sophia" in an apparent attempt to show that Sufism had its origin in Greek thought and thus disqualify the notion that it stems from Islamic backgrounds.

1

surrounding the time of Al-Ghazzāliyy's life, especially the political setting. *I* will then move on to consider his life, education and academic career.

1.1 THE POLITICAL SCENE

The political scene at the time of Al-Ghazzāliyy reflects a disintegrated caliphate. The provincial governors gained considerable powers that left the 'Abbasid Caliph in Baghdad virtually powerless. The Caliphs who ruled during the life of Al-Ghazzāliyy were Al-Qā'im Bi-Amrillāh (d. 467 A.H./1074 C.E.)[4] followed by his grandson, Al-Muqtadī Bi Amrillāh (d. 487 A.H./1094 C.E.).[5] Al-Muqtadī Bi-Amrillah was followed by his son the Caliph Al-Mustazhir Billah (511 A.H./1117 C.E.).[6] It is to be noted that Al-Ghazzāliyy attended the ceremony (*bay'ah*) in which Al-Mustazhir was inaugurated.[7] The presence of Al-Ghazzāliyy at this ceremony, which was noted by the historians, indicates his support of the Caliph which is also manifested in Al-Ghazzāliyy's book *al-Mustazhiriyy fī al-Rad 'ala al-Bāṭiniyyah* which was named after the Caliph.

Furthermore, Baghdad itself came under direct rule by warlords who became known as "Sultans". They presented themselves as *de facto* rulers and restricted the Caliph to dignitary functions (i.e. attending ceremonies). The most important family of Sultans was the Seljuks (*Al-Salājiqah*) who, according to Ibn Kathīr (d. 774 A.H./1372 C.E.) established their reign in Khurasān in 429 A.H./1037 C.E.[8] They moved to Baghdad in 447 A.H./1055 C.E. under Tughrul Beg, their first king.[9] He remained in power until his death in 458 A.H./1065 C.E. His successor was his nephew Alp Arslan who was killed in 465 A.H./1072 C.E.[10] He was

---

4   Ibn Kathīr, *Al-Bidaya wa al-Nihaya* (Beirut: Maktabat al-Ma'arif, n.d.) Vol. XII, p. 110.
5   Ibn Kathīr, Vol. XII, p.146.
6   *Ibid.*, p. 182.
7   *Ibid.*, p. 147.
8   *Ibid.*, p. 44.
9   *Ibid.*, p. 66.
10   *Ibid.*, p. 90.
11   *Ibid.*, p. 139.

followed by his son Malik Shah (d. 485 A.H./1092 C.E.).[11] who had to fight his own half-brother, Tutush in his quest for power.[12] After the death of Malik Shah, the struggle for power within his family continued between his wife Zubeida and his son Mahmūd (d.487 A.H./1094 C.E.), who was only five years old at the time, on the one hand, and his son Barkyaruq (d. 498 A.H./1104 C.E.), who was thirteen years old, on the other. The army fueled this struggle by splitting into two divisions; one sided with Barkyaruq, and the other with Mahmūd. It should be noted that the actual struggle over power was not led by the above mentioned children, but rather by their trustees and older family members: they included Zubeida and vizier Tāj al-Mulk al-Marzubān rival of Nizām al-Mulk. This rivalry led the supporters of Nizam al-Mulk, who were convinced that Tāj al-Mulk played a role in the death of Nizām al-Mulk, to side with Barkyaruq.[13] This dispute was resolved on the battlefield in favour of Barkyaruq who remained Sultan until his death. He was followed by his brother, Muhammad Ibn[14] Malik Shah (d. 511 A.H./1117 C.E.) who ascended to power in 498 A.H./1104 C.E. after another internal struggle, this time with his nephew, Malik Shah Ibn Barkyaruq, grandson of Malik Shah, who was four years old.[15] After the death of Malik Shah, in 485 A.H./1092 C.E., Zubeida demanded that his son Mahmūd, who was five years old at the time, should have the right of appointing governors (*wilāyat al-'ummal*). But even more significantly, the scholars of Baghdad, including Al-Mutatabbib[16] Abū Muhammad Al-Hanafiyy, issued a ruling (*fatwā*) stating that there was nothing wrong in granting this right to the boy, in an unprecedented move. The only exception to this ruling came, we learn, from Al-Ghazzāliyy, who forbade the transfer of such powers to Mahmūd Ibn

---

12 Ibn Kathir, Vol. XII, p. 148.
13 Henri Laoust, *La Politique De Gazali,* (Paris: Librairie Orientaliste Paul Geuthner, 1970) p. 59.
14 Ibn = Arabic for son (of).
15 Ibn Kathir, Vol. XII, pp. 164–180.
16 Literally, the medical practitioner. Many Muslim scholars used to work in areas not related to their scholarly work in order to avoid taking money from those in office. The scholar would acquire a title related to this profession. It could be that Al-Mutatabbib was one of them.

Malik Shah. Fortunately, the Caliph, Al-Muqtadī, adopted Al-Ghazzāliyy's position.[17] Al-Ghazzāliyy's *fatwā* was in accordance with the *Sharī'ah*.

In another *fatwā*; to Yūsuf Ibn Tashafīn (d. 500 A.H./ 1106 C.E.), the Sultan of Al-Maghrib, Al-Ghazzāliyy encouraged this Sultan to unite the divided principalities, by dismissing their kings (*Mulūk al-Tawā'if*) under his rule.[18] The impact of Al-Ghazzāliyy on the political scene went beyond issuing *fatwās*, and writing letters. Both Ibn Khallikān and Ibn Khaldūn reported that Muhammad Ibn 'Abdallah Ibn Tūmart, a student of Al-Ghazzāliyy, established Almohad (*Al-Muwahhidūn*) rule in Al-Maghrib, replacing the state that had been established by Ibn Tāshafīn, which experienced corruption after his death.[19] These *fatwās* are significant in showing the role of Muslim scholars ('*ulamā*') in the political life at the time.

These incidents reveal that Al-Ghazzāliyy enjoyed a prestigious position with those in office at that time which enabled him to send daring letters to the various Sultans and viziers. He reminded them of their duties toward their subjects, and advised them about the affairs of the state. In *The Golden Ingot For Advising Kings* (*Al-Tibr al-Masbūk fi Nasīhat al-Mulūk*), Al-Ghazzāliyy addressed the Sultan Muhammad Ibn Malik Shah and warned him about the injustice that resulted from collecting excessive taxes; he even told him what kind of clothes he could wear and what kind he could not. Moreover, in his Persian letters,[20] Al-Ghazzāliyy provided advice for Fakhr Al-Mulk, and

17 Ibn Kathir, Vol. XII, p. 139.
18 'Abd Al-Amir Al-A'sam, *Al-Faylasuf al-Ghazzaliyy* (Beirut: Dar Al-Andalus, 1981) p. 90.
19 Abu al-Hassan Al-Nadawiyy, *Rijal al-Fikr wa al-Da'wa fi al-Islam*, 7th ed. (Kuwait: Dar al-Qalam, 1985) Vol. I, p. 93.
20 Al-Ghazzaliyy used Arabic and Farsi for writing. His Persian works are few. Some of them we know through translation and secondary sources. It seems that the only major book in Persian that is not translated is *The Al-Chemy of Happiness* (*Kimyay Sa'adat*), which is different from the Arbic (*Kimya' al-Sa'adah*), is the equivalent to *Ihya' 'Ulum al-Din*. Al-Nadawiyy referred to the "Persian letters" in *Rijal al-Fikr wa al-Da'wah fi al-Islam*. The Arabic translation of these letters has been made available by Dr. Nur al-Din Al-Ali: *Fada'il al-Anam min Rasa'il Hujjat al-Islam*.

4

criticized Sultan Sanjar Ibn Malik Shah regarding the welfare of the people.[21] Furthermore, Al-Ghazzāliyy served several times as a special envoy between the Caliph and the Sultan.[22]

In addition, Al-Ghazzāliyy, after his embrace of Sufism which could be interpreted as a withdrawal from public life because of the prevailing corruption, did not accept any gifts from the Sultans. In the chapter on the lawful and the forbidden (*al-ḥalāl wal-ḥarām*) in *Iḥyā' 'Ulūm al-Dīn*, Al-Ghazzāliyy discussed extensively the monetary relationship between the sultans and the people; he concluded by stating that during his time all the monies of the Sultans were acquired unlawfully and thus cannot be accepted.[23] Moreover, he called on people to distance themselves from unjust Sultans, and to avoid those who befriend such tyrants or were of assistance to them. Al-Ghazzāliyy held that these were religious duties (*wājib*).[24]

1.1.1 Al-Ghazzāliyy and the Other Schools of Jurisprudence

In the year Tughrul Beg entered Baghdad there was another event of significance for the life of Al-Ghazzāliyy which sheds light upon the circumstances that he endured. It was during this year that a disturbance took place between the Asha'irites[25] and the Hanbalites.[26] As a result of this disturbance, the Asha'irites were barred from attending Friday ceremonies (*Al-Juma'*) and congregational prayers (*Al-Jamā'āt*).[27]

Al-Ghazzaliyy flourished in this atmosphere of intolerance between the followers of different schools of theology

21 Al-Nadawiyy, Vol. I, p. 191.
22 Ali al-Qarah Daghi, introduction, *Al-Wasit fi al Madhhab*; by Al-Ghazzaliyy (Cairo: Dar al-Islah, n.d.) Vol. I, p. 78.
23 Al-Ghazzaliyy, *Ihya'*, Vol. II, pp. 135–152.
24 Al-Nadawiyy, Vol. I, pp. 189–193.
25 The Asha'irites are theologians who belong to the school of Abu Al-Hasan Al-Ash'ariyy (d. 324 A.H./935 C.E.).
26 The Hanbalites are jurisprudents (*fuqaha'*) who belong to the school of Ahmad Ibn Hanbal (d. 241 A.H./855 C.E.).
27 Ibn Kathir, Vol. XII, p. 66.

and jurisprudence within the Sunnite tradition.[28] He himself was considered an Asha'irite[29] and a doctor of the Shāfi'ite (*Shāfi'iyyah*)[30] school of jurisprudence. Out of his concern, he tried to curb this attitude of intolerance through his writings. In *The Revival Of The Islamic Sciences* (*Ihyā' 'Ulūm al-Dīn*), Al-Ghazzāliyy wrote with great reverence about the most prominent doctors of jurisprudence: "Al-Shāfi'iyy, Mālik, Ahmad Ibn Hanbal, Abū Hanīfah,[31] and Sufiān Al-Thawriyy."[32] The order in which he arranged their names was not chronological: rather Al-Ghazzāliyy arranged them according to the number of their adherents during his own time.[33] Moreover, Al-Ghazzāliyy wanted to emphasize the love and respect that these scholars had for each other; and he wanted the jurists of his time to follow suit. Not only did Al-Ghazzāliyy endorse a policy of tolerance and openness towards other schools of jurisprudence, he also gave priority to some of their rulings over those of al-Shāfi'iyy. For example, he cited numerous rulings of Ahmad Ibn Hanbal.[34] In addition, he accepted the ruling of Abū Hanīfah, agreeing that Al-Shāfi'iyy's position in the case of divorce had a touch of exaggeration (*takalluf*).[35]

Al-Ghazzāliyy also praised Abū Hanīfah for refusing to accept a governmental office that could have made him responsible for all the money of the Caliphate. This refusal led the Sultan to whip Abū Hanīfah twenty times in public. This

28　The scholars who founded these schools never displayed this sort of intolerance. Infact, they were in many cases teachers of one another: Malik Ibn Anas (d. 179 A.H./795 C.E.), founder of the Malikite (*Malikiyyah*) school of jurisprudence taught Al-Shafi'iyy who in turn taught Ibn Hanbal.

29　For a discussion of whether Al-Ghazzaliyy was indeed an Asha'irite, see p. 55.

30　The Shafi'ite school was founded by Muhammad Ibn Idris Al-Shafi'iyy (d 204 A.H./819 C.E.)

31　Abu Hanifah, Al-Nu'man Ibn Thabit (d. 150 A.H./7647 C.E.) founded the Hanafite school of jurisprudence. It is known as the school of personal opinion (*ra'y*). His student, Abu Yusuf (d. 182 A.H./799 C.E.), was a major contributor to this school.

32　Al-Thawriyy, Sufian Ibn Sa'id Ibn Masruq (d. 162 A.H./778 C.E.). Unlike the other schools, his school of law does not exist any more.

33　Al-Ghazzaliyy, *Ihya' 'Ulum al-Din* (Beirut: Dar al-Ma'rifah, n.d.) Vol. I, p. 24.

34　Al-Qarah Daghi, Vol. I, p.163.

35　*Ibid.*, Vol. I, p.162.

6

praise absolves Al-Ghazzāliyy of the charge that he disgraced Abu Hanifah without justification. Now Al-Ghazzāliyy had been accused of disgracing Abu Hanifah by Sultan Sanjar. These accusations were certainly incompatible with the position Al-Ghazzāliyy as stated above; furthermore, he categorically denied such accusations. In fact, they were based upon insults found in copies of Al-Ghazzāliyy's *Al-Mankhūl min Ta'līqāt al-Uṣūl*. However, these insults were forgeries, inserted into his book when it was copied.[36] Furthermore, whenever he mentioned Abū Ḥanīfah's name in the above book, Al-Ghazzāliyy added a supplication (i.e. may Allah be pleased with him) following his name. This supplication was a clear sign of the respect Al-Ghazzāliyy had for Abū Ḥanīfah.[37]

Al-Ghazzāliyy saw that his contemporaries busied themselves studying aspects of jurisprudence that might never be needed during their lifetimes, and preoccupying themselves with the differences between the various schools of jurisprudence. According to Al-Ghazzāliyy, the followers of the different schools of jurisprudence who did such things were unjust to the founders. Instead, Al-Ghazzāliyy suggested that they ought to study medicine in order to be useful.[38]

1.1.2 Al-Ghazzāliyy and the Sects of the Time

The relationship between the Sunnites and the Shi'ites,[39] especially the Rawāfiḍ who lived in the Karakh district of

---

36 These were not only example of forgeries of Al-Ghazzaliyy's work. Al-Ghazzaliyy copies of *Al-Munqidh min al-Dalal* and *Mishkat al-Anwar* were submitted to him for approval (*Ijazah*). He reported the incident to the head (*ra'is*) of Khurasan who imprisoned, and later on deported the person responsible.

37 Al-Qarah Daghi, Vol. I, pp. 159–163.

38 Al-Ghazzaliyy, *Ihya'*, Vol. I, pp. 24–28.

39 Shi'ites (*shi'ah*). Arabic for "supporters of", is a general classification that includes all the different sects that have a position toward 'Ali Ibn Abu Talib, the fourth Caliph and cousin of prophet Muhammad, different than that of the Sunnites. Some of the Shi'ites argue that 'Ali should have been the first Caliph, others adopt an extreme position by claiming that 'Ali has divine attributes. Although Shi'ites started primarily as a political stand, they developed their own theology and jurisprudence.

Baghdad, was also contentious. Almost every year tension used to escalate on the day of 'Ashūrā'[40] which resulted in killings and destruction on both sides. The establishment of a strong Shi'ite political state in Egypt at the hands of the Fatimids[41] in 358 A.H./968 C.E.[42] strengthened the position of the Shi'ites in Baghdad who, in return, had formally acknowledged the Fatimid rulers in Friday ceremonies. This formal acknowledged also spread to Damascus, Medina and Mecca.[43] According to Ibn Al-Athīr's *Al-Kāmil*, the first reconciliation (*sulh*), between the Sunnites and the Shi'ites, took place in 502 A.H./1108 C.E.[44]

Al-Ghazzāliyy was the target of claims that he was a Shi'ite. Sibt Ibn Al-Jawziyy claimed, in *Riyād al-Afhām fī Manāqib Ahl al-Bayt*, that Al-Ghazzāliyy was a Shi'ite for a while, but later on changed his position. According to Dr. Ahmad Al-Shirbasiyy, who seemed to be in favour of Al-Ghazzāliyy's Shi'ism, the Shi'ites considered Al-Ghazzāliyy one of their teachers knowing that he was a Sunnite. He also added that the Shi'ites believed Al-Ghazzāliyy wrote *Risālah Fī Ism Allāh al-A'zam* or *Sharh Jannat al-Asmā'*, a book that praised 'Alī Ibn Abu Ṭālib. Apparently, this book was not written by Al-Ghazzāliyy.[45] In addition, praising and loving

40 Every year, on the 10th of Muharram, the first Arabic month of the lunar year, the Shi'ites commemorate the martyrdom of Al-Hussayn Ibn 'Ali, grandson of prophet Muhammad, and son of 'Ali, the fourth Caliph. The Shi'ites commemorate this event by virtually torturing themselves, since they believe that the Shi'ites of Iraq had betrayed Al-Hussayn when he went to Iraq, after they have promised him support in his quest for power.

41 This name is attributed to Fatima, daughter of prophet Muhammad, and wife of 'Ali Ibn Abu Talib. In 402 A.H./1011 C.E., the scholars of Baghdad stated that the founder of the Fatimids was 'Ubayd Ibn Sa'd Al-Jarmiyy and that he did not descend from the children of 'Ali and Fatima. For further details, see Ibn Kathir, Vol. XI, p. 344.

42 Ibn Kathir, Vol. XI, p. 266.

43 Friday prayer (*Al-Jumu'ah*) is composed basically of two short speeches (*khutab*) and two acts of prostration (*raka'ah*). The acknowledgement mentioned above takes the form of a supplication (*du'a'*) for the sake of the ruler (i.e. asking Allah to guide him) which usually takes place at the end of the second speech before the performance of the two prostrations. This *du'a'* for the ruler became a symbol of alliance.

44 Al-Qarah Daghi, Vol. I, p. 49.

45 Ahmad Al-Sharbasiyy, *Al-Ghazaliyy.* (Beirut: Dar al-Jil, 1975) p. 13.

8

'Ali is not restricted to the Shi'ites: the Sunnites' books are full of such notions.

Furthermore, to refute these accusations[46] one could cite Al-Ghazzāliyy's *fatwā* against the cursing of Yazid Ibn Mu'āwiyah, who was the Caliph at Damascus (reigned 61-63 A.H./680-683 C.E.). The Shi'ites considered Yazid their arch enemy, thinking that he was responsible for the death of Al-Ḥussayn Ibn 'Ali,[47] and thus they curse him. It is not possible that someone affiliated with Shi'ism in any fashion could issue this *fatwā*.[48] Yet, Al-Shirbasiyy maintained that this *fatwā* was not enough to acquit Al-Ghazzāliyy from the allegations that he was a Shi'ite. Al-Shirbasiyy contended that Al-Ghazzāliyy favoured 'Ali's opinion over that of Ibn 'Abbas, in a ruling in jurisprudence; Al-Shirbasiyy thought that Al-Ghazzāliyy had personal preference for 'Ali.[49] It is obvious that this is a case of an *Ad hominem* argument.

The above *fatwā* could be considered a proof that Al-Ghazzāliyy was not a Shi'ite but what if he issued this ruling when he was not a Shi'ite? The answer should emphasis the fact that so far there is nothing to substantiate the claim that Al-Ghazzāliyy was ever a Shi'ite. In fact I could not apprehend why this claim was started.

The sect (*firqah*) that propagated the cause of the Fatimids became known as the Batinites (*Al-Bāṭiniyyah*).[50] Al-Ghazzāliyy listed the names by which they were some-times known as the Qarāmitah, the Qarmatiyyah, the Khur-

---

46 They are considered "accusations" because Sunnites have a tendency to think of Shi'ism as a tradition which involves positions that are not in accordance with Islamic Shari'ah.
47 See footnote # 54.
48 Badawi, pp. 47–49.
49 Al-Sharbasiyy, pp.13-15.
50 The Batinites are a sect that, among other things, believed in an infallible Imam. He is, supposedly, the only one who could interpret the *Shari'ah (Islamic teachings)* and find the esoteric (*batin* and hence *Batiniyyah*) exegesis. They are known by many nicknames which resulted from their internal conflicts and divisions. In addition to the nicknames listed by Al-Ghazzaliyy, others were: Al-Fatimiyyah, Al-Hashashun, Al-Baharah, and Al-A'gha Khaniyyah. For more details, see Al-Nadwah Al—'Alamiyyah Lish-Shabab Al-Islamiyy, *Al-Mawsu'ah al-Muyassarah fi al-Adyan wa al-Madhahib al-Mu'asirah* (Riyad: Matba'at Safir, 1989) pp. 45-52, 395-398.

ramites, the Khurramadinites, the Isma'ilies, the Seveners, the Bābikites, the Muḥammirah, and the Ta'limites.[51] Each of these names emphasized certain aspects of this sect: the founders of the different factions, their beliefs, and, in some cases, the time and place in which they were active.[52] The Batinites posed a threat to the Caliphate and to the Sunni creed. In addition, they had resorted to political assassination.[53] Among those who were killed at their hands was Niẓām Al-Mulk[54] (d. 485 A.H./1092 C.E.),[55] the vizier for Alp Arslan and Malik Shah. He established the famous Niẓāmiyyah colleges[56] which were named after him, and assigned Al-Ghazzāliyy to head the Niẓāmiyyah at Baghdad.[57] Fakhr Al-Mulk, son of Nizam Al-Mulk and vizier for Sanjar in Nishapur, met the same fate as his father in 500 A.H./1106 C.E.[58] Among the many other dignitaries who were systematically assassinated was Abū Al-Qāsim[59] who was killed in Nishapur, where he was a preacher (khātib), in 492 A.H./1098 C.E.[60] He was the son of Imam Al-Haramayn Al-Juwainiyy who was the educator *par excellence* at the time, head of the Niẓāmiyyah college at Nishapur, and teacher of Al-Ghazzāliyy. These assassinations have led

51 Al-Ghazzaliyy, "*Fada'ih al-Batiniyyah wa-Fada'il al-Mustazhiriyyah,*" *Freedom and Fulfillment,* ed and trans. Richard J. McCarthy (Boston: Twayne Publishers, 1980) p.181.

52 The Isma'ilies were Batinites who claimed to be followers of Isma'il Ibn Ja'far Al-Sadiq, the Khurramites from *Khurram,* Farsi for pleasure, advocated hedonism, and the Qaramitah, followers of Qurmut Ibn Al-Asg'ath, established their rule in Al-Bahrayn towards the end of the third century A.H.

53 The English word "assassin" is derived from "Assassin", the Isma'ili sect, from Arabic *hashashin,* hashish-eaters. See *The New Lexicon Webster's Dictionary Of The English Language* (New York: Lexicon Publications, Inc., 1989).

54 His name was Al-Hasan Ibn 'Ali Ibn Ishaq, Abu-'Ali. He was born in Tus, the same birth place of Al-Ghazzaliyy, in 408 A.H./1017 C.E.

55 Ibn Kathir, Vol. XII, p.139.

56 Nizam Al-Mulk built a college in each city in Iraq and Khurasan. Those included Baghdad, Balakh, Nishapur, Harat, Asfahan, Al-Basrah, Marw, Tubristan and Al-Misl. Al-Subkiyy, Vol. IV, p. 314.

57 Taj Al-Din Al-Subkiyy, *Tabaqat al-Shafi'iyyah al-Kubra* (Cairo: 'Isa Al-Babi Al-Halabi & Co., 1964) Vol. VI, p. 197.

58 Ibn Kathir, Vol. XII, p. 167.

59 Abu Al-Qasim Ibn 'Abd Al-Malik (Imam Al-Haramain) Ibn 'Abd Allah (Al-Shaikh Abu Muhammad) Ibn Yusuf.

60 Ibn Kathir, Vol. XII, p. 157.

some Muslim and orientalist scholars to doubt Al-Ghazzā-liyy's account of why he left his position at the Niẓāmiyyah college in Baghdad.[61]

The activities of the Batinites prompted Al-Ghazzāliyy to devote at least seven books and treatises to what appears to be a systematic confrontation of their positions during various stages of his life.[62]

It is understandable that, in this sea of turmoil, struggle, and intolerance, one might not expect any group to be spared. Yet, Watt, an orientalist, said that Christians and Jews had internal autonomy under their heads. He added that "there was practically no religious persecution"; they enjoyed official protection from the Islamic Caliphate until its breakdown at the turn of the century.[63] The presence of Christians and Jews in Khurāsān, during the early life of Al-Ghazzāliyy, enticed him to ask questions crucial for his quest for knowledge.[64] In the *Deliverance from Error*, Al-Ghazzāliyy said:

> The thirst for grasping the real meaning of things was indeed my habit and wont from my early years and in the prime of my life. It was an instinctive, natural disposition

61 See page 142.
62 These books are: 1. *Al-Mustazhiriyy fi al-Rad 'ala al-Batiniyyah*, also known as *Fada'ih al-Batiniyyah wa-Dada'il al-Mustazhiriyyah*. Al-Ghazzaliyy wrote it in support of the 'Abbasid Caliph Al-Mustazhir (d. 512 A.H./1118 C.E.) against the Batiniyyah. 2. *Hujjat al-Haq*, was written in Baghdad but has been lost. Also, both of *Qwasim al-Batiniyyah* and *Al-Darj al-Marqum bi al-Jadawil* which was written in Tus, are lost. For more details see Badawi, *Mu'allafat al-Ghazali*, pp. 85–86 & p. 159. 3. *Qawasim al-Batiniyyah*. 4. *Jawab al-Masa'il al-Arba' allati Sa'alaha al-Batiniyyah bi-Hamadhan*, Al-Ghazzaliyy, "*Al-Manar*" vol. 11 (1908) pp. 601–608. 5. Al-Darj al-Marqum bi al-Jadawil. 6. *Faisal al-Tafriqah bain al-Islam wa al-Zandaqah*. 7. *Al-Qistas al-Mustaqim*, and the section on *Ahl al-Ta'lim* in *Al-Munqidh min al-Dalal* which is a critique of their methodology. Al-Ghazzaliyy, *Al-Munqidh min al-Dalal* which is a critique of their methodology. Al-Ghazzaliyy, *Al-Munqidh min al-Dalal*, eds. Jamil Saliba and Kamil 'Aiyyad, 10th ed. (No. city: Dar al-Andalus, 1981) pp. 117–129. The abovementioned books are listed in chronological order as they appear in Badawi's *Mu'allafat Al-Ghazali*.
63 W. Montgomery Watt, *Muslim Intellectual: A Study of al-Ghazzali* (Edinburgh: The Edinburgh University Press, 1963) p. 8.
64 Al-Ghazzaliyy, *Deliverance from Error*, Jamil Saliba and Kamil 'Ayyad, eds, (No. City: Dar Al-Andalus, 1981), p. 81.

placed in my makeup by Allah Most High, not something
due to my own choosing and contriving. As a result, the
fetters of servile conformism (*taqlid*) fell away from me,
and inherited beliefs lost their hold on me, when I was
quite young. For I saw that the children of Christians
always grew up embracing Christianity, and the children of Jews always grew up adhering to Judaism, and
the children of Muslims always grew up following the
religion of Islam. I also heard the tradition related from
the Messenger of Allah - May Allah's blessing and peace
be upon him - in which he said: "Every infant is born
endowed with the *fitra*:[65] then his parents make him Jew
or Christian or Magian."[66] Consequently I felt an inner
urge to seek the true meaning of the original *fitra*, and
the true meaning of the beliefs arising through slavish
aping of parents, the beginnings of which are sugges-
tions imposed from without, since there are differences
of opinion in the discernment of those that are false.[67]

This mode of questioning and quest for knowledge
continued with Al-Ghazzāliyy until the end of his life.

1.1.3 The Crusades

In addition to the internal conflicts and turmoil, the Islamic Caliphate suffered from the invasions of the Crusaders who were known in medieval sources as the Franks (*Al-
Firanj/al-Firanjah*). They conquered Jerusalem, the third
holy Muslim site,[68] in 492 A.H./1098 C.E.[69] Al-Ghazzāliyy

---

65 Literally, *fitra* means natural disposition. In the above mentioned
    hadith it means that all people are born as Muslims, and hence Islam
    is the religion of *fitra*.
66 This is a part of a *hadith* narrated by Al-Bukhariyy in his *Sahih*. The
    word Magian (*Majusiyy*) means fire-worshipper. This religion was
    spread in Persia. In Islamic Shari'ah, magians were tolerated based on
    the assumption that they could have deviated from a people who
    received a book (i.e. through revelation) (*shubhat kitab*) and thus
    entitled to this tolerance which is a right for the people of the book (*ahl
    al-kitab*), Jews and Christians.
67 Al-Ghazzaliyy, *Freedom and Fulfillment* (*Al-Munqidh min al-Dalal*),
    trans. Richard Joseph McCarthy, S. J. (Boston: Twayne Publishers,
    1980) p. 63.
68 Here I refer to the *hadith* of prophet Muhammad in which he allowed
    muslims to travel to visit three mosques only: Bayt Allah Al-Haram in
    Makkah the mosque of the prophet in Medina, and Al-Aqsa mosque in
    Jerusalem.
69 Ibn Kathir, Vol. XII, p. 156.

12

neither mentioned the Crusaders in his writings nor made clear his position regarding them, and this has proved to be problematic for him. Since the turn of this century, Muslim scholars have criticized his stand and have considered it uncharacteristic of a man of the stature of Al-Ghazzāliyy. In his doctoral dissertation, Dr. Zaki Mubarak blamed Al-Ghazzāliyy's Sufism for the absence of any role that he could have played in calling for *Jihād*:

"Al-Ghazzāliyy had sunk into his retreat (*khalwah*), and was preoccupied with his recitations (*awrād*) not knowing his duty to call for *Jihād*."[70]

In *Abu-Hāmid Al-Ghazzāliyy wa al-Tasawwuf,* 'Abd Al-Rahmān Dimashqiyyah also blames Al-Ghazzāliyy's Sufism. This study lists the position of most contemporary Muslim thinkers.[71] It seems that the only scholar who tried to explain Al-Ghazzāliyy's position in light of Sufism, without blaming him for it, was Dr. Yūsuf Al-Qardawiyy:[72]

"It could be that the excuse of this honorable Imam was his preoccupation primarily with reformation from within, and that internal corruption is responsible for paving (the way) for foreign invasion."[73]

Dr. Al-Qardawiyy acknowledged, however, that Al-Ghazzāliyy's position was "puzzling", especially since Al-Ghazzāliyy wrote about *jihād* in his books of jurisprudence. Dr. Al-Qardawiyy ended his discussion of this issue, by stating "that only Allah knows the reality of his excuse"[74]

It is a fact, however, that Al-Ghazzāliyy did not include a chapter on *jihād* in his major *Ihyā' 'Ulūm al-Dīn,* which he used to teach after returning to Baghdad from his travels,[75]

---

70 Zaki Mubarak, *Al-Akhlaq ind Al-Ghazzaliyy* (Beirut: Al-Maktabah Al-'Asriyyah, n.d.) p. 17. This doctoral dissertation was defended at the Egyptian University on May, 15, 1924. The preface of the publisher, and the introduction of the author, indicate that this dissertation stirred a wave of criticism at the time.

71 'Abd Al-Rahman Dimashqiyyah, *Abu Hamid Al Ghazzaliyy wa al-Tasawwuf* (Riyad: Dar Tibah, 1988) pp. 349–356.

72 Al-Qardawiyy, Yusuf Abdulllah (1926–?). Dean of the college of Shari'ah and Islamic Studies at the University of Qatar, he is one of the most renowned jurists of the Islamic world today.

73 Yusuf al-Qardawiyy, *Al-Imam Al-Ghazzaliyy Bayn Madihih wa Naqidih* (Al-Mansurah: Dar al-Wafa', 1988) pp. 172–174.

74 Al-Qardawiyy, p. 174.

75 Al-Subkiyy, Vol. VI, p. 200.

which included Jerusalem just before the Crusaders reached it. In addition, he chose to continue the solitary life for about ten years after Jerusalem was captured.

In my opinion, however, Al-Ghazzāliyy's silence on this matter can be seen in a different light. This requires a more careful understanding of the meaning of *jihād*. The literal meaning of *jihād* is "effort", "striving" or "struggle". The translation of *jihād* as "holy war" is incorrect; there is no equivalent use in Arabic language.[76] In the Qur'an and the Sunnah, *jihād* is understood to have more than one meaning. One meaning denotes fighting (*qitāl*). The other meaning, which is overlooked by many, is the ethical and moral *jihād*. However, in jurisprudence, all four schools[77] defined the meaning of *jihād* as fighting.[78]

In what might express one of his views toward *jihād*, Al-Ghazzāliyy quoted Abū Al-Dardā', one of the companions of prophet Muḥammad [S.A.A.S].[79] who said: "He who thinks that seeking knowledge is not *jihād*, has a defect in his opinion and reason".[80] Moreover, in *Kitāb Al-Adhkār wa-Al-Da'awāt* (the "Book of Remembrance and Supplication" in *The Revival of Islamic Sciences*, Al-Ghazzāliyy cited two traditions of prophet Muḥammad [S.A.A.S.] that elevated the reward for the performance of *dhikr* (remembrance) to the level of *jihād* or even better[81] In addition, Ibn Kathir narrates that the people of Baghdad were indifferent to the

76 Bernard Lewis, *The Political Language of Islam* (Chicago: The University of Chicago Press, 1988) pp. 70–75.
77 The Hanifite, the Malikite, the Shafi'ite and the Hanbalite.
78 'Abdallah 'Azzam, *fi al-Jihad Adab wa-Ahkam* (No City: Matbu'at al-Jihad, 1987) pp. 2–3.
79 Short for *Salla Allahu 'Alayhi Wa Sallam* (May Allah's peace be upon him).
80 Al-Ghazzaliyy, *Ihya'*, p. 9.
81 The first tradition, which starts with "*Ma 'Amal Ibn Adam min 'Amal Anja Lahu min 'Adhab Allah min Dhikr Allah 'Azza wa-Jall...* etc.," had been narrated by Mu'adh Ibn Abu Jabal. Ibn Abu Shaybah and At-Tabaraniyy verified this tradition and said that it has a "good" chain of narrators (*isnaduhu hasan*). The second tradition, which starts with "Ala unbi'akum Bi Khayri A'malakum wa-Azkaha ... etc." had been narrated by Abu Al-Darda'. Al-Tirmidhiyy, Al-Hakim and Ibn majah verified this tradition and said that it has a "sound" chain of narrators (*isnaduhu sahih*). See Al-Ghazzaliyy, *Ihya' 'Ulum al-Din*, Vol. I, p. 295.

14

effort of jurists, including Ibn 'Aqīl[82] who tried to mobilize them.[83] Al-Ghazzāliyy must have been aware of what was going around him, and acted accordingly.

Moreover, Al-Ghazzāliyy's correspondence with the authorities and his criticism of their policies which were not in accordance with Islamic Shari'ah are direct applications of a tradition of prophet Muḥammad [S.A.A.S.] in which he said: "The greatest *Jihād* is (saying) a word of truth in front of an unjust Sultan."[84]

In my opinion, Al-Ghazzāliyy realized that the Islamic Caliphate at the time was corrupt and filled with social and ideological trends that ran against Islamic Shari'ah. I think he was convinced that the disease was within the state, and that the Crusaders were nothing but the symptoms. Al-Ghazzāliyy understood that the core of the issue was moral. To solve this problem, he wanted to educate people and to revive the role of the Shari'ah ad its aims (*maqāṣid*). But, the period during which Al-Ghazzāliyy withdrew from public life can not be justified in the light of Islamic Shari'ah. Any act that resembles monasticism (*rahbāniyyah*) was rejected by the Qur'an and the Sunnah.[85] The Qur'an considered monasticism an innovation (*bid'ah*) that was not required from the monks (Sura *al-Ḥadīd* 57:27).

1.2 HIS EARLY LIFE

His full name was Muhammad Ibn Muhammad Ibn Mu-

---

82   'Ali Ibn 'Aqil Ibn Muhammad (431 A.H./1039–513 A.H./1119 C.E.). He was the head of the Hanbalites at Baghdad and a contemporary of Al-Ghazzaliyy. He was another exception to the prevailing tense relations between the different schools of jurisprudence. Ibn Kathir, Vol. XII, p. 184.

83   Ibn Kathir, Vol. XII, p. 156.

84   *"Inna A'zama al-Jihad Kalimata Haqqin inda Sultanin Ja'ir"*.

85   In the Qur'an, there are verses that praises Christian monks for their humbleness and acceptence of Allah's revelation (al-Qur'an, Sura *al-Ma'idah* 5:82); yet there are also verse that criticize many of them in relationship to financial affairs (al-Qur'an, Sura *al-Taubah* 9:34). In the Sunnah, prophet Muhammad prohibited 'Uthman Ibn Maz'un from monasticism saying to him, "Oh 'Uthman, monasticism is not required from us; am I not an example for you?" This hadith has been narrated by Ahmad Ibn Hanbal in his *Musnad*, 6: 226.

hammad Ibn Aḥmad al-Ṭūsiyy (the Tusite), Abū Hāmid,[86] Al-Ghazzāliyy. He bore the title of respect Hujjat Al-Islam (proof of Islam) for the role he played in defending Islam against the trends of thought that existed at the time.[87] He was born in Tus in 450 A.H./1058 C.E. Tus was a city of Khurasan near Meshhad in Iran today. It was composed of two adjacent towns: Nūqān and Tabarān. His father was a wool spinner (*ghazzāl*)[88] and thus, relative to this profession, Al-Ghazzāliyy acquired this name with a stressed "z". Many medieval scholars accepted this form of Al-Ghazzāliyy's name.[89] Those who say that the correct form is "Al-Ghazaliyy" with unstressed "z" base their judgement on the idea that "Al-Ghazāliyy" is derived from the word Ghazalah, supposedly, one of the villages that surround Tus. In this case, "Al-Ghazāliyy" would mean the Ghazalite. However, according to Ibn Al-Sam'āniyy (d. 506 A.H./112 C.E.),[90] a contemporary of Al-Ghazzāliyy, the people of Tus denied the existence of the village of Ghazalah when he asked them about it.[91] Among those who were also called "Al-Ghazzāliyy"[92] were his brother Ahmad (d. 520 A.H./1126 C.E.), and the brother of Al-Ghazzāliyy's grandfather, Ahmad Ibn Muhammad (d. 435 A.H./1043) C.E.). The latter also had Abu Ḥāmid as an honorific title. He was a scholar and teacher of Abū 'Alī Al-Faḍl Ibn Muhammad Ibn 'Alī Al-Faramdhiyy (d. 477 A.H./1048 C.E.). Al-Faramdhiyy played a major role in shaping Al-Ghazzāliyy's Sufism.[93]

---

86 This is an honorific title (*kunyah*). Many Shafi'ite scholars held this *kunyah*, which literally means "father of Hamid." Al-Ghazzaliyy did not have any sons. Murtada Al-Zubaydiyy, *Ithaf al-Sadah al-Mutaqin bi-Sharh Asrar Ihya' 'Ulum al-Din*, (Beirut: Dar Ihya' Al-Turath al-'Arabiyy) Vol. I, p. 18.

87 Taj Al-Din Al-Subkiyy, *Tabaqat al-Shafi'iyyah al-Kubra*, 'Abd Al-Fattah Muhammad Al-Hilw and Mahmud Muhammad al-Tanahiyy, eds., (Cairo: Matba'at 'Isa al-Babi al-Halabi & Co., 1968). Vol. VI, p. 191.

88 Al-Subkiyy, Vol. VI, p. 193.

89 They include Al-Nawawiyy, Ibn Al-Athir, Al-Dhahabiyy, and Ibn Khallikan. Muhammad Ibn Muhammad Al-Husayniyy Murtada Al-Zubaydiyy, *Ithaf Al-Sadah al-Muttaqin bi-Sharh Asrar Ihya' 'Ulum al-Din* (Beirut: Dar Ihya' Al-Turath al-'Arabiyy, n.d.) p. 18.

90 Ibn Kathir, Vol. XII, p. 174.

91 Ibn Al-Sam'aniyy, *The Genealogies* (*Al-ansab*): Al-Zubaydiyy, p. 18.

92 In this dissertation, I refer to Muhammad as Al-Ghazzaliyy, and to his brother Ahmad, by his first name, as a metter of convenience.

93 Al-Subkiyy, Vol. VI, p 209.

Although Al-Ghazzāliyy was born in Tus, which is rightly considered non-Arabic land, there were voices advocating the possibility that Al-Ghazzāliyy was of Arabic origin.[94] Whether Al-Ghazzāliyy was an Arab or not does not make much difference. Ibn Khaldun (d. 809 A.H./1406 C.E.) stated "that most Muslim scholars were not Arabs, and in some fields all of them were *'Ajam* (non-Arabs).[95] Such scholars used Arabic in their writings because it was *lingua franca* of their world.

Before his death, Al-Ghazzāliyy's father entrusted him and his brother Ahmad to a Sufi friend. He asked him to spend whatever little money he left behind, to teach them reading and writing. When the money was finished, the Sufi asked them to join a school as students so that they might subsist.[96] According to Al-Subkiyy, schools used to provide room, board and a stipend.[97]

1.3   HIS EDUCATION AND ACADEMIC CAREER

1.3.1 Formal Education

As mentioned above, Al-Ghazzāliyy and his brother Ahmad, learned to read and write at the hand of their Sufi trustee. Although no dates are available about Al-Ghazzāliyy's early education, the normal age to begin school was eleven.[98] Al-Ghazzāliyy was eleven in 469 A.H./1069 C.E. It could be during this time that he began his study of jurisprudence at Tus where his teacher was Ahmad Ibn Muhammad Al-Radhakaniyy. Al-Ghazzāliyy's next station was Jurjān where he wrote *Al-Ta'liqah* from the lectures of Abū Al-Qasim Al-Isma'iliyy Al-Jurjāniyy.[99] On his way

94   Al-Zubaydiyy,Vol. I, p. 18 and Al-Sharbasiyy, p. 21.
95   Ibn Khaldun, *Al-Muqaddimah*, (Beirut: Dar al-Qalazm, 1984), p. 543.
96   Al-Subkiyy, Vol. VI, pp. 193–194.
97   Al-Qarah Daghi, Vol. I, p. 69.
98   Watt, *Muslim Intellectual*, p. 21.
99   According to As-Subkiyy, Vol. VI, p. 195. Al-Ghazzāliyy's teacher in Jurjan was Abu Nasr Al-Isma'iliyy. His full name was Muhammad Ibn Ahmad Ibn Ibrahim Ibn Ismail (d. 405 A.H./1014 C.E.) The actual teacher full name was Isma'il Ibn Mas'adah Ibn Iams'il Ibn Ahmad Ibn Ibrahim Ibn Isma'il (d. 477 A.H./1084 C.E.). It is obvious

back to Tus, his belongings including *Al-Ta'liqah* were stolen by bandits. Al-Ghazzaliyy followed them and appealed to their commander to return him the books for which he had "travelled in order to listen, to write and know their contents".[100] The commander laughed at Al-Ghazzaliyy because he claimed to know the contents of the books, yet he was striped of the knowledge the moment they took the books from him. Al-Ghazzaliyy took back his books and decided to memorize them, so he could never be deprived of his knowledge again. Al-Ghazzaliyy's journey to Jurjan must have occurred before 474 A.H./1074 C.E., since he spent three years in Tus memorizing the books he brought back with him before leaving to Nishapur.[101] In 470 A.H./ 1077 C.E., Al-Ghazzaliyy went to Nishapur, where he studied at the Nizamiyyah, under Imam Al-Haramayn, Al-Juwainiyy, until his death in 478 A.H./1085 C.E. During his stay at the Nizamiyyah, Al-Ghazzaliyy learned and excelled in the Shafi'ite Jurisprudence, comparative jurisprudence (*'Ilm al-Khilaf*), fundamentals of jurisprudence (*Usul al-Fiqh*), fundamentals of religion (*Usul al-Din*), logic and philosophy. In the field of philosophy Al-Ghazzaliyy read Al-Farabiyy (d. 345 A.H./950 C.E.) and Ibn Sina (Avicenna) (d. 429 A.H./1037 C.E.).[102] Also, he read the letters of the Brethren of Purity (*Ikhwan al-Safa*).[103] Al-Ghazzaliyy ranked very high among the students of the Nizamiyyah ; Al-Juwainiyy used to ask Al-Ghazzaliyy to assist in lecturing to the other students, even in his own presence. Al-Ghazzaliyy began writing his books during the life of Al-Juwainiyy, which according to Al-Subkiyy, might have been a source of discomfort to his teacher.[104]

that Abu Nasr was the cousin of Abu Al-Qasim's grandfather. Many orientalists and Muslim scholars copied the mistake of Al Subkiyy. Farid Jabre, S. J. said in *Mideo*, Vol. I, p. 77, that it was Abu Al-Qasim who taught Al-Ghazzaliyy. Badawi, *Mu'allafat Al-Ghazali*, p. 4.

100   Scholars, including Al-Ghazzaliyy, used to dictate their books.
101   Al-Subkiyy, Vol. VI, p. 195.
102   We know this from Al-Ghazzaliyy's writings about them first in *Maqasid al-Falasifah* and later on in his critique of philosophy *Tahafut al-Falasifah*.
103   These are fifty one letters of an underground group of philosophers who called themselves the Brethren of Purity. In these letters they attempted to reconcile philosophy and Shari'ah. Al-Zubaydiyy, p. 28.
104   Al-Subkiyy, Vol. VI, p. 196.

18

1.3.2 Teaching at the Nizāmiyyah, The "Spiritual Crisis"

After the death of Al-Juwainiyy, Al-Ghazzāliyy went to the Camp (*Al-Mu'askar*), to see vizier Nizām al-Mulk, whose court was a meeting place for scholars. There, Al-Ghazzāliyy debated with other scholars and won their respect. After about six years at Al-Mu'askar, Nizām Al-Mulk assigned Al-Ghazzāliyy to teach at the Nizāmiyyah of Baghdad. He lectured there between 484 A.H./1091 C.E. and 488 A.H./ 1095 C.E.[105] This position won him prestige , wealth, and "respect that even princes, kings and viziers could not match,"[106] According to the Hanbalite scholar Ibn Al-Jawziyy (d. 597 A.H./1200 C.E.) who studied at the hands of Al-Ghazzāliyy's student judge Ibn Al-'Arabiyy, Al-Ghazzāliyy came to Baghdad directly from Asfahān where the Camp must have been located.[107]

At the Nizāmiyyah, several hundred students used to attend the lectures of Al-Ghazzāliyy. Some of those students became famous scholars, judges, and few became lecturers at the Nizāmiyyah of Baghdad itself.[108] Also scholars like Ibn 'Aqīl and Abū Al-Khattāb, among the heads of the Hanbalite school of jurisprudence, attended his lectures and incorporated them in their writings.[109]

The end of Al-Ghazzāliyy's career at the Nizāmiyyah of

105 Al-Subkiyy, Vol. VI, pp. 196–197.
106 Al-Zubaydiyy, Vol. I, p. 7.
107 Ibn Al-Jawziyy, *Al-Muntazam fi Tarikh al-Muluk wa al-Umam*, (*Hayderabad: Da'irat al-Ma'arif al-'Uthmaniyyah*, 1939) Vol. IX, p. 55.
108 They included: Judge Abu Nasr Al-Khamqariyy (d. 544 A.H./1149 C.E.): Abu Bakr Ibn Al-'Arabiyy al-Malikiyy (d. 545 A.H./1150 C.E.) who was quoted frequently in criticism of Al-Ghazzaliyy: Abu 'Abdullah Shafi' Ibn 'Abd Ar-Rashid Al-Jiliyy Al-Shafi'iyy (d. 541 A.H./1146 C.E.), whose lectures were attended by Ibn Al-Jawziyy: Abu Mansur Sa'd Ibn Muhammad Al-Bazzar (d. 539 A.H./1144 C.E.), who taught at the Nizamiyyah,: Imam Abu Al-Fath Ahmad Ibn 'Ali Ibn Burhan (d. 518 A.H./1124 C.E.), who taught at the Nizamiyyah for a short period: and Abu 'Abdullah Ibn Tumart, founder of Al-Muwahhidun state in Al-Maghrib, among many others. Al-Shirbasiyy made a mistake in listing Abu Hamid Al-Isfarayiniyy (d. 406 A.H./1015 C.E.), who was one of the heads of the Shafi'ites, among the students of Al-Ghazzaliyy. See Al-Shirbasiyy, p. 32.
109 Al-Shirbasiyy, p. 31.

Baghdad was unexpected. The circumstances surrounding this event became known as the "spiritual crisis"[110] of Al-Ghazzāliyy. Al-Ghazzāliyy discussed the reason that prompted him to quit his position in his autobiographical work, *Deliverence from Error (Al-Munqidh min al-Dalāl)*, in the section of Sufism. The aim of this book was to show Al-Ghazzāliyy's quest for knowledge. After discussing the methods of Al-Mutakallimūn,[111] the philosophers and the Batinites respectively, Al-Ghazzāliyy chose the method of the Sufis as the right method for the acquiring of knowledge. This method had prerequisites; one should abandon all worldly attachments. Al-Ghazzāliyy thought that, in order to implement this , he should "shun fame, money and to run away from obstacles".[112] He made it clear that any deed that was not for the sake of Allah,[113] was an obstacle. Al-Ghazzāliyy scrutinized his activities, including teaching, and decided that his motivation was not for the sake of Allah.[114] Al-Ghazzāliyy wanted to abandon those obstacles but the temptation was very strong. He spent six months struggling to stop teaching, until he no longer had a choice. Of this Al-Ghazzāliyy said:

> "For nearly six months beginning with Rajab, 488 A.H. July, 1095 C.E.), I was continuously tossed about between the attractions of worldly desires and the impulses towards eternal life. In that month the matter ceased to be one of choice and became one of compulsion. (Allah) caused my tongue to dry up so that I was prevented from lecturing. One particular day I would make an effort to lecture in order to gratify the hearts of my following, but my tongue would not utter a single word nor could I accomplish anything at all."[115]

110   *Al-A'sam,* p. 42: Al-Shirbasiyy, p. 34: *Dimashqiyyah,* p. 43.
111   Muslim theologians who incorporated logic in their subject matter, which became known as *'Ilm al-Kalam.*
112   Al-Ghazzaliyy, *Deliverence,* p. 134.
113   I used the word "Allah" instead of "God" because the latter has various connotations, in different religions and cultures, that might not represent the Islamic concept.
114   Al-Ghazzaliyy, *Deliverance,* p. 134.
115   Algazali, "Deliverance from Error," *Philosophy in the Middle Ages,* eds. Arthur Hyman, and James J. Walsh (Indianapolis: Hackett Publishing Cp., 1987) . 277.

The fact that Al-Ghazzāliyy could not speak caused him grief, which eventually effected his ability to digest food. Soon Al-Ghazzāliyy's health deteriorated and the physicians gave up any hope and stated that the only way to cure him was by solving his psychological problems. Realizing his impotence, and worsening situation, Al-Ghazzāliyy "sought refuge with Allah who made it easy for his heart to turn away from position and wealth, from children and friends."[116] He distributed his wealth retaining only as much as would suffice him and his children. In public, he declared that he was going to make pilgrimage to Makkah, while in fact, he was planning to go to Syria. Al-Ghazzāliyy had this plan because he was convinced that the Caliph and the scholars of Baghdad would not understand his position; he was afraid that they might prevent him from leaving.[117] Al-Ghazzāliyy asked his brother Aḥmad to replace him at the Niẓamiyyah,[118] and left Baghdad with the intention never to return.[119]

Although Al-Ghazzāliyy used clear and simple language in describing the reason why he left the Niẓamiyyah, there were some contemporary scholars who used Al-Ghazzāliyy's account of that event to "diagnose" his sickness.[120] Al-Ghazzāliyy described in great details his physical and spiritual conditions. It seems that those details invited some contemporary scholars to leave the realm of philosophy to medicine in their attempt to diagnose Al-Ghazzāliyy. Although it is not the aim of this book to define what the job of philosophy is, looking for symptoms in autobiographical works, is not philosophy *per se*. One can not but criticize and reject such unphilosophical attitudes.

Al-Ghazzāliyy's declared motives for his departured from Baghdad in *Deliverance From Error* have been challenged by two scholars. Duncan Black Macdonald argued that Al-Ghazzāliyy left Baghdad because he felt that he was *persona non grata* with the Sultan Barkyaruq.[121] According to Macdonald, this was because Al-Ghazzāliyy sided with

116   Al-Gazzaliyy, *Deliverance*, p. 278.
117   Al-Ghazzaliyy, *Deliverance*, p. 137.
118   Al-Zubaydiyy, Vol. I, p.7.
119   Al-Ghazzaliyy, *Delivenrence*, p. 137.
120   Al-Shirbasiyy, p. 37.
121   Watt, p. 140.

Tutush (d. 488 A.H./1095 C.E.), uncle and rival of Bark-yaruq. In fact Al-Ghazzāliyy mentioned that this opinion was in circulation in *Deliverance from Error*. This opinion, which goes back in history to the time of Al-Ghazzāliyy, contradicts Al-Ghazzāliyy's account of his relationship with those in authority at the time. It is quite clear, rather, that he was courted by them.[122] Besides, if his only goal was to disappear from Baghdad in order to escape political difficulties, he could have done so without going to the trouble of becoming a Sufi.

The other challenge to Al-Ghazzāliyy's account was set forth by Farid Jabre who claimed that Al-Ghazzāliyy fled Baghdad for fear of assassination by the Batinites.[123] The criticisms of Macdonald's opinion also apply here. In addition, one could argue that if it were true that Al-Ghazzāliyy feared for his life, he should have looked for places   located far away from the influence of the Batinites. However, he went to Damascus and Jerusalem which were under the direct influence of the Fatimids. Furthermore, at the end of his journey, Al-Ghazzāliyy returned to Ni-shapur, which was very close to the strongholds of the Batinites, during the peak of political assassinations.[124] Thus it is untenable that Al-Ghazzāliyy's fear of assas-sination could have played any role in his departure from Baghdad. His own account, on the other hand, is perfectly comprehensible.

Al-Ghazzāliyy's abandonment of almost everything that he possessed and his choice of the spiritual path of Su-fism (*tarīqah*) should not come as a surprise. He read the books of Sufis such as Abū Ṭalīb Al-Makkiyy's *Qūt al-Qulūb* (Food of the Hearts), the books of Al-Harith Al-Muhāsibiyy, and the fragments of Al-Junayd, Al-Shibliyy, and Abū Yazīd Al-Bistāmiyy.[125] Al-Ghazzāliyy's position was consis-tent with those of the above mentioned Sufis. He chose their methodology as the one that could best fulfill his quest for knowledge. Al-Muhāsibiyy (d. 243 A.H./857 C.E.), for exam-

122   Al-Ghazzaliyy, *Deliverance*, 137.
123   Watt, p. 140.
124   Watt, pp. 140–143.
125   Al-Ghazzaliyy, *Deliverance*, p. 131.

ple, withdrew from public life and died in want.[126] Likewise, Al-Junayd (d. 298 A.H./910 C.E.), a student of Al-Muḥasībiyy, had doubts whether he was worthy to give lectures.[127] Al-Shibliyy (d. 334 A.H./946 C.E.), a student of Al-Junayd, was the governor of Dunbawind, canton of Rayy, also renounced the world and asked of the inhabitants immunity for his past conduct. He then submitted his resignation.[128] Al-Bisṭāmiyy (d. 261 A.H./874 C.E.) stated that he gained knowledge of the world by means of a hungry belly.[129] Following suit, Al-Makkiyy (d. 386 A.H./996 C.E.) advocated self-mortification: he lived for a considerable time on nothing but wild herbs.[130] Their influence on Al-Ghazzāliyy is unmistakable.

Al-Ghazzāliyy's internal struggle might have been triggered by the visit of Abū Al-Ḥusayn Ardashir Ibn Manṣūr Al-'Abbādiyy to the Niẓamiyyah in 486 A.H./1093 C.E. His preaching, which Al-Ghazzāliyy attended, was so influential that "more than thirty thousand men and women were present at his circles, many people left their livelihood, many people repented and returned to mosques, wines were spilled and instruments of play (i.e. music) were broken."[131]

1.3.3 The Journeys of Al-Ghazzāliyy

It was a part of the path of the Sufi to travel from one place to another and to visit tombs of good people. Visiting cemeteries are intended to help the Sufi purify his soul, since the sight of the graves teaches one a lesson about the temporal and limited nature of this life.

Based upon Al-Ghazzāliyy's account in *Deliverance from Error*, his trip, after leaving Baghdad in 488 A.H./1095 C.E., could be outlined as covering the following cities in

126 Ibn Khallikan. *Wafayat al-A'yan wa Anab' Abna' al-Zaman*, tans. B. Mac Guckin De Slane: The John J. Burns Library, Boston College, Chestnut Hill, MA 02167 (Paris: Printed for the Oriental Translation Fund of Great Britain And Ireland, 1843) Vol. I, p. 365.
127 Ibn Khallikan, Vol. I, p. 338.
128 *Ibid.*, Vol. I, p. 511.
129 *Ibid.*, Vol. I, p. 662.
130 Al-Ghazzaliyy, *Deliverance*, p. 131.
131 Ibn Kathir, Vol. XII, p. 144.

chronological order: Damascus (where he stayed "close to two years",[132] Jerusalem, Hebron, Makkah and Madinah.[133] He later returned to Baghdad[134] in Jumada Al-Akhirah, 490 A.H./June, 1097 C.E.[135] From there he went to Tus and lived in seclusion (*khalwa*), except when he had to attend to family affairs.[136] Al-Ghazzāliyy ended his seclusion, which lasted for eleven years,[137] to teach at the Nizamiyyah of Nishapur[138] in 499 A.H./1106 C.E. His stay in Nishapur was rather short. he returned to Tus where he remained until his death on Monday, Jumada al-Akhirah, 505 A.H./December 18, 1111 C.E.[139]

There have been other accounts of the route Al-Ghazzāliyy took in his journey; they advocate the notion that he visited Alexandria in Egypt on his way to Yusuf Ibn Tashāfin, and that he returned when he learned that Ibn Tashāfin had died.[140] All other accounts confirm that Al-Ghazzāliyy was in Khurasan, a district in Persia, in 500 A.H./1106 C.E., the year in which Ibn Tashafin died.[141] The idea that Al-Ghazzāliyy was in Egypt may be refuted on two accounts. His student, Ibn Al-'Arabiyy saw him, after returning from his journey, in the wilderness of Baghdad in 491 A.H./1097 C.E. In addition, Al-Ghazzāliyy's account that he was in Nishapur, Khurasan, in Dhu al-Qi'dah, 499 A.H./July 1106,[142] is a clear indication of the falsity of such claims.

According to Al-Subkiyy, Al-Ghazzāliyy left Baghdad in 488 A.H./1095 C.E., and went to perform pilgrimage in Makkah, before he went to Damascus in 489 A.H./1096 C.E. In Damascus, he stayed for a few days as a *faqir* (literally poor, another way of referring to a Sufi) before heading to Jerusalem, where he remained for awhile. From Jerusalem

132 Al-Ghazzaliyy, *Deliverance*, p. 138.
133 *Ibid.*, pp. 137–139.
134 Al-Subkiyy. Vol. VI, p. 200.
135 Watt, p. 201.
136 Al-Ghazzaliyy, *Deliverance*, p. 138.
137 *Ibid.*, p. 159.
138 Al-Zubaydiyy, Vol. I, p. 8.
139 Al-Subkiyy, Vol. VI, p. 201.
140 Al-Zubaydiyy, Vol. I, p. 8.
141 Badawi, p. 23.
142 Al-Ghazzaliyy, *Deliverance*, p. 159.

he returned to Damascus. There he chose the western minaret of the Umayyad mosque as his place of seclusion.

From there he returned to Baghdad where he preached, and lectured on his *Ihyā' 'Ulum al-Dīn* for awhile.[143] It must be noted that the order of the journey does not correspond to that of Al-Ghazzāliyy.

In *Deliverance from Error*, Al-Ghazzāliyy states that he stayed in Damascus almost two years. He used to spend his days in seclusion and isolation by locking himself inside the minaret of the mosque of Damascus. For the duration of his stay there, he kept himself busy purifying his soul, polishing his morals, and cleansing his heart to make remembrance (*dhikr*) of Allah, in the fashion he grasped from the books of the Sufis.[144]

When Al-Ghazzāliyy left Damascus for Jerusalem, he continued to live in isolation. He used to enter the Rock (*Al-Sakhrah*)[145] wherein he locked himself. Then, after visiting the tomb of prophet Ibrahim [a.s.] in Hebron, he went to perform pilgrimage to the Ka'bah[146] in Mekkah and to visit Madinah, where prophet Muhammad [S.A.A.S.] was buried.

At this stage, Al-Ghazzāliyy missed his children.[147] He returned home, to Tus after a brief stay in Baghdad at the Ribat[148] of Abū Sa'id Al-Naysaburiyy, in front of the Nizamiyyah.[149] In Tus, he continued to live in seclusion although his seclusion was interrupted from time to time because of family affairs.[150] Eleven years elapsed between

143 Al-Subkiyy, Vol. VI, pp. 197–200.
144 Al-Ghazzaliyy, *Deliverance*, p. 138.
145 This "Rock" is located in the yard of Al-Aqsa mosque in Jerusalem. There is a mosque built on that location; it is called Dome of the Rock. Muslims believe that prophet Muhammad travelled from Makkah to Al-Aqsa mosque in a night journey. Al-Qur'an 17:1. From the position of that "Rock", prophet Muhammad [S.A.A.S.] ascended to heavens, before returning to Makkah; all this with the help of *Jibril* (Gabriel). This event is known as the *Isra'* and *Mi'raj*. In contemporary Islamic political thought, this event, among other things, is used to support the idea of the Islamization of Jerusalem. Hence it has a spiritual value that led Al-Ghazzaliyy to visit it in his quest for truth.
146 The Ka'bah is the house that has been built by prophet Ibrahim and his son prophet Isma'il (Ishmael).
147 Al-Ghazzaliyy, *Deliverance*, p. 138.
148 Lodge for the Sufis where they can have free room and board.
149 Al-Qarah Daghi, Vol. I, p. 122.
150 Al-Ghazzaliyy, *Deliverance*, p. 139.

25

Al-Ghazzāliyy's departure from Baghdad to the end of his life of isolation.[151]

Al-Ghazzāliyy's journeys had many consequences. He wrote *Iḥyā' Ulūm al-Dīn* and *Al-Risālah al-Qudsiyyah fī al-'Aqā'id*. In Hebron, he pledged three things: not to accept money from any Sultan, not to visit any of them, and never to debate any person. Al-Ghazzāliyy fulfilled these pledges. For money, he depended on his estate in Tus; its income provided him with his need.[152] Most importantly, he came to know "without doubt (*yaqīn*) that the Sufis are the (true) dwellers (*sālikūn*) on the path of Allah, their conduct is the best, and their method is the best method."[153]

Al-Ghazzāliyy ended his seclusion, in 499 A.H./1105 C.E., at a request from the vizier Fakhr Al-Mulk to teach at the Nizamiyyah of Nishapur.[154] He agreed to return to teaching after "consulting with masters of the hearts[155] who agreed that he could leave his seclusion."[156]   To indicate that there was no contradiction between leaving the Nizamiyyah of Baghdad and joining that of Nishapur, Al-Ghazzāliyy said that at the first he taught sciences that brought about fame, but at the latter, he taught knowledge that led to deserting such fame. He justified his move by quoting several verses from the Qur'an,[157] that made preaching, the job of the prophets, a priority, even if discomfort was the consequence. Furthermore, Al-Ghazzāliyy said that the timing of this coincides with the beginning of the fifth century A.H., which he considered a good omen.[158] According to a *hadīth*, prophet Muḥammad [S.A.A.S.] said that Allah sends to this nation (Muslim), at the head of each hundred years, someone to renew (*yujaddid*) its religion.[159]   Al-Ghazzāliyy believed that he was the renovator (*mujaddid*) of that century.

151   Al-Ghazzāliyy, *Deliverance*, p. 159
152   Al-Qarah Daghi, Vol. I, p. 118.
153   Al-Ghazzāliyy, *Deliverence*, p. 139.
154   Al-Qarah Daghi, Vol. I, p. 123.
155   Arabic=*arbab al-qulub*, by which Al-Ghazzāliyy meant the Sufis.
156   Al-Ghazzāliyy, *Deliverance*, p. 159.
157   Al-Qur'an 29:1, 6:24, and 36:11.
158   Al-Ghazzāliyy, *Deliverence*, pp. 158–159.
159   This *hadīth* was narrated by Abu Dawud, Al-Hakim, and Al-Bayhaqiyy.

The exact duration of Al-Ghazzāliyy's teaching at the Niẓamiyyah of Nishapur is not known. It is believed though that he left after the assassination of the vizier Fakhr al-Mulk Ibn Niẓām Al-Mulk, by a Batinite, on the day of 'Ashura', the 10th of Muharram, 500 A.H./1106 C.E.[160]

Subsequently Al-Ghazzāliyy returned to Tus, where he built a lodge for the Sufis (*khānaqāh*) and a school next to his house. He had about one hundred and fifty students. There were attempts, by vizier Aḥmad Ibn Niẓām Al-Mulk (d. 544 A.H./1149 C.E.), to convince Al-Ghazzāliyy to return to the Niẓamiyyah of Baghdad after the death of its teacher, Ilkiya Al-Harasiyy (d. 504 A.H./1110 C.E.), who was Al-Ghazzāliyy's colleague during the days of Al-Juwainiyy. Al-Ghazzāliyy declined the offer.[161]

1.3.4 Al-Ghazzāliyy and the Science of Hadīth

Al-Ghazzāliyy has been criticized for his weakness in the science of *hadith*. It appears that in that milieu jurists, like himself neglected to a certain degree this science because they considered the scholars of *hadith* below the level of jurists. Al-Rāziyy (d. 313 A.H./925 C.E.) said, "As for the people of *hadith*, they memorize the traditions of the Messenger of Allah, may Allah's peace and prayers be upon him, but they are not capable of reasoning and debate. Every time jurists present them with a question or a problem they fail to answer and get "puzzled"."[162] However, the position of the jurists led scholars of *hadīth* to eventually adopt a similar position.

Moreover, there were many scholars who considered devoting one's life to seeking *hadith* and narrating it a worldly activity unless the goal was for the sake of Allah. Abū Ṭālib Al-Makkiyy (d. 386 A.H./996 C.E.) narrated in *Qūt Al-Qulūb*, which Al-Ghazzāliyy mentioned in *Al-Munqidh min al-Dalāl* as one of the sources that shaped his thought about Sufism,[163] that Abū Sulaymān al-Dāraniyy

---

160 Badawi, p. 25.
161 Al-Qarah Daghi, Vol. I, pp. 134–136.
162 Muhammad Hasan Hitu, Introduction, *Al-Mankhul min Ta'liqat al-Usul*, by Al-Ghazzaliyy (Damascus: Dar al-Fikr, 1970) p. 4.
163 Al-Ghazzaliyy, *Al-Munqidh*, p. 131.

said: "a man who seeks *Hadith*, gets married or travels to find a job is a worldly person".[164] One could only add that if this was the position of the Sufis, the position of Al-Ghazzaliyy should not come as a surprise.

Though Al-Ghazzaliyy was an outstanding scholar in many fields of knowledge, ignoring the Science of *hadith* can not be justified because it led to the inclusion of unsound narrations in his writings. This science (*'ilm mustalah al-hadith*) had developed, as an independent field of study, a century before his birth. At least four major books on *'ilm mustalah al-hadith* were written during that time.[165] Moreover, in the last paragraph of his book *Qanun al-Ta'wil*, Al-Ghazzaliyy confessed that his knowledge in the science of

hadith was little.[166]

In addition, the large number of narrators (*muhaddithun*) indicates the importance of this field which in return explains the criticism to Al-Ghazzaliyy regarding his weakness in narrating *hadith*. According to Al-Khatib Al-Baghdadiyy (d. 463 A.H./1071 C.E.) in *Tarikh Baghdad*, Baghdad was the home of more than five thousand[167] scholars of hadith during the first five centuries A.H.[168]

Like all jurists and scholars of the time. Al-Ghazzaliyy was introduced to the science of *hadith* as part of his education. Yet it appears that he did not study this science as an independent subject. Critics of Al-Ghazzaliyy pointed

164 Abu Talib al-Makkiyy, *Qut al-Qulub* (Dar Sadir: No Place, N.D.) Vol. I, p. 135.

165 These were 1. *Al-Muhaddith al-Fasil bayn al-Rawi wa al-Wa'i* by Al-Ramharamziyy (d. 360 A.H./964 C.E.). 2. *Ma'rifat 'Ulum al-Hadith* by Al-Hakim al-Naysaburiyy (d. 405 A.H./1014 C.E.). 3. *Al-Mustakhraj 'ala Ma'rifat 'Ulum al-Hadith* by Abu Na'im Al-Asbahaniyy (d. 430 A.H./1038 C.E.). 4. *Al-Kifayah fi 'Ilm Al-Riwayah* by Al-Khatib al-Baghdadiyy (d. 463 A.H./1070 C.E.). See At-Tahhan, p.10

166 Al-Ghazzaliyy, *Ma'arij al-Quds fi Ma'rifat Al-Nafs* and *Qanun al-Ta'wil* (Cairo: Maktabat al-Jindi, 1968) p. 246.

167 The actual number of entries in *Tarikh Baghdad* were 7831 of which 32 were women scholars. It should be noted that Al-Baghdadiyy did not include the scholars who were still alive at the time which means that the number of scholars was still higher.

168 Munir-ud-din Ahmed, *Muslim Education and the Scholar's Social Status up to the 5th Century Muslim Era in the Light of "Tarikh Baghdad"*, Sami Al-Saqqar, trans. and ed. (Riyad: Dar al-Marrikh, 1981) p. 20.

to this issue as something that undermined his works, especially *Ihyā' 'Ulūm al-Dīn*, because it included "weak"[169] and forged (*mawdū'*) narrations. Al-Subkiyy wrote a whole chapter in which he classified all the forged narrations that were without proper *sanad* (chain of narrators), that appeared in the *Ihyā'*. Their number was more than nine hundred.[170] It must be noted that Al-Subkiyy, in his verification of these narrations, considered the *matn* (text) of the *hadīth* as it appeared in the *Ihyā'* as a whole; some of these narrations included parts that are sound. As a practical precaution, in order to be aware of the status of the hadith, one should use an edition of the *Ihyā'* that has Al-'Irāqiyy's (d. 806 A.H./1404 C.E.) verification (*takhrīj*) in the margin.[171]

The reporting of a "weak" narration, which has many levels, was not rejected altogether by all scholars of *hadīth*. Dr. Al-Tahhan states that there were scholars who allowed the use of such narration in preaching, but never in *'aqidah* (creed), or in jurisprudence. He added that Al-Thawriyy and Ahmad Ibn Hanbal were among those who allowed such usage. Moreover, this *hadīth* should be narrated in a "weakened" (*tad'īf*)[172] form.[173] The scholars who rejected the "weak" narrations altogether include Al-Bukhariyy, Muslim, Yahyā Ibn Ma'īn (d. 233 A.H./835 C.E.), Ibn Hazm (d. 456 A.H./1064 C.E.), and Al-Ghazzāliyy's student, the judge, Ibn Al-'Arabiyy. Among the contemporaries, Ahmad Muhammad Shākir, and Muhammad Nāsir Al-Dīn Al-Albaniyy held the latter position. In *al-Bā'ith al-Hathīth*, a commentary on

169 A *hadīth* is considered weak (*da'īf*) when it lacks any of the conditions that are necessary to render it *hasan* (good). An example of these conditions is that the chain of narrators (*sanad*) should not include any one who is not *'adl*, which means "trustworthy", in a regulated sense. A *hadīth* that is classified *hasan* is still one degree below the level of a narration that is *sahīh* (sound).

170 Al-Subkiyy, Vol. VI, pp. 287–388.

171 'Abd Al-Rahim Ibn Al-Husayn al-'Iraqiyy, *Al-Mughni 'an Haml al-Asfar fi al-Asfar fi Takhrij ma fi al-Ihya' min al-Akhbar.*

172 The *hadith* should not be introduced by the clause "prophet Muhammad said", which provides a false impression of a true statement. Reporting a "weak" narration should start with a form close to indirect speech in English grammer (e.g. it has been said /narrated/ reported that prophet Muhammad ... etc.).

173 Mahmud al-Tahhan, *Taysir Mustalah al-Hadith* (Riyad: Maktabat al-Ma'arif, 1981) p. 49.

Ibn Kathīr's *Ikhtisar 'Ulūm al-Hadīth*, Shākir explained the position of the early Muslim Scholars who permitted the use of "weak" narrations by stating that during the time of those scholars (eg. Ahmad Ibn Hanbal), narrations were divided into two basic categories, *sahīh* and *da'īf*. The category of *hasan*, which was advanced by Al-Tirmidhiyy (d. 279 A.H./880 C.E.), was not yet distinguished from sound narrations. It follows that those scholars were actually permitting the use of the *hasan* not the *da'īf*.[174]

It is important to mention that Abū Tālib Al-Makkiyy adopted the position of Ahmad Ibn Hanbal in narrating "weak" *hadīth*. The difference between him and Al-Ghazzāliyy is that he wrote a chapter in *Qūt al-Qulūb* in which he defended the use of a *hadīth da'īf*.[175]

Towards the end of his life, Al-Ghazzāliyy started studying the narrations of prophet Muhammad [S.A.A.S.] He read Al-Bukhāriyy's *Sahīh* and Muslim's *Sahīh*.[176] According to Abū Al-Qāsim Ibn 'Asākir, Al-Ghazzāliyy studied Al-Bukhāriyy's *Sahīh* at the hands of Abū Sahl Muhammad Ibn 'Abd Allāh Al-Hafsiyy. Also, Al-Sam'āniyy reports that Al-Ghazzāliyy studied Al-Bukhariyy's *Sahīh* and Muslim's *Sahīh* at the hands of Abū Al-Fityān 'Umar Ibn Abū Al-Hasan Al-Rawasiyy Al-Tūsiyy. Furthermore, 'Abd Al-Ghāfir Ibn Ismā'īl Al-Khātib Al-Farisiyy (d. 551 A.H./1156 C.E.), who visited Al-Ghazzāliyy several times before and after he changed his way of life to Sufism, narrated that it came to his knowledge that Al-Ghazzāliyy studied the *Sunan* of Abū Dawūd Al-Sijistaniyy at the hands of Abū Al-Fath Al-Hākimiyy Al-Tūsiyy.[177]

The importance of Al-Ghazzāliyy's study of the science of *hadīth* can be found in the question of whether he changed his method again. The answer to this question will be discussed later on in this book.[178]

174 Yusuf Al-Qardawiyy, *Kayfa Nata'amal ma' al-Sunnah al-Nabawiyyah* (Al-Mansurah: Dar al-Wafa', 1990) pp. 74–75.
175 Al-Makkiyy, Vol. I, pp. 176–178.
176 Al-Subkiyy, Vol. VI. p. 210.
177 *Ibid.*, Vol. IV, p. 212.
178 See page 224.

1.4 THE CREED OF AL-GHAZZĀLIYY

Creed (*'aqidah*) has been always a sensitive issue in Islamic circles. The only generation of Muslims that was spared differences in opinion in this respect was the companions (*ṣaḥābah*) of the prophet [S.A.A.S.][179] They were considered the ancestors (*salaf*) of the Muslims, and their creed was accepted by virtually every Muslim.[180] Thus, the creed of those ancestors (*'aqīdah salafiyyah*) became a reference point when creed was in question. To indicate that there was no problem with creed during the first generation of Muslims, Al-Ghazzāliyy asserted in *Al-Iqtisād fī Al-I'tiqād* that "the companions of the prophet [S.A.A.S.] did not discuss, teach or write about creed".[181] Furthermore, Al-Ghazzāliyy added that the companions were preoccupied with jurisprudence.[182]

In addition, Al-Maqriziyy stated in his *Khitat* that if any Arab has asked prophet Muhammad [S.A.A.S.] about the divine attributes, it should have been narrated in the books of *hadīth.* Furthermore, Al-Maqriziyy added that:

"If anyone looks carefully in the books of *hadīth* and the statements about the companions (*al-āthār al-salafiyyah*) he would know that there were neither sound nor weak *hadīths* that a companion of the prophet [S.A.A.S.] ever asked him about the meaning of anything that Allah [S.W.T.] has described himself with in the Qur'an, despite the fact that the companions were numerous."[183]

There were many examples before and after the time of

179   Ibn Al-Qaiyyim, *Ijtima' al-Juyush al-Islamiyyah,* 'Awwad 'Abdullah Al-Mu'attaq, ed. (Riyad: Matabi' Al-Farazdaq Al-Tijariyyah, 1988) pp. 118–131.

180   By Muslims here I refer to what became known as "*ahl al-sunnah*" (people of the sunnah). Also, they are known as "*ahl al-sunnah wa al-jama'ah*" (people of the sunnah and the group). As for the sects and groups that were rooted in Islam and had a different position than that of the above, Al-Baghdadiyy listed seventy major branches of them in an apparent attempt to relate this number to a narration of prophet Muhammad in which he professed that his people will be divided into seventy branches.

181   Al-Ghazzaliyy, *Al-Iqtisad fi al-I'tiqad* (Cairo: Maktabat al-Jindi, 1972) p. 16.

182   Al-Ghazzaliyy, *Al-Iqtisad,* p. 20.

183   Muhammad Abu Zahrah, *Tarikh al-Madhahib al-Islamiyyah* (Cairo: Dar al-Fikr al-'Arabiyy, n.d.) p. 98.

Al-Ghazzāliyy that reflect the way different schools (e.g. *al-Ashā'irah*)[184] and scholars (e.g. Ibn Taymiyyah), were treated whenever there was any doubt or claims regarding their creed, even if these claims were politically motivated.

I have chosen Ibn Taymiyyah, a leader of the Hanbalite school of jurisprudence who flourished two centuries after Al-Ghazzāliyy and was one of his critics, as an example. He was considered the leader of the *Salafiyyah* school, yet he was accused of incorporating anthropomorphic elements into his *'Aqīdah Wāsitiyyah*. Two councils were convened to verify the claims about his book. In the first one, which was held in Damascus, he was acquitted of the charges. In the second, which took place in Cairo, he was unjustly convicted and sentenced to prison for an indefinite period.[185]

As discussed above,[186] the Ashā'irites, who were almost exclusively Shafi'ites, were denied the right to attend congregational and Friday prayers because of the way they presented the beautiful names (*al-asmā' al-ḥusnā*) of Allah. Out of more than ninety nine names,[187] Al-Ghazzāliyy followed the footsteps of the Ashā'irites and used their method of *Kālam* (theological argumentation).[188] It should be noted that Al-Ash'ariyy himself and Al-Baqillāniyy (d. 403 A.H./ 1112 C.E.) followed the path of the *salaf* in the way they understood Divine attributes. It was the later Ashā'irites

---

184   Followers of Al-Ash'ariyy, Abu al-Hasan 'Ali Ibn Isma'il (260–324

     A.H./873-935 C.E.). He was a Mu'tazilite but returned to the method of the *salaf* at later stage in his life and renounced the Mu'tazilites.
185   Merlin Swarz, "A seventh-century (A.H.) Sunni creed: The 'Aqidah Wasitiya of Ibn Taymiya," *Humaniora Islamica* 1 (1973):102.
186   See page 17.
187   It is a common mistake to restrict the names of Allah to ninety nine names. In fact, there are more than the above mentioned number. Although they are called "names" (*asma'*) as in al-Qur'an, Sura *al-A'raf* 7:180, they are also called attributes (*sifat*) (i.e. the Merciful). In discussing the verses in the al-Qur'an that include such "attributes", one refer to these verses as *ayat al-sifat*.
188   Al-Ghazzaliyy discussed the following subject matters: life and omnipotence (*al-hayah wa al-qudrah*), knowledge (*al-'ilm*), will (*al-iradah*), hearing and sight (*al-sam' wa al-basar*), and speech (*kalam*). Al-Ghazzaliyy, "Qawa'id al-'Aqa'id fi al-Tawhid" *Majmu'at Rasa'il al-Imam Al-Ghazzaliyy* (Beirut: Dar al-Kutub al-'Ilmiyyah, 1986) Vol. II, pp. 124–127.

who chose to discuss the subject matter of a few attributes as representative for their importance, and they adopted the method of metaphorical interpretation (*ta'wil*) in order to avoid questions of anthropomorphism (*tajsim*). Those who belong to the latter include Al-Ghazzāliyy and Al-Rāziyy. (d. 606 A.H./1209 C.E.)[189]

The Ashā'irites got their method from their rivals, the theologians (*al-Mutakallimūn*). This method, which was intended to defend Islamic Shari'ah against philosophy in the first place, contained several philosophical terms such as the word "essence" (*jawhar*) and "accident" (*'ard*). It is the use of such philosophical words that upset traditional scholars before and after the time of Al-Ghazzāliyy. His contemporary, Ibn 'Aqīl, head of the Hanbalite school at the time, said about this subject:

> "I assure (you) that the companions (of the Prophet S.A.A.S.) died without knowing the (terms) "essence" and "accident". So, if you would like to be like them you can, but if you think that the method of *al-Mutakallimūn* is better than the method of Abū Bakr and 'Umar,[190] this would be the worst of your opinions."[191]

Based on his use of the above mentioned method, Al-Ghazzāliyy was "accused" of being an Ash'ārite by the Salafiyyah school.[192] There were many Muslim scholars who considered him so; they have used neutral language in classifying him as an Ash'arite. Among those we find the medieval scholars Al-Subkiyy and Al-Zubaydiyy who stated that to judge what someone believes belongs to Allah. He also added that after reviewing most of the works of Al-Ghazzāliyy and the books of his contemporaries who saw him, he reached the conclusion that Al-Ghazzāliyy "was most probably an Ash'ārite".[193] In addition, among the contemporaries we find that Sulaymān Dunya is very supportive

189   Ibn al-Qaiyyim, p. 120.
190   Abu Bakr, 'Abdullah Ibn abu Quhafah, the first Caliph, and 'Umar Ibn Al-Khattab, the second Caliph.
191   Ibn Al-Jawziyy, *Talbis Iblis* (Beirut: Dar al-Kutub al-'Ilmiyyah, 1949) p. 85.
192   Dimashqiyyah, p. 89.
193   Al-Zubaydiyy, p. 30.

of the idea that Al-Ghazzāliyy was an Asha'irite. In fact, Dunya said that Al-Ghazzāliyy advocated Asha'irism in *Al-Iqtiṣād fī al-I'tiqād.*[194]

A rather different opinion came from a medieval Muslim scholar. This time from Ibn Rushd (Averroes) (d. 595 A.H./ 1198 C.E.) the great critic of Al-Ghazzāliyy. Regarding the Asha'irism of Al-Ghazzāliyy Ibn Rushd stated in *Fasl al-Maqal fima Bayn al-Ḥikmah wa al-Sharī'ah min Ittiṣal* that Al-Ghazzāliyy maintained a relative position and that he did not commit himself to any one school and that "he was an Asha'irite with the Asha'irites, a Sufi with the Sufis and a philosopher with the philosophers". Among the contemporaries a similar position is held by Dimashqiyyah who says that Al-Ghazzāliyy was an Ash'āirite only when he addressed the general public (*al-'awām*).[195]

A strong position against the Ash'arism of Al-Ghazzāliyy was advanced by George Makdisi. In his article "The Non-Ash'arite Shāfi'ism Of Ghazzāliyy,"[196] Makdisi states that Al-Ghazzāliyy was not an Ash'arite for a number of reasons. The first one was that Al-Ghazzāliyy never declared himself an Ash'ārite. Yet this argument has the same weight as one saying that Al-Ghazzāliyy never denied being an Ash'arite. The second argument was based on the idea that the deed of the Nizamiyyah college insisted in having the Shafi'ite *Uṣūl al-Fiqh* as the official position that should be taught. According to Makdisi, Al-Shāfi'iyy founded this method against the method of *Kalām.* Makdisi also adds that the professors of the Nizamiyyah distanced themselves from the Ash'arites. As for his position towards Al-Ghazzāliyy's *al-Iqtiṣād fī al-I'tiqād*, Makdisi says, after confirming that Al-Ghazzāliyy followed the Ash'arite method in writing this book, that "this work does not represent Ghazzāliyy's own inner convictions".[197]

In my opinion, the reality about Al-Ghazzāliyy's position regarding the Ash'arite method can be deduced from the

194 Dimashqiyyah, p. 94.
195 Dimashqiyyah, pp. 94–98.
196 George Makdisi, "The Non Ash'arite Shafi'ism Of Ghazzali," *Reveu des Etudes Islamiques* 54 (1986) pp. 239–257.
197 Makdisi, pp. 244–249.

34

"appearances" which for us are restricted to his works, since we do not have access to his "inner convictions". Whether Al-Ghazzāliyy was or was not an Ash'arite, he certainly used that methodology. It appears that he used the Ash'arite methodology or *Kalām*, but not blindly. In his introduction to *Faisal al-Tafriqah bayn al-Islām wa al-Zandaqah*, Al-Ghazzāliyy criticized those Ash'ārites who thought that deviating from the method of Al-Ash'āriyy, no matter how little, was heretical.[198] It is rather important to know that Al-Ghazzāliyy referred to Al-Ash'ariyy in his earlier writings as "our teacher" (*shaykhunā*) which could be an important factor in determining the relationship between the two especially if we know that on the same page where Al-Ghazzāliyy quotes Al-Ash'ariyy he quotes another scholar without referring to him as "*shaykhunā*".[199] Towards the end of his life, Al-Ghazzāliyy wrote *Iljam Al-'Awām 'an 'Ilm al-Kalām* in which he criticized the method of the Ash'arites and *Kalām*. In addition there are numerous places in *The Revival of Islamic Sciences* where he criticized *Kalām*. In the book of knowledge (*kitāb al-'ilm*), which is the first of forty chapters of the *Ihyā'*, not only Al-Ghazzāliyy criticized *kalām* but he also listed it along with unacceptable innovations (*bida'*) of which children who were reaching maturity should be protected.[200]

Al-Ghazzāliyy's position on many other controversial subjects (e.g., logic) will be addressed as they unfold in this book. The idea that Al-Ghazzāliyy's theory of knowledge has developed throughout his life, shall provide an explanation, and not necessarily a defence, to many of the raised questions. The following chapters will discuss this idea.

198   Ibn Al-Jawziyy, *Talbis Iblis* (Beirut: Dar al-Kutub al-'Ilmiyyah, 1949) p. 85.
199   Al-Ghazzāliyy, *Al-Mankhul*, p. 36.
200   Al-Ghazzāliyy, *Ihya'*, Vol. I, p. 15.

Chapter TWO

AL-GHAZZĀLIYY'S THEORY OF KNOWLEDGE AS A STUDENT (465–478 A.H./1072–1085 C.E.)

This chapter deals with Al-Ghazzāliyy's writings as a student and how these writings could be related to his epistemological development during the above mentioned years which ended with the death of his most important teacher Al-Juwainiyy in 478 A.H./1085 C.E. During these years Al-Ghazzāliyy wrote two major books; *Al-Ta'līqah fī Furū' al-Madhhab* (Notes on the Branches of the (Shāfi'īte) School of Jurisprudence) and *Al-Mankhūl min Ta'līqat al-Uṣūl* (The Sifted from the Notes on the Fundamentals of Jurisprudence).[1] In addition, it deals with Al-Ghazzāliyy's later work *Al-Munqidh min al-Dalāl*(Deliverance from Error) in which he projected in clear terms his thoughts knowledge during the same period.

2.1 *AL-TA'LĪQAH*

Al-Ghazzāliyy wrote his first book, *Al-Ta'līqah*, when he travelled to Jurjan to study at the hands of Abū-Nasr Al-Ismā'īliyy. It seems that this book was simply a collection of notes on the lectures that he attended during the above mentioned journey.[2] *Al-Ta'līqah* was lost and our knowledge

---

1 The word *Ta'līqah* is translated by J.G. Hava, S.J. as 'marginal notes' or as 'appendix of a book': *Al-Fara'id al-Durriyyah* (Beirut: Dar Al-Mashriq, 1972) p. 495. I think that Al-Ghazzaliyy intended this word, which was used in its singular form *'Ta'līqah'* in the title of the first book and in its plural form *'Ta'līqat'* in the second, to indicate that these notes were taken from the lectures of his teacher (i.e Al-Isma'iliyy) when he was a student.
2 Al-Subkiyy, Vol. IV, p. 195.

of it is restricted to secondary sources. These sources provide a simple historical account of the book without dealing with its contents except simply mentioning that it was about *fiqh* according to the Shāfi'īte school of jurisprudence.[3]

2.2 *AL-MANKHŪL*: THE QUESTION OF AUTHENTICITY

The only surviving book that could have been written during this period was *Al-Mankhūl min Ta'līqāt al-Usūl*. At least one orientalist and one medieval Muslim scholar doubted that *Al-Mankhūl* was written by Al-Ghazzāliyy. The former, Brockelmann, claimed in his *Geschichte der Arabischen Litteratur* that *Al-Mankhūl* was written by one of Al-Ghazzāliyy's students without specifying the reason that led him to such claim. The latter was Ibn Ḥajar Al-Haytamiyy (d. 973 A.H./1565 C.E.) who said in his book *Al-Khayrāt Al-Ḥisān Fī Manāqib Al-Nu'mān* that *Al-Mankhūl* could not have been written by Al-Ghazzāliyy because it included harsh criticism of Abū Ḥanīfah while Al-Ghazzāliyy praised him in *Iḥyā' 'Ulūm al-Dīn*. Yet, it seems that Ibn Ḥajar Al-Haytamiyy was not sure of his position because he narrated a defense of Al-Ghazzāliyy by Ḥanifites who explained that these insults were committed by Al-Ghazzāliyy when he was a student and thus forgivable.[4] One could only add, as discussed in the previous chapter, that Al-Ghazzāliyy denied insulting the person of Abū Ḥanīfah and declared all such insults as forged additions to his book.[5] The possibility of altering the works of any scholar at the time was enormous due to the fact that these works were copied manually.

The authenticity of *al-Mankhūl* could be proven beyond doubt from the cross-references that Al-Ghazzāliyy made to *Al-Mankhūl* in his book *Al-Mustaṣfā*, which he wrote after returning to teaching at the Nizamiyyah of Nishapur, at the request of some students of jurisprudence who wanted him to write a book on the fundamentals of jurisprudence (*usūl al-fiqh*) that would include "more details than *Al-*

3 Al-Zubaydiyy, p. 41.
4 Badawi, pp. 7–9.
5 Muhammad Hasan Hitu, *Introduction, Al-Mankhul min Ta'liqat al-Usul*, by Al-Ghazzaliyy (Damascus: Dar al-Fikr, 1970) pp. 31–33.

38

Mankhūl which is concise and brief."[6]

There remains the question whether *al-Mankhūl* was written before or after the death Al-Juwainiyy. The historiographers (e.g. Al-Subkiyy) maintained that Al-Ghazzāliyy wrote this book during the life of his teacher.[7] On the other hand, there were those who claimed that Al-Ghazzāliyy used to write a supplication (*du'ā'*) right after the name of Al-Juwainiyy.[8] This supplication, *rahimahu Allāh* (i.e. may Allah be merciful to him) usually indicates that the person who's name was mentioned is deceased. The contradiction between those two positions could be resolved by pointing to the concluding paragraph of *Al-Mankhūl* in which Al-Ghazzāliyy stated that "this is the completion of *Al-Mankhūl min Ta'līqat al-Uṣūl* after omitting the extras." In addition, Al-Ghazzāliyy said that he restricted (himself) to whatever Al-Juwainiyy - may Allah be merciful to him - has mentioned in his lectures."[9] It is apparent that at least Al-Ghazzāliyy wrote the original text of this book when he attended the lectures of Al-Juwainiyy. The fact that he omitted the "extras" might indicate that he wrote a modified version of this book after the death of his teacher which explains the presence of the above mentioned supplications in the text of *Al-Mankhūl.*

It should also be noted that Al-Ghazzāliyy's later work in *usūl al-fiqh* (i.e. *Al-Mustasfā*) reflects a different approach to the fundamentals of jurisprudence which exemplified the originality of Al-Ghazzāliyy's writings after the death of Al-Juwainiyy. Accordingly, I would argue that *Al-Mankhūl* does not fit into the works of the later Al-Ghazzāliyy that portrayed an independent scholar and thus it could have been written only at an earlier stage (i.e. as a student).

Moreover, the above position towards Abū Ḥanīfah was explained in another way. In the introduction to a critical edition of *al-Mankhūl*, Hito showed that Al-Ghazzāliyy was simply reiterating the position of Al-Juwainiyy, his teacher, in *Mughīth Al-Khalq Fī Tarjīh Al-Qawl*

---

6 Al-Ghazzaliyy, *Al-Mustasfa min 'Ilm al-Usul* (Bulaq: Al-Matba'ah al-Amiriyyah, 1322 A.H.) Vol. I, p.4.
7 Al-Subkiyy, Vol. IV, p. 225.
8 Hitu, p. 35.
9 Al-Ghazzaliyy, *Al-Mankhul*, p. 504.

Al-Haqq[10] in which he ranked the Shāfi'ite school of jurisprudence higher than that of Abū Ḥanīfah. Al-Ghazzāliyy wrote a section at the end of *al-Mankhūl* in which he praised Al-Shāfi'iyy and criticized other jurists including Abū Ḥanīfah.[11] Also, many books (eg. Al-Baghdadiyy's *Tārīkh Baghdād*) which were written during that period included harsh critfcism of Abu Ḥanīfah and yet no one denied that these books belonged to their authors.[12]

2.2.1 *Uṣūl al-Fiqh*

The fundamentals of jurisprudence (*uṣūl al-fiqh*), the subject matter of *Al-Mankhūl*, deals with the methodology by which the different questions of jurisprudence are answered. Historically, *uṣūl al-fiqh* was the outcome of a struggle between the traditionalists (*Ahl Al-Hadīth*) who's methodology was based on a more or less literal interpretations of the texts of the Shari'ah, and the Hanafite jurists who allowed reasoning to play a more decisive role in determining the laws of the Shari'ah. The latter became known as the rationalists (*Ahl al-Ra'y*). Although tension ran high between both schools, the *Ahl Al-Ḥadīth* agreed with *Ahl Al-Ra'y* on the necessity of having recourse to reason if the texts of the Shari'ah contained no specific reference to whatever case they had.[13] The dispute between these two schools was not resolved until Al-Shāfi'iyy wrote *Al-Risālah* in which he reconciled the two positions by establishing the methodology that later on became known as *uṣūl al-fiqh*.[14] It is a commonly accepted fact that all works in *uṣūl al-fiqh* written after *al-Risālah* were dependent on it.

Following Al-Shāfi'iyy's lead there were many books written in this field. Of these, Imam Al-Juwainiyy wrote *Al-*

---

10 It should be noted that the originality of this book was doubted.

Although it was listed by Ibn Khallikan as one of Al-Juwainiyy's books, it was not listed by Ibn Kathir among the books of Al-Juwainiyy. Ibn Kathir, Vol. XII, p. 128.

11 Hitu, p. 32.

12 Hitu, p. 32.

13 Taha Jabir Al-'Alwani, *Usul al-Fiqh al-Islami*, edrs. Yusuf Talal De Lorenzo and A.S. Al-Shaikh-Ali (Herndon: The International Institute of Islamic Thought, 1990) p. 31.

14 Hitu, pp. 3–5.

40

Burhān and Al-Ghazzāliyy wrote four books: *Al-Mankhūl, Tahdhib al-Uṣūl* (which is lost), *Shifā' al-Ghalil fī Bayān Masālik al-Ta'lil*, and *al-Mustaṣfā.*[15]

In *al-Mankhūl*, Al-Ghazzāliyy ranked jurisprudence as the most important field of knowledge. Yet, he stated that jurisprudence was a branch (*far*) that could not be totally apprehended without understanding and mastering the fundamental (*aṣl*).[16] It is a clear message that promoted the study of *uṣūl al-fiqh* for those who were interested in studying jurisprudence. In the introduction of *Al-Mankhūl*, Al-Ghazzāliyy reduced the sources of knowledge to those declared to be the fundamentals of jurisprudence according to the school he belonged to (i.e. Shāfi'īte). Although all schools list the Al-Qur'an, the Sunnah and the consensus of the companions of the Prophet s.a.w. as the basic sources for knowledge of the Shari'ah, these schools differed in their position regarding the role of *Ijtihād*. Similiar to the position of Al-Juwainiyy, Al-Ghazzāliyy did not consider criteria that were derived from *Ijtihād* as peremptory (*qaṭ'iyy*) and thus could not be considered as part of the fundamentals of jurisprudence; he would still use such criteria in verifying the validity of certain arguments.[17]

In the introduction of *Al-Mankhūl*, Al-Ghazzāliyy stated that the fundamentals of jurisprudence aimed at knowing the peremptory proofs regarding the requirements of the Shari'ah. In addition he defined the sources of which the predictions (*muqaddamat*) of the fundamentals of jurisprudence were derived as *'Ilm al-Kalām* (scholastic theology),[18] *Fiqh* (jurisprudence) and language,[19] It should be noted that these sources are exactly the same as those of

---

15 Hitu, pp. 8–9.
16 Al-Ghazzaliyy, *Al-Mankhul*, p. 3.
17 *Ibid.*, pp. 4–5.
18 *'Ilm al-Kalam*, literally the science of talk or speech, but here it refers to scholastic theology. *Ilm al-Kalam* is the method originally used in *tawhid* (theology) by Abu Hasan Al-Ash'ariyy. He was followed by his student Ibn Mujahid who in turn was followed by Al-Baqillaniyy and after him by Imam Al-Haramayn Al-Juwainiyy before it reached Al-Ghazzaliyy. Scholars who followed this method became known as *Mutakallimun* (philosopher-theologians). The inclusion of Aristotelian logic in this method led to sharp criticism and rejection from scholars who belonged to different schools. Rejection of logic and labeling it *haram* (prohibited) is still advocated by many.
19 Al-Ghazzaliyy, *Al-Mankhul*, pp. 3–4.

41

his teacher Al-Juwainiyy in his book *al-Burhān.*[20]

The importance of *'Ilm al-Kalām* in the development in Al-Ghazzāliyy's thought can be traced to one of its sources: Aristotelian logic. Al-Ghazzāliyy incorporated logic as a distinct subject in his writings. He renamed many Aristotelian logical categories; it seems that he did so in order to overcome the rejection of logic prevailing at the time. In addition, he attempted to show that these logical categories could be derived from the al-Qur'an and the Sunnah.[21] A more detailed discussion of Al-Ghazzāliyy's confirmed contribution to logic and its inclusion in *Usūl al-Fiqh* will follow when I discuss *Al-Mustasfā min 'Ilm al-Usūl.*[22]

2.2.2 *Al-Qiyās (analogical reasoning)*

On the question of *qiyās* (analogical reasoning), al-Ghazzāliyy stated that the companions of the Prophet [S.A.A.S.] used analogical reasoning without hesitation in solving problems when there is no direct text in the Qur'an and the Sunnah to address them.[23] The context in which Al-Ghazzāliyy presented his arguments to support his position regarding analogical reasoning indicates that he was on the defensive. It is a clear sign that there were those who opposed the use of *qiyās* in the Shari'ah. In fact, Al-Ghazzāliyy discussed the position of the various schools of jurisprudence and sects towards *qiyās.*

In the chapter on analogical reasoning (*kitāb al-qiyās*),

---

20 Al-'Alwani, p. 49.
21 One famous example that Al-Ghazzaliyy cited in his book was the Hadith in which prophet Muhammad [S.A.A.S.] asked Mu'adh Ibn Jabal when he sent him to Yemen, "What are you going to use for judgement? He answered, "The book of Allah." He (the prophet) said, "What if you do not find (what you are looking for)"? He answered, "Then by the Sunnah of Allah's messenger-May Allah's peace and prayers be upon him." Then he said, "What if you do not find (what you are looking for)"? He (Mu'adh) said, "I will use my opinion (*ajtahidu ra'yiy)*". He (the prophet) said, "Praise Allah who guided the messenger of the messenger of Allah." This Hadith was narrated by Ahmad, Abu-Dawud and Al-Tirmidhiyy who stated that the chain of narrators of this Hadith is incomplete. In addition, Al-Bukhariyy said that this Hadith is not sound, but nevertheless there were those who considered it sound. Al-Ghazzaliyy, *Al-Mankhul,* p. 331.
22 See this discussion on page 145.
23 Al-Ghazzaliyy, *Al-Mankhul,* p. 328–332.

Al-Ghazzāliyy stated that *qiyās* was divided into purely rational (*'aqliyy*) and into that which was deduced from the Qur'an and the Sunnah (*shar'iyy*).[24] Most of the scholars of jurisprudence accepted both forms of *qiyās*. The Ḥanbalite school of jurisprudence rejected the *'aqliyy* and accepted the *shar'iyy*. On the other hand, a school like the Dāwūdiyyah[25] rejected the *qiyās shar'iyy* in favour of the *qiyās 'aqliyy*. Moreover, Al-Ghazzāliyy discussed the position of several sects including Al-Mu'tazilah which its leaders either rejected the *qiyās shar'iyy* totally or most of it.[26] In addition, one should note that the Zahirites were the only school of jurisprudence which rejected *qiyās*. A good example of this rejection can be seen in the writings of Ibn Ḥazm.

2.2.3 Al-Ghazzāliyy's Position on Science and Reason in *Al-Mankhūl*

Al-Ghazzāliyy devoted a chapter in *Al-Mankhūl* to a discussion of the nature of the sciences (*al-Kalām fī Ḥaqā'iq al-'Ulūm*). It should be noted that Al-Ghazzāliyy's use of the word "sciences" is general and not restricted to the natural or physical sciences; it covers all subjects of knowledge including those of the Shari'ah. He started this chapter by criticizing the position of the Sophists (*Ṣūfistā'iyyah*) regarding knowledge because "they denied the possibility of knowing things in themselves". Al-Ghazzāliyy added that "one should not debate them because they denied sensibles (*al-mahsūsāt*)".[27] What Al-Ghazzāliyy meant was that there was no point in starting a debate with them because they have rejected the senses which include hearing without which there could be no debate in the first place.

---

24 Al-Ghazzaliyy, *Al-Mankhul*, p. 324.
25 The Dawudiyyah, also known as Al-Zahiriyyah, followers of Dawud Ibn 'Ali Ibn Khalaf (d. 270 A.H./883 C.E.) who established a school of jurisprudence that only accepted the literal meaning of the Qur'an and the Sunnah.
26 Al-Nazzam (d. 221 A.H./836 A.D.) rejected *qiyas shar'iyy* totally. This position of al-Nazzam is similar to the position of most of Al-Khawarij and most Al-Rawafid. Abu Hashim Al-Jubba'iyy rejected most of *qiyas shar'iyy*. Al-Ghazzaliyy, *Al-Mankhul*, pp. 324–326.
27 Al-Ghazzaliyy, *Al-Mankhul*, pp. 34–35.

On the definition of science ('ilm), Al-Ghazzāliyy listed six different definitions including those of four famous scholars along with his arguments which undermined them all. Al-Ghazzāliyy had a peculiar position towards science: he thought that "science cannot be defined" (*inna al-'ilma la ḥadda lah*). Moreover, he explained that science could be known and that "our inability to define (science) does not indicate our ignorance about the same science". To explain his point, Al-Ghazzāliyy said that it would be similar to his being asked to define Musk perfume; while knowing what it is,   he would not be able to do so (i.e. provide a definition [*ḥadd*] of it). In addition, he maintained that science could be distinguished in classification from opinion (*ẓann*) and skepticism (*shakk*).[29]

Al-Ghazzāliyy divided the sciences or knowledge[30] into eternal (*qadīm*) and accidental (*ḥadīth*). Eternal knowledge is that of Allah (i.e. knowledge which Allah possesses). This knowledge has no beginning and it encompasses all information.[31] Furthermore, "it cannot be described neither as acquired nor as necessary (*walā yusaf bikawnihi kas biyyan walā ḍaruriyyan*)".[32] Al-Ghazzāliyy divided accidental knowledge into immediate (*hajmiyy*)[33] and theoretical (*naẓāriyy*). The *hajmiyy* is that knowledge which one has to (*yaḍtarru*) know with the beginning of reason (*bi awwal al-'aql*), like knowing the existence of the self (*wujūd al-dhat*), pains and pleasures. On the other hand, theoretical knowledge, which is acquired, is the result of sound thinking (*an-naẓar al-ṣaḥiḥ*).[34]

28   They are: Abu Al-Hasan Al-Ash'ariyy, Abu Al-Qasim Al-Iskafiyy (d. 452

A.H./1060 C.E.) who was one of Imam Al-Haramayn's teachers, Ibn Fawrak (d. 406 A.H./1015 C.E.) and Al-Baqillaniyy whom Al-Ghazzaliyy refer to as the Judge. Al-Ghazzaliyy, *Al-Mankhul*, pp. 36–39.

29   Al-Ghazzaliyy, *Al-Mankhul*, p. 40.

30   Al-Ghazzaliyy used science ('ilm) and knowledge (*ma'rifah*) to indicate the same concept. Al-Ghazzaliyy, *Al-Mankhul*, p. 38.

31   The scope of Allah's knowledge, whether it encompasses all knowledge including details or not, led Al-Ghazzaliyy to dispute the position of philosophers like Al-Farabi and Ibn Sina who claimed that Allah's knowledge did not comprise details (*juz'iyyat*) and eventually declared their position as sacrilegious.

32   Al-Ghazzaliyy, *Al-Mankhul*, p. 42.

33   The root of this word is *hajama* which literally means "came about or attacked suddenly". It seems that Al-Ghazzaliyy here used it to indicate that this kind of knowledge takes place quickly.

44

On the essence of reason (*māhiyyat al-'aql*), Al-Ghazzāliyy listed the definitions of jurists, Sufis and philosophers; he was not critical regarding all of them. Al-Bāqillaniyy said that the essence of reason is knowing what is possible and what is not. Al-Ghāzzaliyy rejected this definition saying that someone who was unaware of the possible and the impossible could still be rational (*'āqil*). In addition, Al-Harith Al-Muhāsibiyy, said that reason was an instinct (*gharīzah*). This definition was mentioned without any comment. Moreover, Al-Ghazzāliyy listed what he called the philosophers' definition without any comment.[35] He said that the philosophers defined reason as the state in which the brain is prepared for the emanation (*fayd*)[36] of the soul. The most important definition here is that of Al-Ghazzāliyy himself. He defined reason as "the qualification which enables the qualified (person) to perceive knowledge and to think about the cognizable".[37]

Al-Ghazzāliyy had a peculiar classification of knowledge. The rank of each aspect of knowledge depended on necessity (*darūrah*) and intuition (*badīha*): the closest to necessity and intuition would be the the clearest and thus ranked first. The following are Al-Ghazzāliyy's ten levels of knowledge in the order they appear in *Al-Mankhūl*

1. The knowledge of the existence of the self (*al-'ilm bi wujūd al-dhat*), pain and pleasure.

2. Knowing the impossibility of the agreement of contradictions.

---

34 Al-Ghazzaliyy, *Al-Mankhul*, pp. 42–43.

35 Al-Ghazzaliyy's usage of the term "philosophers" comprises Greek and Muslim philosophers such as Ibn Sina and Al-Farabi. Al-Ghazzaliyy provided a more detailed account of the philosophers in *Tahafut Al-Falasifa* (The Destruction of the Philosophers) and *Al-Munqidh Min Al-Dalal.*

36 Emanation (*fayd*) is a neo-Platonic idea that was entertained by various Muslim philosophers and especially by al-Farabi. The fact that Al-Ghazzaliyy left this notion without comment could be explained by stating that Al-Ghazzaliyy studied philosophy on his own when he was in Baghdad, long after he wrote *Al-Mankhul.* One should be aware of the use of another word to indicate emanation which is *sudūr.*

37 Al-Ghazzāliyy, *Al-Mankhul*, pp. 44–45.

3. Knowing the sensibles (*al-maḥsūsāt*).

4. The knowledge that results from more than one source reporting the same news (*akhbār al-tawātur*).

5. Understanding a message (*khiṭāb*), and the ability to perceive conditions that indicate shyness, anger and fear.

6. Knowledge of crafts and industries.

7. Knowledge of theories (*naẓāriyyāt*).

8. Knowing of the mission of the messengers (of Allah).[38]

9. Knowledge of miracles.

10. Knowledge that results from narrations (*sam'iyyāt*) which is "similar to imitation (*taqlīd*)."[39]

Analyzing the above list, one can see that Al-Ghazzāliyy's approach was developmental. He started with the clearest and most necessary notion of knowledge and proceeded in the direction of the more complex. The first level was the realization of the existence of the self which he associated with pain and pleasure. The second level of knowledge was logical necessities. In listing the first two levels of knowledge before the senses, Al-Ghazzāliyy indicated that these two levels were innate. However, in his *Al-Munqidh min al-Dalāl*, the first two notions were not mentioned. Instead, the senses were ranked first.[40] This shows that Al-Ghazzāliyy was refining his sources of knowledge due to his continued reflection and interest in epistemology. The changes in themselves are clear indications of the developmental aspect of his

---

38 It should be noted that the eighth level indicates knowledge of the necessity of having messengers and thus differs from the fourth level which is concerned with knowledge that is transmitted from those messengers through multiple chains of narrators.
39 Al-Ghazzaliyy, *Al-Mankhul*, pp. 46–48.
40 Al-Ghazzaliyy, *Al-Munqidh*, p. 144.

46

theory of knowledge.

According to Al-Ghazzāliyy, the fourth source of knowledge, *akhbār al-tawātur*, was a result of a logical necessity and a conventional agreement. The logical necessity came from the notion that it is unlikely for a large number of independent narrators of the same news (i.e. hadith) to lie about it.[41] In the language of the scholars of Hadith, the above idea is called "the impossibility of (having) a conspiracy to lie" (*istiḥālat al-tawātu' 'ala al-kadhib*). The conventional aspect came in answer to the following question: how many narrators were needed in order to render a narration as *mutawātir*?[42] The importance of this source of knowledge could be realized from the fact that Muslim scholars regarded a *hadīth* which was considered *mutawātir* on the same level as the Qur'an in terms of certitude.

The fifth kind of knowledge was analytical. Al-Ghazzāliyy was not the only one to talk about analytical knowledge that resulted from written texts; he also talked about analytical knowledge that could be derived from facial expressions. While he did not provide examples of the former, he listed shyness, anger and fear as examples of the latter. The sixth and seventh level could be described as the practical and theoretical knowledge respectively.[43]

The last three kinds of knowledge, which included knowing the mission of the prophets, miracles and knowledge that was based on authority (*taqlīd*), were all directly related to religion. *Taqlīd* differs from *khabar al-tawātur* in the methodology one adopts in verifying the transmitted knowledge; in the case of *taqlīd* there is an uncritical acceptance of knowledge (i.e. hadith), while in *khabar al-tawātur* one is critical about the methodology of transmitting the hadith. In addition, *taqlīd* or knowledge of miracles could be related to *khabar al-āhad* where the number of narrators

---

41   To qualify for acceptance, those narrators should meet very strict criteria in moral character and memory. Al-Tahhan, *Mustalah al-Hadith*, p. 109.

42   A hadith is considered *mutawatir* if it was narrated by at least ten narrators in each generation (*tabaqah*). In addition, the circumstances of these narrators should be such that it is impossible for them to conspire to lie (*istihalat tawatu'hum 'ala al-Kadhib*). Al-Tahhan, *Mustalah al-Hadith*, pp. 17–18.

43   Al-Ghazzaliyy, *Al-Mankhul*, p. 47.

is less than that of *khabar at-tawatur*. Al-Ghazzāliyy's listing
of the knowledge of miracles as a separate entity might
indicate his early preoccupation with this idea, although he
did not explain his own position until he responded to the
Muslim philosophers' notion of causality in *Tahāfut al-
Falāsifah* (The Incoherence of the Philosophers).[44] By classifying *taqlīd* as the last kind of knowledge, Al-Ghazzāliyy
hinted that he considered it the least clear on his list. It
should come as no surprise, therefore, that the first source
of knowledge that he gave up before his period of skepticism
was *taqlīd*.[45]

Al-Ghazzāliyy later revised this list and came up with
a list of thirteen categories of knowledge that were used by
the philosophers as premises in the section on logic in his
Maqāsid al-Falāsifah (The Aims of the Philosophers) which
he wrote in Baghdad when he assumed his professorial
position at the Nizāmiyyah. Al-Ghazzāliyy listed these
categories in the following order:

1. *Al-Uwwaliyyāt* (logical necessities): e.g., knowing that
    "the whole is greater than the part".

2. *Al-Mahsūsāt* (sensibles): e.g., "the light of the moon
    increases and decreases".

3. *Al-Tajrībiyyāt* (experimentals): they result from the senses
    and reason together, e.g., "the fire burns".

4. *Al-Mutawātirāt* (knowledge related by a group of narra-
    tors): "like our knowledge of the existence of Egypt and
    Makkah without seeing them".

5. *Al-Qadāyā al-Latī Qiyāsātuha fī al-Tab' Ma'ahā* (the
    cases that include their proofs within): premises that
    were treated as logical necessities because their
    proofs were forgotten with time as the premise "two is
    half four" which originally was known through the
    proof "the half is one of two parts of a whole that is
    equal to the other".

44   For a full discussion of Al-Ghazzaliyy's understanding of causality and
     miracles see page 85.
45   See Al-Ghazzaliyy, *Al-Munqidh*, p. 77.

48

6. *Al-Wahmiyyāt* (hypothetical): like the premise "it is impossible for something to exist if one cannot point to it and it is described as being neither inside nor outside this world".

7. *Al-Mashhūrat* (famous): as in the case of "lying is bad". Al-Ghazzāliyy said that this category comprised conventional notions that were good for practical reasons. He added that if there were a man who was rational yet not accustomed to anything, he might reject famous premises.

8. *Al-Maqbūlāt* (acceptables): premises that were accepted by virtue of the position of the person who provided them (i.e. scholars).

9. *Al-Musallamāt* (agreeables): premises that were agreed upon between two parties.

10. *Al-Mushabbihāt* (similars): premises that only appeared to be corresponding to *al-Uwwaliyyāt*, *al-Tajribiyyāt* or *al-Mashhūrat* but in reality they were not.

11. *Al-Mashhūrāt Fī-Al-Zāhir* (those that appear to be famous): premises that were accepted as true upon hearing them, but rendered false upon reflecting on them.

12. *Al-Maznunāt* (probables): premises that were accepted as true with the "feeling that the opposite is possible".

13. *Al-Makhīlāt* (imaginatives): premises that were known to be false yet they were influential psychologically.[46]

In *Mi'yār al-'Ilm fī al-Mantiq* (The Criterion of Science in Logic), Al-Ghazzāliyy maintained basically the same list as above except for the addition of a new category which was *Al-Hadsiyyāt* (intuitions). He explained the knowledge that resulted from intuition as that which "cannot be proved,

---

46 Al-Ghazzaliyy, *Maqasid al-Falasifah*, Sulaiman Dunya, ed. (Cairo: Dar al-Ma'arif Bi-Misr, 1961) pp. 102–109.

cannot be doubted and cannot be shared with others through education". Al-Ghazzaliyy did not provide examples of this kind of knowledge, but he hinted that it is similar to the case of knowledge that is acquired by "taste" *dhawq*. He maintained that one could only lead the student to the path that he chose, but it is up to the student's ability to achieve such knowledge.[47]

Moreover, Al-Ghazzāliyy discussed the differences between the senses, whether they are on the same level or whether some rank higher than others. He cited several positions without stating his own thought on this subject. It should be noted that in *Al-Munqidh min al-Ḍalāl* (*Deliverance from Error*), which he wrote towards the end of his life, Al-Ghazzāliyy became very clear about this issue; he ranked the senses on different levels in the order of their development and by virtue of this classification they were listed as sources of sensible knowledge.[48]

Al-Ghazzāliyy concluded his classification of knowledge by stating that there were no differences between the sciences once knowledge is acquired, regardless of how difficult the subject of the science was.[49] This view of Al-Ghazzāliyy regarding the equality of the sciences, once they are achieved, is compatible with his position regarding his interchangeable use of the terms "science" and "knowledge".[50] Nevertheless, one could still find contradiction on the surface between the above notion and the fact that Al-Ghazzāliyy listed various levels of knowledge in different texts, a procedure that started with *Al-Mankhūl* and continued through out his life. It is rather obvious that in such lists, he classified different categories of sciences leaving the impression that some are more scientific than others. As to the changes in the number of these categories, one can attribute them to the development in his understanding of the concept of science which could be attributed partially to his exposure to philosophy.

47   Al-Ghazzaliyy, *Mi'yar al-'Ilm fi al-Mantiq*, Ahmad Shams Al-Din, ed. Beirut: Dar Al-Kutub Al-'Ilmiyyah, 1990) p. 182.
48   Al-Ghazzaliyy, *Al-Munqidh*, pp. 144–145.
49   Al-Ghazzaliyy, *Al-Mankhul*, p. 48.
50   See footnote 30.

50

2.2.4 The Sources of Knowledge

Prior to stating his position on the sources of knowledge, Al-Ghazzāliyy cited some positions that were circulating at the time. He started with Al-Hashawiyyah[51] who's view was that the sources of knowledge were restricted to the Qur'an and the Sunnah without any role for reason. Al-Ghāzzaliyy said that this position was obviously false.[52] Although one could understand the background of Al-Ghazzāliyy's statement regarding the Hashawiyyah, it was insufficient on his part not to provide a full account of his position. Of course, there is the possibility that Al-Ghazzāliyy thought it was self-evident.

In addition, he listed the ideas of those who restricted the sources of knowledge to the senses, the stance of the ˙Indian philosophers who thought that the sources were thinking and meditation and the position of those who considered inspiration (*ilhām*) as the source of knowledge. The latter position was based upon the idea that all knowledge belonged to Allah in the first place and then it is passed to human beings. Furthermore, he mentioned the opinion of Al-Qalanisiyy who restricted the source of knowledge to reason (*'aql*) without rejecting the senses. For him, the function of the senses is to perceive, but it is reason that knows at the time the senses perceive (i.e. light). The meaning of this is that Al-Qalanisiyy saw the senses as tools that cannot comprehend what they perceive on their own. He tried to support his argument by giving an example of a child who perceives the perceptibles without knowing what they are for his lack of reason.

Al-Ghazzāliyy brought the above discussion to an end by asserting that rational discernment (*mīz*) was the source of knowledge. He held that there is a level of discernment that belonged to animals which did not yield any knowledge.[53] Al-

---

51 Al-Hashawiyyah was a sect that accepted only the literal meaning of the verses of the al-Qur'an and Hadiths that mentioned Allah in language that would add corporeal attributes to Allah. Al-Ghazzaliyy, *Al-Mankhul*, p. 49.

52 Al-Ghazzaliyy, *Al-Mankhul*, p. 50.

53 *Ibid.*

Ghazzāliyy used the term "rational discernment" to distinguish human discernment from the ability of animals to discern[54] between things following their instincts. In addition, he ranked discernment higher than other faculties in *Al-Mankhūl*. In his latter work *Al-Munqidh*, he ranked discernment, which he called *tamyiz*, higher than the senses but lower than reason.[55]

Al-Ghazzāliyy held that there were two ways to acquire knowledge, with or without instruments of mediation (*wasā'it*). According to Al-Ghazzāliyy, there were three kinds of media: the senses which were the source of the sensibles (*al-mahsūsāt*), the "look" of the mind which was the source of the rational (*al-'aqliyyāt*) and the consistency of habits (*ittirād al-'adāt*) which enables one to know the meaning of messages. The latter was important for Al-Ghazzāliyy in defining the notion of causality and thus explaining miracles which needed two media: reason and habits. Al-Ghazzāliyy used these ideas in proving the possibility of miracles in support of the concept of prophecy. He said that through reason one could find that the miracle is an activity of an inventor and maker who is in control. He added that it was through custom or habit that miracles indicate the veracity of the Prophet [S.A.A.S.][56]

2.2.5 Al-Ghazzāliyy's Theory of Language

In a long section of *Al-Mankhūl*, Al-Ghazzāliyy discussed the theories concerning the origin of languages. He listed two major views about how languages evolved. The first advocated the idea that language, like any other knowledge, came from Allah directly. Those who held this view based their thought upon a verse in the Qur'an which says that Allah had taught Adam all the names.[57]   The second opinion asserted that languages were conventional. Those of the first stance refuted the latter position by declaring the word "conventional" paradoxical.

---

54 Al-Ghazzaliyy used the same Arabic term *tamyiz* (discernment) for both human beings and animals.
55 Al-Ghazzaliyy, *Al-Munqidh*, p. 145.
56 Al-Ghazzaliyy, *Al-Mankhul*, p. 51.
57 "*Wa'allama Adama al-asma'a kullaha ...*" al-Qur'an, Sura *al-Baqarah*

2:31.

Al-Ghazzāliyy brought this discussion to a culmination by reconciling the two positions together. It could be that language at its beginning was conventional; this conventional beginning could have been made possible by other creatures who were created before Adam. Al-Ghazzāliyy maintained that the above mentioned verse "appeared" to indicate the non-conventionality of language but it was not decisive.[58]

2.3 DELIVERANCE FROM ERROR
(Al-Munqidh min al-Dalāl)

According to Al-Subkiyy, Al-Ghazzāliyy spent about eight years (470-478 A.H./1077-1085 C.E.) in Nishapur with Al-Juwainiyy.[59] At the time Al-Juwainiyy died Al-Ghazzāliyy was at least 20 years old. The importance of these dates and Al-Ghazzāliyy's age stem from an account of Al-Ghazzāliyy's thought in his autobiographical work *Al-Munqidh min al-Dalāl* which, although written towards the end of his life, included useful information about the development of his epistemology during his early life which fits the frame work of this chapter. At the beginning of *Al-Munqidh*, he describes his state of mind starting with the prime of his youth when he "reached puberty *(al-bulūgh)*, before becoming twenty", until he became more than fifty years old.[60] It is obvious that his timeframe covers the period when Al-Ghazzāliyy wrote his book *Al-Mankhūl min Ta'līqāt al-Usūl.*

In *al-Munqidh*, Al-Ghazzāliyy showed that early in his life he was aware of the differences between the various religions, sects and schools of jurisprudence. This awareness prompted him to "investigate the creed of every sect and to explore the secrets of every denomination". In addition, he studied the Batinites, Zahirites, philosophers, dialectical theologians *(mutakallimūn)*, Sufis and Manicheans *(zanādiqa)*.[61] Al-Ghazzāliyy realized at a very early stage that

58 Al-Ghazzaliyy, *Al-Mankhul*, pp. 70–71.
59 Al-Subkiyy, Vol. VI, p. 196.
60 Al-Ghazzaliyy, *al-Munqidh*, p. 79.
61 *Zanadiqah* also means atheists, but generally in medieval sciences it referred to Manicheans who were not atheists.

one major reason for these differences was authority. For him it was parents and teachers who were responsible for such differences. Al-Ghazzāliyy saw that "children of Christians were raised as Christians, children of Jews were raised as Jews and children of Muslims were raised as Muslims".[62]

As a result, Al-Ghazzāliyy wanted to prescind from the knowledge that was based on the authority of parents and teachers. He had "a thirst to perceive the reality of things" which led him to break away from imitating others. Al-Ghazzāliyy realized that in order to reach truth, he needed to "seek the reality of knowledge, as it is"?[63]

2.4 CONCLUSION

Comparing the language of *al-Mankhūl* to that of *Al-Munqidh*, one finds a big difference. In *Al-Mankhūl*, Al-Ghazzāliyy's basic interest in knowledge was mainly as a jurist. He concentrated on technical issues that were part of or related to *uṣūl al-fiqh*. One example of a technical issue was Al-Ghazzāliyy's discussion of the conditions of the narrators of Hadith. He said that the narrator has to be a rational adult Muslim who could be male or female, free or a slave. For a narrator who fits these conditions, only questions of immorality render his/her narration unacceptable.[64] Another issue that Al-Ghazzāliyy dealt with was the position of Islamic Shari'ah towards the Shari'ah of the prophets before Islam. The question that underlines this area of discussion is whether Muslim jurists should consider previous Shari'ah as another source in addition to the Qur'an, Sunnah, consensus of the companions of the prophet [S.A.A.S.], which later on became the consensus of the scholars, and *qiyās* (analogy). He started by discussing whether prophet Muhammad [S.A.A.S.] was following any previous Shari'ah before he became a prophet. After setting forth the positions for several other scholars, Al-Ghazzāliyy brought the issue to a culmination by stating that one cannot consider the Shari'ah of past religions as a source of Islamic Shari'ah because there was no reference to such notions in

62 Al-Ghazzaliyy, *Al-Munqidh*, pp. 78–82.
63 *Ibid.*, p. 82.
64 Al-Ghazzaliyy, *Al-Mankhul*, p. 257.

the Sunnah of prophet Muḥammad [S.A.A.S.][65]

It should not come as a surprise that, as a student, Al-Ghazzāliyy imitated his teacher Al-Juwainiyy, a position that he acknowledged at the end of *Al-Mankhūl*. Although he differed in very few cases from his teacher in *Al-Mankhūl*, his originality in *uṣūl al-fiqh* was manifested in his later work *Al-Mustaṣfā* where logic played a major role in his *uṣūl*.

In *Al-Munqidh*, Al-Ghazzāliyy is preoccupied with truth in itself. He did not refer to jurisprudence or the *uṣūl*. While *uṣūl al-fiqh*, and thus *Al-Mankhūl*, was supposed to solve differences in jurisprudence, it was differences in belief that prompted Al-Ghazzāliyy to search for truth. His awareness, during the early stages of his life, of the different creeds of people started him on his first stage of a long journey of systematic skepticism which lasted until the climax of his quest for knowledge during his last days at the Niẓāmiyyah of Baghdad.

Al-Ghazzāliyy's critical thinking and regard to general questions of truth and knowledge, while apparent in *Al-Munqidh* is absent from *Al-Mankhūl*. The fact that these two books reflected different areas of interest in Al-Ghazzāliyy's early life might appear contradictory. One question that might surface as a result of these two areas is: how could someone like Al-Ghazzāliyy, who was investigating the general notions of knowledge and their sources as stated in *Al-Munqidh*, proceeded to verify the particular as the case in *Al-Mankhūl?*

There could be one answer, I argue, that explains the above mentioned positions. Al-Ghazzāliyy maintained two lines of thought since the days of youth until the last years of his life. The first line of thought, which represents Al-Ghazzāliyy's quest for knowledge, is best illustrated in the following lines from the introduction of *Al-Munqidh*:

"In the bloom of my life, from the time I reached puberty before I was twenty until now, when I am over fifty, I have constantly been diving daringly into the depths of this profound sea and wading into its deep water like a bold man, not like a cautious coward. I would penetrate far

65 Al-Ghazzaliyy, *Al-Mankhul*, pp. 231–234.

into every murky mystery, pounce upon every problem, and dash into every mazy difficulty. I would scrutinize the creed of every sect and seek to lay bare the secrets of each faction's teaching with the aim of discriminating between the proponent of truth and the advocate of error, and between the faithful follower of tradition and the heterodox innovator."[66]

Al-Ghazzāliyy reaffirmed the early beginning of this search for truth and the source of this quest for knowledge in the same introduction. He said:

"The thirst for grasping the real meaning of things was indeed my habit and wont from my early years and in the prime of my life. It was an instinctive, natural disposition placed in my makeup by God (Allah) Most High, not something due to my own choosing and contriving. As a result, the fetters of servile conformism (taqlīd)[67] fell away from me, and inherited beliefs lost their hold on me, when I was still quite young."[68]

Although the above quotations showed the time frame of the first line of thought, which covered Al-Ghazzāliyy's life as a student, it remains that there were no books written by the student Al-Ghazzāliyy, that reflected this independent approach to knowledge and truth. There were many works (e.g. *Al-Munqidh min al-Dalāl*) by the later Al-Ghazzāliyy that embodied this investigative course that he undertook in pursuit of knowledge and truth in what could be called the area of universals.

The second line of thought is represented in Al-Ghazzāliyy's works in fields like jurisprudence. Although the first line of thought must have influenced the way Al-Ghazzāliyy approached areas like *fiqh* by having that independent spirit which led him not to be a conformist to previous writings in such fields, one cannot claim that these

---

66 Al-Ghazzaliyy, *Freedom and Fulfillment* (*Al-Munqidh min al-Dalal*), Richard Joseph McCarthy, tr. (Boston: Twayne Publishers, 1980) p. 62.
67 For Al-Ghazzaliyy, conformism or *taqlid* meant uncritical acceptance of knowledge and belief at the hands of parents and teachers by virtue of their authority.
68 Al-Ghazzaliyy, *Freedom*, p. 63.

works were reflecting the first line of thought because they were concerned with particulars. Unlike a reductionist, he addressed these areas of particulars as if there was no relationship between the general notions of knowledge, which he put under investigation, and these particular fields.

The fact that Al-Ghazzāliyy kept working in the particular fields of the Shari'ah indicates that he was never in doubt about the true validity of the premises which were derived from the Qur'an and the Sunna. In fact, he continued lecturing on these subjects even at the Nizamiyyah of Baghdad, when he was going through what I like to call the climax of his mental discourse regarding the first line of thought.[69]

Al-Ghazzāliyy's continuous inquiry into both universals and particulars is interesting because on the surface they seem incompatible. One could see that Al-Ghazzāliyy had an obvious, spontaneous interest in the first. It prompted a good deal of reflection throughout his life. The difficulty is in the question: why did he pursue the second? Part of the answer could be found in Al-Ghazzāliyy's formal education which started with training in the particulars (e.g. *fiqh*). Another partial answer comes from the fact that there was common interest in these particular sciences, especially in jurisprudence. In addition, Al-Ghazzāliyy pursued his interest in the particulars as a teacher who was expected, and thus there is a sense of duty, to lecture on such topics. All of these aspects and probably more provided the motivation for such pursuit of knowledge in the particulars. Moreover, one could think that once Al-Ghazzāliyy achieved universal knowledge, he found that his interest in the particulars was in line with his interest in the universals. In addition, there is a sociological element in this equation, where a scholar in the Islamic world is unlikely to be accepted without being deep rooted and having strong interest in the particulars.

69   Al-Ghazzaliyy, *Al-Munqidh*, p. 136.

Chapter THREE

AL-GHAZZALIYY'S QUEST FOR KNOWLEDGE: THE FIRST PERIOD OF PUBLIC TEACHING (478–488 A.H./1085–1095 C.E.)

This chapter deals with Al-Ghazzāliyy's writings from the time of the death of Al-Juwainiyy in 478 A.H./1085 C.E. until he abandoned his professorial position at the Niẓāmiyyah of Baghdad in 488 A.H./1095 C.E.

During this period, Al-Ghazzāliyy wrote at least twenty books in addition to the written rulings (*fatāwā*) that he issued during the same period. These writings, many of which were lost or remain in manuscript form,[1] covered several subjects including jurisprudence (*fiqh*), debates (*munāẓarah*) in *fiqh*, fundamentals of jurisprudence (*Uṣūl Al-Fiqh*), philosophy, politics and creed (*'aqīdah*). In this chapter, I shall concentrate on his works in areas that pertain to his quest for true knowledge directly (i.e. philosophy). Others will be treated briefly.

In addition, it is necessary to also treat Al-Ghazzāliyy's *Al-Munqidh min al-Ḍalāl* in this chapter. Although this work was written during the second period of public teaching (499 A.H./1106 C.E.–503 A.H./1110 C.E.), it includes one of the most important accounts on his thought during the period leading to his departure from Baghdad. This account covers his skepticism in addition to his analysis of the me-

---

1 The writings that were lost include *Al-Muntahal fi 'Ilm al-Jadal Ma'akhidh al-Khilaf, Tahsin al-Ma'akhidh, Al-Mabadi' wa al-Ghayat, Hujjat al-Haq* and *Qawasim al-Batiniyyah*. The manuscripts comprise *Al-Basit, Khulasat al-Mukhtasar wa Naqawat al-Mu'tasar, Shifa' al-Ghalil fi al-Qiyas Wat-Ta'lil, Fatawa, Ghayat al-Ghawr fi Dirayat al-Dawr* and *Al-Ma'arif al-'Aqliyyah wa Lubab al-Hikmah al-Ilahiyyah.*

thodologies of the four "classes of seekers": the dialectical theologians (*Al-Mutakallimūn*), the esoterics (*Al-Bāṭiniyyah*), the philosophers and the *Sufis*. The pertinence of these issues to Al-Ghazzāliyy's development during this decade will be examined in detail in this chapter.

3.1 ON *FIQH, MUNĀẒARAH AND UṢŪL AL-FIQH*

Al-Ghazzāliyy's works in jurisprudence and the related subjects show his continuing interest in this field, an interest which started in his student days. Although these works reflect a certain development in Al-Ghazzāliyy's perspective on jurisprudence, he remained throughout faithful to the Shāfi'īte school of jurisprudence.

3.1.1 On Jurisprudence

Al-Ghazzāliyy wrote several books of *fiqh*, according to the Shāfi'īte school, during the time regarded by Maurice Bouyges as the first period of his public teaching (478–488 A.H./1085–1095 C.E.).[2] These books, which were considered his first writings, include *Al-Basīṭ, Al-Wasīṭ, Al-Wājiz* and *Khulāsat Al-Mukhtaṣar*. In addition, he issued tens of separate rulings (*fatāwā*) in the area of *fiqh*. One hundred and ninety of these rulings were gathered in one manuscript which remains unpublished.[3]

Ibn Khallikān stated that Al-Ghazzāliyy borrowed the names of the first three books, in the same order, from Al-Wāḥidiyy Al-Mufassir[4] (d. 468 A.H./1074 C.E.) who wrote three books on the interpretation of the Qur'an.[5]

These three books of Al-Ghazzāliyy were practically the same as one another. The first in the series was *Al-Basīṭ* (The Simple). Realizing that this book included unnecessary details and examples which made it difficult for

2 Badawi, p. xvi.
3 *Ibid.*, p. 46.
4 'Ali Ibn Hasan Ibn Ahmad Ibn 'Ali Ibn Buwayh Al-Wahidiyy. He died in Nishapur when Al-Ghazzaliyy was stuyding there, which explains the borrowing.
5 Ibn Kathir, Vol. II, p. 114.

students to read, Al-Ghazzāliyy decided to write a shorter version which he called *Al-Wasīt* (The Median). According to him, *Al-Wasīt*, which was written as a textbook, is half the size of *Al-Basīt*. In addition, Al-Ghazzāliyy set forth a rule for writing when he explicitly said that "deciding the goal (of a book) should be according to the ability of the student".[6] This rule reflects Al-Ghazzāliyy's exceptional talent as an educator. Later on, Al-Ghazzāliyy wrote a further abridgement which he named *Al-Wajīz* (The Concise).

The fourth book that Al-Ghazzāliyy wrote on jurisprudence during this period was *Khulāsat Al-Mukhtasar* (The Extract of the Compendium). This book was simply an abridgment of the *Mukhtasar* of Al-Muzaniyy (d. 264 A.H./878 C.E.).[7] Al-Murtada Al-Zubaydiyy stated that Al-Ghazzāliyy did not work directly on the original book of Al-Muzaniyy, but rather on an intermediate work which was also an abridgment written by Al-Juwainiyy (d. 438 A.H./ 1047 C.E.), father of Imam Al-Harāmayn Al-Juwainiyy, teacher of Al-Ghazzāliyy.[8] According to Al-Ghazzāliyy, this book was his smallest contribution to jurisprudence.[9]

The contributions of Al-Ghazzāliyy in *fiqh* are to be expected. After all, his position at the Nizāmiyyah school was given only to scholars of the Shāfi'īte school of jurisprudence. It was apparent from his writings in *fiqh* that they were intended as textbooks. Al-Ghazzāliyy dedicated most of his time to teaching and writing. He used his "spare time" to pursue the goal that he designated for himself: his quest for true knowledge.[10]

3.1.2 On the Methods of Debate

Al-Ghazzāliyy wrote four books on debates in the field of jurisprudence *Al-Muntahal fī 'Ilm al-Jadal, Ma'ākhidh al-*

---

6 Al-Ghazzaliyy, *Al-Wasīt*, Ali Muhyid-Din Al-Qarah Daghi, ed. (Cairo: Dar al-Nasr li al-Tiba'ah al-Islamiyyah, 1984) Vol. I, p. 296.
7 Abu Ibrahim Isma'il Al-Muzaniyy, a companion of al-Shafi'iyy. The full title of his book is *Mukhtasar min 'Ilm al-Imam al-Nafis Muhammad Ibn Idris*.
8 Abu Muhammad 'Abdallah Ibn Yusuf Al-Juwainiyy.
9 Badawi, p. 31.
10 Al-Ghazzaliyy, *Al-Munqidh*, p. 95.

Khilāf Lubāb al-Naẓar and *Taḥsīn al-Ma'ākhidh* were all written as a result of a trend dominant in his time. Concerning that trend, he said in *Mi'yār al-'Ilm*:

> "Because aspirations during our age were almost exclusively inclined to jurisprudence, I was led to write
> books in the methods of debate. (*al-Munāẓara*).[11]

The fact that Al-Ghazzāliyy wrote many books on debate, and that he spent much time in debating others at the "Camp" of Niẓām Al-Mulk, show his personal interest in debates which could not be considered, strictly speaking, part of his quest for knowledge. Al-Ghazzāliyy held that unless the debating parties adhered to etiquette of debate (*adab al-munāẓarah*) as he outlined in his books,   these debates would lead to animosity and hatred.[12] It seems that Al-Ghazzāliyy did not consider debate to be a very positive activity. Indeed, when his visited the tomb of prophet Ibrāhīm [a.s.] in Hebron after his departure from Baghdad, which marked a new era in his thought, Al-Ghazzāliyy despised debating and made a pledge never again to debate with anyone.[13]

3.1.3 On the Fundamentals of Jurisprudence

On *Uṣūl al-Fiqh*, Al-Ghazzāliyy wrote two books during the same period: *Al-Mabādi' Wal-Ghāyat* and *Shifā' Al-Ghalīl fī Al-Qiyās wa al-Ta'līl*. The first book was lost, and what little information there is about it comes from two references in other writings of Al-Ghazzāliyy. Badawi claimed the subject of *Al-Mabādi' wa al-Ghāyāt* was *uṣūl al-fiqh*. Such a claim was disputed, but given the scant information, it is virtually impossible to settle the debate regarding even its subject matter.

There are many manuscripts of the second book, *Shifā' al-'Alīl fī al-Qiyās wa al-Ta'līl*, which was edited by

11 Al-Ghazzaliyy, *Mi'yar al-'Ilm*, p. 27.
12 Qadri Hafiz Tuqan, *Al-'Ulum 'ind al-'Arab* (Beirut: Dar Iqra', 1983) p. 189.
13 Qarah Daghi, vol. I, p. 118.
14 This book was published by Dar al-Irshad in Baghdad in 1971. Qarah Daghi, p. 202.

Ḥamad Al-Kābisī.[14] Although this book was unique in comparison to other books on the fundamentals of jurisprudence, still it did not rise to the level which *al-Mustaṣfā* reached later. The latter incorporated logic as a separate entity, which marked an especially important stage in the development of Al-Ghazzāliyy's thought. A full account of *al-Mustaṣfā* will be provided in chapter six.

3.2 AL-GHAZZĀLIYY'S SKEPTICISM

In *Al-Munqidh min al-Ḍalāl*, Al-Ghazzāliyy stated that he broke away from conformism (*taqlīd*) which he understood as accepting knowledge as true based upon the authority of parents and teachers. He found this authority to be unreliable because it could not be the case that parents were providing true knowledge while at the same time being responsible for the differences among children (i.e. among the rearing of Jews, Christians or Muslims).[15]

As a result, Al-Ghazzāliyy sought to distinguish between true and false knowledge. To do that, he realized that he should determine the nature of true knowledge. In a statement that reflected his appreciation of mathematics, Al-Ghazzāliyy said that primary knowledge should be indubitable in the same way as mathematics (eg. ten is greater than three).[16]

Next, Al-Ghazzāliyy scrutinized all his cognitions in search for knowledge that would meet the previous description, but he found himself devoid of any such knowledge except in the case of sensibles (*al-ḥissiyyāt*)[17] and the self evident truths (*al-ḍarūriyyāt*).[18] Although these two areas appeared clear and assuring, Al-Ghazzāliyy wanted to

15 Al-Ghazzaliyy, *al-Munqidh*, pp. 81–82.
16 Al-Ghazzaliyy, *al-Munqidh*, p. 82.
17 In his translation of *al-Munqidh min al-Dalal*, *Freedom and Fulfillment*, R. J. McCarthy used "sense-data" to translate "*al-hissiyyat*". It was Bertrand Russell who was first to use "sense-data" linguistically to express the contents of sensations. For Russell, there is an element of immediacy associated with the concept of "sense-data" which Al-Ghazzaliyy's idea of sensibles (*hissiyyat*) lacks. Thus, I have departed from McCarthy's translation.
18 Al-Ghazzaliyy, *Freedom and Fulfillment* (*al-Munqidh*), p. 64

make sure that he did not have a false sense of security
like the one he had previously with knowledge that he received from parents and teachers.[19]

With great seriousness, Al-Ghazzāliyy started meditating on sensibles and self evident knowledge. He wanted
to see whether he could doubt them. As a result, he
concluded:

> "This protracted effort to induce doubt (*tashakkuk*)
> finally brought me to the point where my soul would
> not allow me to admit safety from error even in the
> case of sensibles. It began to give ground to doubt
> (*tattasi'u lishshak*) and to say: Whence comes your
> reliance on sensibles?"[20]

In a rather beautiful style, Al-Ghazzāliyy presented
these reflections in the form of dialogue with his personified soul which brought to his attention examples from
sight, the strongest of the sensibles, in order to prove that
he could not rely on the senses. One example was the case of
shadow where sight "looks at shadow and sees it standing
still and motionless and judges that motion must be
denied. Then due to experience and observation, an hour
later it (the soul) knows that the shadow is moving, and that
it did not move in a sudden spurt, but so gradually and
imperceptibly that it was never completely at rest". His
soul showed him that on this and similar sensibles, the
sense-judge (*ḥākim al-ḥiss*) deemed them to be true. But
soon, the reason-judge (*ḥākim al-'aql*) "refutes it and re-
peatedly gives it the lie in an incontrovertible fashion".[21]

After doubting sensibles, Al-Ghazzāliyy describes himself as provisionally thinking that he could only trust
rational data (*al-'aqliyyāt*) which belong to primary truths
(*al-uwwaliyyāt*). These primary truths would consist of
mathematical and logical truths. He said:

> "My reliance on sensibles has also become untenable.
> Perhaps, therefore I can rely only on those rational data

---

19 Al-Ghazzaliyy, *Al-Munqidh*, p. 83.
20 Al-Ghazzaliyy, *Freedom and Fulfillment*, p. 64. See also, Al-Ghazzaliyy,
    Al-Munqidh, p. 84.
21 Al-Ghazzaliyy, *Freedom and Fulfillment*, pp. 64–65.

64

which belong to the category of primary truths, such as our asserting that 'Ten is more that three' and 'One and the same thing cannot be simultaneously affirmed and denied' and 'One and the same thing cannot be incipient and eternal, existent and nonexistent, necessary and impossible'".[22]

At this stage, as Al-Ghazzāliyy found himself trusting rational data, a challenge was posed by the sensibles which also showed up as a personified character. It addressed Al-Ghazzāliyy and disputed his acceptance of rational data. Its argument was based upon drawing similarities between his previous acceptance of sensibles and his later approval of rational data as the only trustworthy knowledge. Al-Ghazzāliyy's doubt of sensibles was the outcome of the presence of a higher faculty, namely, the judge of reason. Why then could it not be the case that there were yet another judge higher than that of reason which, if manifested, would render reason doubtable? "The sensibles" also argued, even though this other judge was not revealed, this did not indicate the impossibility of its existence.[23]

Al-Ghazzāliyy next described himself as puzzled and not knowing what to say. "The sensibles" reinforced its position by appealing to dreams where it said:

"Don't you see that when you are asleep you believe certain things and imagine certain circumstances and believe they are fixed and lasting and entertain no doubts about that being their status? Then you wake up and know that all your imaginings and beliefs were groundless and unsubstantial. So while everything you believe through sensation or intellection in your waking state may be true in relation to that state, what assurance have you that you may not suddenly experience a state which would have the same relation to your waking state as the latter has into your dreaming in relation to that new and further state? If you found yourself in such a state, you would be sure that all your rational beliefs were unsubstantial fancies."[24]

Al-Ghazzāliyy considered that the latter state might

22 Al-Ghazzaliyy, *Freedom and Fulfillment*, p. 65.
23 *Ibid.*, p. 85.
24 *Ibid.*, p. 65.

be the one that the Sufis claim as theirs. They alleged to "see, in their states, conditions that are not compatible with rational data".[25]   In addition, he cited a part of a verse from the Qur'an whose meaning could be translated as, "We have removed your veil and today your sight is acute."[26] For Al-Ghazzāliyy, this verse indicated that one would see things differently after death and, thus, life could be nothing but a long dream of which one could wake up only after death.

Al-Ghazzāliyy tried to find a solution to this complex situation, but he could not. He stated that any proof used would consist of primary knowledge that was already doubted. Unable to find an answer, Al-Ghazzāliyy said that he found himself in a state of skepticism which lasted close to two months.[27]

During these two months, Al-Ghazzāliyy described his situation as that of a skeptic who denied the possibility of knowledge, as indicated in the title of this chapter of *Al-Munqidh*: "The Avenues for Sophistry and the Denial of the Sciences" (*Madākhil al-Safsatah wa Jahd al-'Ulūm*).[28] He said that he contained this skepticism within himself, giving it neither utterance nor composition.[29] It indeed appears true that he did not allow his skepticism to influence his lectures or writing. Thus, Al-Ghazzāliyy maintained two lines of intellectual activity: the first was in pursuit of true knowledge and the second was within conventional areas of study.

Al-Ghazzāliyy described his state of skepticism as a "sickness", the remedy for which "was not the result of arranging proofs or organizing words." Rather, he claimed that he was healed by "a light (*nūr*), that Allah Most High cast into (his) chest". At this stage, Al-Ghazzāliyy regained his trust in logical necessities. He added that "this light was the key to most of the cognitions (*ma'ārif*).[30]

25 Al-Ghazzaliyy, *Al-Munqidh*, p. 85.
26 Al-Qur'an, Sura *Qaf* 50:22.
27 Al-Ghazzaliyy, *Al-Munqidh*, pp. 85–86.

28 *Ibid.*, p. 83.
29 *Ibid.*, p. 86.
30 *Ibid.*, p. 86.

In a language that could only be described as that of Sufism, Al-Ghazzāliyy defended the possibility of knowledge through unveiling (*kashf*), which was the outcome of divine illumination. By *kashf*, he meant attaining knowledge directly (i.e. from Allah). Therefore, he wrote "whoever restricts the unveiling of truth to formulated proofs has indeed strained the broad mercy of Allah.[31]

3.3 SKEPTICISM AND THE CLASSES OF SEEKERS

The section of Al-Ghazzāliyy's skepticism in *Al-Munqidh* is extremely important for any attempt to comprehend the development in Al-Ghazzāliyy's thought. This is especially true because he placed this section before the chapter on the classes of seekers (*Aṣnaf Al-Ṭālibīn*) in which he described the next phase of his quest for true knowledge in a fragmented frame of time.[32] As such, the section of skepticism forms the background to his assessment of the classes of seekers.

In his search for the methodology that leads for true knowledge. Al-Ghazzāliyy looked into the belief and creed of every sect and group, including Manichaeans[33] (*zanādiqah*), where he sought the background of this position which he considered so bold.[34] Eventually, after being relieved of skepticism, he narrowed his search to four groups: the dialectical theologians, the esoterics, the philosophers and the *Ṣūfīs*.[35] Before analyzing each of these groups in detail, he listed and described each of them briefly:

31 Al-Ghazzaliyy, *Freedom and Fulfillment*, p. 66.
32 Al-Ghazzaliyy spent three years studying philosophy and six months in his "spiritual crises" which took place right before he left the Nizamiyyah of Baghdad at the end of 488 A.H./1095 C.E. By deducting three and half years, to which one should add the time Al-Ghazzaliyy spent in studying and writing about the dialectical theologians (*Al-Mutakallimun*) and the esoterics (*Al-Batiniyyah*), I would say that Al-Ghazzaliyy's skepticism took place after his arrival at the Nizamiyyah of Baghdad in 484 A.H. 1091 C.E.
33 Another possible meaning for *zanadiqah* is "nihilists", and another is "dualists", for the Manichaeans to whom the term *zanadiqah* was frequently used were throughgoing dualists.
34 Al-Ghazzaliyy, *Al-Munqidh*, pp. 79–81.
35 *Ibid.*, p. 89.

1. The dialectical theologians (*Al-Mutakallimūn*), who claim, (*yadda'ūn*) that they are men of independent judgment and reasoning.

2. The esoterics (Batinites), who allege (*yaz'umūn*) to be the unique possessors of learning and the privileged recipients of knowledge acquired from the Infallible Imam.

3. The philosophers, who allege (*yaz'umūn*) that they are the men of logic and apodictic demonstration.

4. The Sufis, who claim (*yadda'ūn*) to be the familiars of the divine Presence and the men of mystic vision and illumination.[36]

Careful attention to the language that Al-Ghazzāliyy used in this classification reveals that he regarded the four independent groups as actually forming two pairs. He used only two verbs in expressing what the groups had to say. He applied the verb "*yadda'ūn*" (claim), which is neutral, to *Al-Mutakallimūn* and the Sufis, but the verb "*yaz'umūn*" (allege), which has a subtle negative tone, to the Batinites and the philosophers. It is evident, therefore that Al-Ghazzāliyy had already taken a position that was favourable to two of the four groups. Furthermore, Al-Ghazzāliyy was convinced that only one of these four groups must have the methodology that leads to true knowledge and if not, he believed that his case was hopeless. He felt that he was compelled to proceed in his quest because there was no way to return to conformism. Al-Ghazzāliyy maintained that once someone becomes conscious of his status as a conformist, it becomes imperative for this person to be independent and to search for true knowledge on his own. It should be noted that Al-Ghazzāliyy exempted from this obligation a conformist (*muqallid*) who is not aware of himself as being one.[37]

---

36 For this part of *Al-Munqidh*, I have used the translation of McCarthy with slight changes pertaining to the words 'claim' and 'allege'. *Freedom and Fulfillment*, p. 67.
37 Al-Ghazzaliyy, *Al-Munqidh*, pp. 89–90.

3.4 ON DIALECTICAL THEOLOGY ('ILM AL-KALĀM)

After going through the period of skepticism, Al-Ghazzāliyy continued his quest for true knowledge. He first considered the dialectical theologians, the first of the classes of seekers (aṣnāf al-ṭālibīn).[38] The roots of Dialectical theology (kalām), or Islamic Scholasticism as it is sometimes called, emerged early in Islamic history but gained considerable momentum with the introduction of Greek philosophy in the eighth and ninth centuries.[39]

Al-Ghazzāliyy was familiar with the methodology and the notions that Al-Mutakallimūn dealt with because of his close ties with the Asha'irites. The latter were the heirs of Kalām when the Mu'tazilites surrendered their leadership of Islamic theology to what might be called the Salafiyyah school which was headed by Aḥmad Ibn Hanbal (d. 241 A.H./855 C.E.).[40] Al-Ghazzāliyy studied 'Ilm al-Kalām, read the books of their scholars and finally wrote about the subject. What he found was that the aim of al-Mutakallimūn differed from his. They aimed at the preservation of the creed of the Sunnites. He was searching for that group which aimed at truth without resorting to conformism, of which Al-Mutakallimūn were not devoid.[41]

Al-Ghazzāliyy admitted that Al-Mutakallimūn were successful in attaining their goal which was defending the Shari'ah, but also that they attempted to study the true nature of things. As a result, they researched the notions of substances and accidents, yet without reaching the ultimate goal (al-ghāyah al-quṣwā) in this field. Al-Ghazzāliyy explained the latter position by stating that "since that (studying Aristotelian categories) was not the

---

38 Al-Ghazzaliyy, *Al-Munqidh*, p. 89.

39 Majid Fakhry, *A History of Islamic Philosophy* (New York: Columbia University Press, 1970) p. 56.

40 The Mu'tazilites and Ahmad Ibn Hanbal were rivals for a long time. The issue at stake was the question whether the Qur'an, being the word of Allah, was created or eternal? The Mu'tazilites, who were politically influential during the reign of Al-Ma'mun (d. 223 A.H./ 833 A.D.) and the subsequent two caliphs, advocated the notion that the Qur'an was created, a position declared heretical by Ibn Hanbal. Fakhry, pp. 79–80.

41 Al-Ghazzaliyy, *Al-Munqidh*, p. 91.

aim of their (*Al-Mutakallimūn*) science, their search did not achieve the ultimate goal in it".[42] The interpretation of "ultimate goal" here could be understood in Aristotelian terms. The general meaning of Al-Ghazzāliyy's argument is that the dialectical theologians did not reach complete understanding of the Aristotelian categories.

Al-Ghazzāliyy's conflict with *Al-Mutakallimūn* resulted from their appropriation of arguments from the theses of their antagonists. Of this Al-Ghazzāliyy said:

> "But in so doing (protecting religion) they relied on premises which they took over from their adversaries, being compelled to admit them either by uncritical acceptance, or because of the Community's consensus (*ijmā'*), or by simple acceptance deriving from the Qur'an and the Traditions. Most of their polemic was devoted to bringing out the inconsistencies of their adversaries and criticizing them for the logically absurd consequences of what they conceded. This, however, is of little use in the case of one (i.e. Al-Ghazzāliyy) who admits nothing at all except the primary and self-evident truths."[43]

It is clear that at this stage Al-Ghazzāliyy restricted his acceptance to primary and self-evident truths and denied the same status to the sources of Islamic Shari'ah: the Qur'an, Traditions and the consensus of the companions of the Prophet [S.A.A.S.][44] This fact shows that Al-Ghazzāliyy was consistent in his position. He wanted to find an objective truth that would "provide an effective means of dispelling entirely the darkness due to the bewilderment about the differences dividing men".[45]

3.5 AL-GHAZZĀLIYY'S ENCOUNTER WITH PHILOSOPHY

According to *Al-Munqidh min al-Dalāl*, Al-Ghazzāliyy stated

---

42 Al-Ghazzaliyy, *Al-Munqidh*, p. 93.
43 Al-Ghazzaliyy, *Freedom and Fulfillment*, pp. 68–69.
44 The consensus of the companions of the prophet became, in later generations, the consensus of the scholars (*Ijma' al-'Ulama'*) at any given time.
45 Al-Ghazzaliyy, *Freedom and Fulfillment*, p. 69.

that in his quest for true knowledge he started studying philosophy after he was done with *'Ilm al-Kalām* (which did not provide the remedy for which he was looking). In his introduction to the section on philosophy he outlined his approach to this new field. He wanted to pursue the science of philosophy to a level higher than that of the most knowledgeable in the field. Only then, he argued, could one know the intricate depths of the science.[46]

Al-Ghazzāliyy was aware that he could not rely on secondary sources, such as those of *al-Mutakallimūn*, in order to study philosophy. For him, their books included fragmented philosophical words that were complex and contradictory to one another. Instead, he decided to read books of philosophy directly without the assistance of a teacher. Although he was teaching three hundred students at the Nizāmiyyah of Baghdad and writing in the Islamic revealed sciences at the same time, in his spare time Al-Ghazzāliyy was able to master philosophy in less than two years. He continued reflecting on it for almost another year.[47] He reached the level where he became so familiar with the measure of its precisions as well as its deceits, deceptions and delusions, that he had no doubt about his thorough grasp of it.[48]

As a result of his study he wrote two books: *Maqāsid Al-Falāsifah* (The Aims of the Philosophers) and *Tahāfut al-Falāsifah* (The Incoherence of the Philosophers). It was Al-Ghazzāliyy's intention to write a book which would encompass the thought of the philosophers without criticizing or adding anything to it. This book was to be followed by another (i.e. *Tahāfut al-Falāsifah*) that would include his critique of the contents of the first one. It was this latter work that prompted Ibn Rushd[49] to write (around 576 A.H./1180 C.E.), *Tahāfut al-Tahāfut* (The Incoherence of the Incoherence) which constituted a

46 Al-Ghazzaliyy, *al-Munqidh*, p. 94.
47 *Ibid.*, pp. 94–95.
48 Al-Ghazzaliyy, *Freedom and Fulfillment*, p. 70.
49 The full name of Ibn Rushd, who is known in Latin as Averroes, was Abu al-Walid Muhammad Ibn Ahamd Ibn Muhammad Ibn Rushd. He was born in 520 A.H./1126 C.E. and died 595 A.H./1198 C.E.

systematic rebuttal of Al-Ghazzāliyy's critique of this melange of Greco-Islamic Philosophy.[50]

Maqāṣid Al-Falāsifah (which according to Brockelmann
was written in 488 A.H./1095 C.E.)[51] was a pioneer work
in its attempt to deliberately present an
objective
account of the thought of adversaries without the inclusion
of the author's ideas. Al-Ghazzāliyy wanted to introduce
philosophy as the philosophers knew it. Of this objective,
he said:

> "I thought that I should introduce, prior to the *Tahāfut*,
> a concise account that will include the story of their
> aims (*maqāṣid*) which will be derived from their logical,
> natural and metaphysical sciences, without distinguish-
> ing between what is right and what is wrong, without
> additions and along with that they believed as their
> proofs."[52]

The works of Al-Ghazzāliyy began to be translated
into Latin before the middle of the twelfth century C.E.[53]
Of these, *Maqāṣid Al-Falāsifah* was so influential in Latin
Europe that Fr. Manuel Alonso listed forty four theologians
and philosophers, including St. Thomas Aquinas who himself referred to this book thirty one times.[54]

In *Maqāṣid al-Falāsifa*, Al-Ghazzāliyy divided the
sciences of the philosophers into four major categories:
mathematical (*al-riyāḍiyyāt*), logical (*al-manṭiqiyyāt*),
natural (*al-ṭabi'iyyāt*) and metaphysical (*al-ilāhiyyāt*).[55] He
listed politics, economy[56] and ethics as subdivisions under
metaphysics. In *Al-Munqidh min al-Dalāl*, he listed politics
and ethics as major sections along with the first four.[57]

50 Fakhry, p. 307.
51 Badawi, p. 53.
52 Al-Ghazzaliyy, *Maqasid al-Falasifah*, p. 31
53 M. Saeed Sheikh, *Islamic Philosophy* (London: The Octagon Press,
    1982) p. 107.
54 Manuel Alonso: "*Influencia de Algazel en el mundo latino*", *Al-Andalus*,
    Vol. XXIII, Fasc. 2, pp. 371–380. Madrid, 1958. See Badawi, pp. 56–58.
55 Al-Ghazzaliyy, *Maqasid al-Falasifah*, p. 31.
56 For "economy". Al-Ghazzaliyy used *tadbir al-manzil*, management of the
    house, the literal Arabic translation of *oikonomia* in Greek. The contem-
    porary Arabic translation of economy as a science is *Iqtisad*.
57 Al-Ghazzaliyy, *Al-Munqidh*, p. 100.

Regarding mathematics, Al-Ghazzāliyy thought that it dealt with geometry and arithmetic. Neither of these subjects contradicted reason. As a result, Al-Ghazzāliyy did not think that he ought to include a detailed account of mathematics in his book.[58] This way of treating mathematics shows that reason was the criterion that Al-Ghazzāliyy applied when he entertained philosophy.

Al-Ghazzāliyy's basic position regarding metaphysics was that most of what the philosophers believed in this field was contrary to the truth (al-haq). The correct ideas were seldom included. On the other hand, in logic he thought that mistakes were very rare. The philosophers only differed with their Muslim counterparts, whom Al-Ghazzāliyy called *Ahl al-Haq* (people of truth), in the terminology, not in the meanings. As for natural science, he held that it comprised a melange of true and false notions.[59]

Al-Ghazzāliyy's judgement regarding metaphysics needs some clarification. In *Tahāfut al-Falāsifah*, he held that there were mistakes in translating the works of Aristotle which led to distortions and changes in the Arabic texts. These mistakes prompted the Islamic philosophers to interpret the philosophical texts in a fashion that caused conflict amongst themselves. In addition, he restricted his discussion of philosophy to the books of Al-Fārābi and Ibn Sīnā. Since Al-Fārābi's metaphysics was basically a melange of Neo-Platonism and Aristotelianism, one can see the roots of Al-Ghazzāliyy's position that what the philosophers believed in this field is contrary to the truth.[60]

Al-Ghazzāliyy defined logic as "the law (qānūn) that distinguishes a sound premise and analogy from a false one, which leads to the discernment of true knowledge".[61] In addition, he reviewed all the subjects of logic including induction (istiqrā'). He held that induction could be correct only if all parts were covered; if one part could possibly be different, then induction in this case could not yield true knowledge. To prove his point, he used the following argument:

58 Al-Ghazzāliyy, *Maqasid al-Falasifah*, pp. 31–32.
59 *Ibid.*, p. 32.
60 Al-Ghazzāliyy, *Tahafut*, pp. 76–77.
61 Al-Ghazzāliyy, *Maqasid al-Falasifah*, p. 36.

Every animal is a human being, mare, etc.

Every human being moves his lower jaw when he chews.

Every mare moves its lower jaw when it chews.

And every (animal) other than these two moves its lower jaw when it chews.

The conclusion: every animal moves its lower jaw.

Al-Ghazzāliyy said that if one animal differs, as is the case with the crocodile which moves its upper jaw, then the conclusion does not yield true knowledge. So, by parts he means members of the same species or group as in the case of "mare", "human being" and "crocodile". Al-Ghazzāliyy maintained that induction was suitable for matters of jurisprudence (*fiqhiyyāt*), but not for true knowledge.[62] This suggests that Al-Ghazzāliyy accepted induction for practical reasons, but not as a source of true knowledge.

In addition to his review of logic in *Maqāṣid al-Falāsifah*, Al-Ghazzāliyy wrote several books on logic during this period. He wrote *Mi'yār al-'Ilm fī Fann al-Manṭiq* (The Criterion of Knowledge in the Art of Logic), *Miḥak al-Naẓar fī al-Manṭiq* (The Touch-Stone of Reasoning in Logic) and *Mīzān Al-'Amal* (The Balance of Action).[63]

It was argued that the first book, *Mi'yār al-'Ilm fī Fann al-Manṭiq*, was the last part of *Tahāfut al-Falāsifah*. Unlike Ibn Sīnā who began his *Al-Ishārāt wa al-Tanbīhāt* with a discussion of logic,[64] Al-Ghazzāliyy stated that he was going to write the *kitāb*[65] of *Mi'yar al-'Ilm* at the end of *Tahāfut al-Falāsifah*. One can see that whether they comprise one or two books depends on how to interpret the word *kitāb*. If it is interpreted as chapter, then there is one book; if it is interpreted as book then there are two.

62 Al-Ghazzaliyy, *Maqasid al-Falasifah*, pp. 89–90.
63 Badawi, p. xvi.
64 Al-Ghazzaliyy, *Mi'yar al-'Ilm*, Ahmad Shams Al-Din, ed. (Beirut: Dar al-Kutub al-'Ilmiyyah, 1990) p. 11.
65 The word *kitab* is used in classical Arabic literature to indicate, among many other meanings, either a book or a chapter.

Regardless of the latter issue, Al-Ghazzāliyy placed *Mi'yār al-'Ilm* "after" the *Tahāfut* in order that those who were already familiar with logic could commence with his criticism of philosophy directly. For those who did not understand the vocabulary that he used in responding to the philosophers, Al-Ghazzaliyy instructed them to start with *Mi'yar al-'Ilm.*[66]

Despite the fact that Al-Ghazzāliyy wanted his presentation of metaphysics and logic in the *Tahāfut* and *Mi'yār al-'Ilm* to be different from their order in Ibn Sīnā's *al-Ishārāt wa al-Tanbīhāt,* Marmura argues that "much of the account of demonstration in the *Mi'yār* seems to be a faithful summary of Avicenna's *Demonstration (Al-Ishārāt)* which in turn is an exposition and an enlargement of Aristotle's *Posterior Analytics".*[67]

There was yet another purpose for *Mi'yār al-'Ilm.* Al-Ghazzāliyy intended that the relationship between logic and thought to be analogous to that between meter (*'arūḍ*) and poetry. For him, the theoretical sciences (*al-'Ulum al-nazāriyyah*), which correspond to "thought" in the above analogy, were not innate but rather acquired (*mustaḥṣalah*). Al-Ghazzāliyy realized that the process of acquiring knowledge resulted in many mistakes in reasoning which required a criterion for science (*mi'yār li al-nazar*) which corresponds to logic.[68]

One of the most important claims in *Mi'yār al-'Ilm* was Al-Ghazzāliyy's assertion that, in every person, there were three judges: a sensible-judge (*ḥākim ḥissiyy*), an imaginative-judge (*ḥākim wahmiyy*)[69] and a rational-judge (*ḥākim 'aqliyy*). He declared the rational-judge to be the only correct one.[70] This suggests that *Mi'yār al-'Ilm* must have been written after the end of his two months of

---

66 Al-Ghazzaliyy, *Tahafut al-Falasifah,* Sulaiman Dunya, ed. (Cairo: Dar al-Ma'arif, 1972) p. 85.
67 Michael Marmura, "Ghazali and Demonstrative Science," *Journal of the History of Philosophy,* III (1965): 189.
68 Al-Ghazzaliyy, *Mi'yar,* p. 26.
69 Al-Ghazzaliyy defined the judge of illusion in terms of its false judgement such as denying the existence of a being that one "cannot point to its direction", which indicates a being that is spaceless.
70 Al-Ghazzaliyy, *Mi'yar,* p. 29.

skepticism for only then had he regained his trust in logical necessities.[71]

The language that Al-Ghazzāliyy used in his introduction to discuss the above position in *Mi'yār al-'Ilm* was somewhat similar to the one he used later on in *Al-Munqidh min al-Ḍalāl*. In *Al-Munqidh*, Al-Ghazzāliyy portrayed the different faculties, including the senses, discernment and reason according to their natural evolution in the human being. But he did not mention the imaginative-judge and restricted himself to the sensible-judge and the rational-judge.[72] The idea of *al-ḥākim al-waḥmiyy* was not an original idea of Al-Ghazzāliyy. He borrowed the concept, along with that of the imaginative (*khayāliyyah*) and thinking (*mufakkirah*) powers, from the philosophers.[73] He differed from the philosophers, however by attempting to justify his usage of these concepts through texts of the Shari'ah (the Qur'an and the Sunnah) or even with *Āthār*.[74]

The second book on logic, *Miḥak al-Nazar fī al-Mantiq*, was written as a shorter, refined version of *Mi'yar al-'Ilm fī Fann al-Mantiq* which was not circulated when it was written because it needed some clarification.[75]

At the end of *Mi'yār al-'Ilm*, Al-Ghazzāliyy stated his intention to write a book which would provide a criterion for action (*Mīzān Al-'Amal*)[76] just as *Mi'yār al-'Ilm* was a criterion for knowledge.[77] Al-Ghazzāliyy reiterated the same concept in his introduction to *Mīzān al-'Amal* where he discussed happiness. For him, there were two conditions for the attainment of happiness: knowledge and action. He said that he intended to discuss the action

71 Al-Ghazzaliyy, *Al-Munqidh*, p. 86.
72 *Ibid.*, pp. 83–85.
73 Al-Ghazzaliyy, *Tahafut*, pp. 252–253.
74 *Athar* indicates narrations about the early generations of Muslims. These *athar* were never considered as part of the Shari'ah. An example of Al-Ghazzaliyy's use of *athar* was an account about Abu Bakr, the first Caliph, on page 32 of *Mi'yar al-'Ilm*.
75 Al-Ghazzaliyy, *Miḥak al-Nazar fī al-Mantiq*, Muhammad Badr al-Din al-Na'saniyy, ed. (Beirut:Dar An-Nahdah al-Hadithah, 1966) p. 145.
76 The literal translation of *Mizan al-'Amal* is *The Balance for Action*.
77 Al-Ghazzaliyy, *Mi'yar*, p. 334.

which leads to happiness in a way that transcended conformism (*taqlīd*) in accordance with the conditions he set forth in *Mi'yār al-'Ilm*, and planned to begin it with a brief summary of the fundamentals of his criterion of knowledge.[78]

Al-Ghazzāliyy stated that happiness consisted in the life hereafter; i.e., the eternal.[79] Thus he revealed his sympathy with the position of the Sufi leaders regarding eternal happiness, who held that happiness should not be thought of merely as the attainment of paradise or the avoidance of hellfire. They considered such aspirations crass, since there was a more honorable aim.[80] Al-Ghazzāliyy explained this aim as unveiling (*kashf*) divine matters through divine inspiration (*ilhām*). He stated, citing the case of the Qur'an, that knowledge is never conveyed directly from Allah to human beings; this act takes place indirectly (eg. by angels).[81] The position of the Sufi leaders, however, contradicts the Qur'an which considers seeking paradise or the avoidance of hellfire to be legitimate.[82] By agreeing with the Sufi leaders, Al-Ghazzāliyy's position could be interpreted as contradictory to that of the Qur'an. It should be noted that Al-Ghazzāliyy, under the influence of Sufism, differed with the Qur'an and the Sunnah if these texts are to be taken literally.

In addition to his emphasis on the correlation between happiness and the noetic elements in *kashf*, as he explained above, Al-Ghazzāliyy said that the happiness of anything lies in its perfection. He understood this perfection, in the case of the human beings, to be perceiving the reality of the intelligibles (*ma'qūlāt*), as they are in themselves (*'alā ma hya 'alayh*), without the interference of imagination and the sensibles.[83] It appears that he was hinting at divine inspiration as a source of knowledge that is not hindered by imagination or sensibles.

Al-Ghazzāliyy maintained that in order to receive this divine inspiration, one should purify his soul from what-

---

78 Al-Ghazzaliyy, *Mizan al-'Amal*, Sulaiman Dunya, ed. (Cairo: Dar al-Ma'arif Bi-Misr, 1964) p. 179.
79 Al-Ghazzaliyy, *Mizan*, p. 180.
80 *Ibid.*, p. 185.
81 *Ibid.*, p. 205.
82 Al-Qur'an, Sura *al-Anbiya'* 21:90, and Sura *al-Sajdah* 32:16.
83 Al-Ghazzaliyy, *Mizan*, pp. 195–196.

ever lust he has. After conquering bodily lust and freeing himself from slavery, one should start spiritual exercise (*riyāḍah*).[84] To support his argument on the purification of the soul, Al-Ghazzāliyy quoted a verse from the Qur'an which promises success for the one who purifies her/his soul.[85]

If someone does not receive such divine inspiration, Al-Ghazzāliyy asserted that this person is to be blamed. To explain this, he provided the following metaphorical example:

"There is nothing in the colored picture to prevent it from being reflected in iron; the veil is in the rust and in the

lack of a polisher to clean it."[86]

Similarly, Al-Ghazzāliyy went on to say, not only should one polish the the mirror by cleaning the dirt if he would like it to reflect pictures, but he should also face it in the direction of what he would like this mirror to reflect.[87] By "mirror" Al-Ghazzāliyy meant the soul, by "dirt", wordly desires and by "picture", divine knowledge.

Al-Ghazzāliyy believed in the possibility of changing human behavior. He thought that if it was possible to change the nature of animals (i.e. taming them), then one must not deny human beings the same possibility.[88] He stated that human beings have the potential to reach the level where they can acquire truth. If they strive hard enough against their desires, they can reach the level of the angels. And if they allow dirt to accumulate on the mirror of the soul, by following their desires, they join the ranks of the animals.[89]

To change one's character, one should attain virtue which could be achieved in two ways. The first is through what Al-Ghazzāliyy called human education (*ta'allum bashariyy*) which involves the will and needs time and

84   Al-Ghazzaliyy, *Mizan*, pp. 196–197.
85   Al-Qur'an, Sura *al-Shams* 91:9.
86   Al-Ghazzaliyy, *Mizan*, p. 208.
87   *Ibid.*, p. 218.
88   *Ibid.*, p. 247.
89   *Ibid.*, p. 218.

practice according to the ability of the person involved. The second way takes place through "divine grace (*jawd ilāhiyy*) where the human being becomes knowledgeable at birth as 'Īsā Ibn Maryam (Jesus son of Mary [a.s.]) and Yaḥyā Ibn Zakariyya [a.s.] in addition to the other prophets. Also, it was said that this (knowledge) might be given to non-prophets".[90]

Al-Ghazzāliyy's discussion of virtue is clearly Aristotelian in its inspiration, with many concepts that can be traced back to *Nicomachean Ethics*. He stated that the soul has two powers: the rational (*al-'aqliyyah*) and the practical intellect (*al-'aql al-'amaliyy*). The first one is responsible for receiving "theoretical practical wisdom" (*al-ḥikmah al-'amaliyyah al-nazariyyah*)[91] which he defined as truths that are absolute and do not change because of time or place. The second is the practical intellect which attains moral wisdom (*al-ḥikmah al-khuluqiyyah*). This moral wisdom is related to the lower part of the soul which Al-Ghazzāliyy defined as that which addresses the concerns of the body.[92]

Al-Ghazzāliyy believed that all virtues could be classified under four major categories - wisdom, courage, chastity and justice. He maintained that a virtue is a median (*wasaṭ*) that falls between two vices: excess and deficiency. Similar to the position of Aristotle, Al-Ghazzāliyy exempted justice from the above rule, stating that justice has only one extreme which is injustice.[93]

Mīzān al-'Amāl can be placed in the development of Al-Ghazzāliyy's epistemology by means of his statement about the composition of this book - namely, that most of what is in *Mīzān al-'Amal* is based upon the Sufi way. In response to a previous question about whether Al-Ghazzāliyy's account of Sufism in this book reflects his own

90 Al-Ghazzaliyy, *Mizan*, p. 257.
91 Aristotle distinguished between "theoretical" and "practical wisdom". Nevertheless, we can see that Al-Ghazzaliyy was inspired by Aristotle's discussion of these two concepts; he departed from Aristotle by bringing these two categories together. See Aristotle, *Nicomachean Ethics*, Martin Ostwald, trans, and ed. (Indianapolis: Bobbs-Merill Educational Publishing, 1983) pp. 147–173.
92 Al-Ghazzaliyy, *Mizan*, p. 265.
93 *Ibid.*, p. 264–273.

belief, he said that he was only reporting it.[94] Neverthe-less, one can see his inclination towards Sufism in many places.

Al-Ghazzāliyy ended *Mīzān al-'Amal* in the same way he started it. There was a lengthy yet very important invitation to abandon conformism (*taqlīd*):

> "Do not look at the (available) schools (as sources of knowledge), and seek truth through research, so you will have your own school. Do not be like a blind person imitating a leader who guides you to a way, while you are surrounded by a thousand leaders similar to yours, who are telling you that he rushed you into danger and that he misled you away from the right path. You will eventually know the injustice of your leader. There is no salvation except in independence."[95]

Al-Ghazzāliyy added that it would be good enough if the above words lead the reader to doubt his inherited belief, so he may begin searching for truth because "doubts lead to the truth, and he who does not doubt, does not look, and he who does not look does not see, and he who does not see lingers blind and astray".[96]

3.6 AL-GHAZZĀLIYY'S CRITIQUE OF PHILOSOPHY

After Al-Ghazzāliyy reported the core of philosophy as he understood it in *Maqāsid al-Falāsifah*, he followed with, *Tahāfut al-Falāsifah*. The latter was written basically as a critique of the metaphysics of the ancient (i.e. Greek) philosophers.[97] Although Al-Ghazzāliyy mentioned Aristotle's name in particular,[98] he restricted his criticism to whatever Al-Fārabī (d. 339 A.H. /950 C.E.)[99] and Ibn Sīnā

94   Al-Ghazzaliyy, *Mizan*, p. 358.
95   *Ibid.*, p. 409.
96   *Ibid.*
97   Al-Ghazzaliyy, *Tahafut*, p. 75.
98   *Ibid.*, p. 76.
99   The full name of Al-Farabi, who was known in Latin as Alpharabius, was Muhammad Ibn Muhammad Ibn Tarkhan Ibn Uzlagh Abu Nasr Al-Farabi. He was born at Wasij, a village near Farab, in 257 A.H./870 C.E.

80

(d. 428 A.H./1037 C.E.)[100] incorporated in their philosophies.[101] Of the issues they dealt with, he commented on twenty: sixteen in metaphysics and four in the natural sciences.[102] He listed these issues as follow:

1. The refutation of their theory of the eternity of the world.

2. The refutation of their theory of the incorruptibility of the world and of time and of motion.

3. The demonstration of their confusion in saying that Allah is the agent and the maker of the world in His product and act, and the demonstration that these expressions are in their system only metaphors without any real sense.

4. Showing that they are unable to prove the existence of a creator of the world.

5. To show their incapacity to prove Allah's oneness and the impossibility of two necessary existents both without a cause.

6. To refute their denial of attributes.

7. To refute their claim that nothing can share with the First its genus, and be differentiated from it through a specific difference, and that with respect to its intellect the division into genus and specific difference cannot be applied to it.

8. To refute their theory that the existence of the First is simple, namely that it is pure existence and that its existence stands in relation to no quiddity and to no

---

100 The full name of Ibn Sīna was Abu 'Ali Al-Husayn Ibn 'Abdullah Ibn Sīna. His Latin name was Avicenna. He was born in 370 A.H./980 C.E.
101 Al-Ghazzaliyy, *Tahafut.* pp. 77–78.
102 *Ibid.,* pp. 86–87.

essence, but stands to necessary existence as do other beings to their quiddity.

9. To show their incapacity to prove that the First is incorporeal.[103]

10. To prove their incapacity to demonstrate that the world has a creator and a cause, and that in fact they are forced to admit atheism.

11. To show the incapacity of the philosophers to prove what they believe: that the First (i.e. Allah) knows other things besides His own self, and that He knows the genera and the species in a universal way.

12. On the impotence of the philosophers to prove that Allah knows Himself.

13. To refute those who affirm that Allah is ignorant of the individual things which are divided in time into present, past and future.

14. To refute their proof that heaven is an animal moving in a circle in obedience to Allah.

15. To refute the theory of the philosophers about the aim which moves heaven.

16. To refute the philosophical theory that the souls of the heavens observe all the particular events of this world.

17. The denial of a logical necessity between cause and effect.

18. The importance of the philosophers to show by demon-

103 Simon Van Den Bergh wrongly translated *Fi ta'jizihim 'an bayan anna al-Awwal laysa bijism* as "To refute their proof that the first is incorporeal." Averroes, *Tahafut al-Tahafut*, Simon Van Den Bergh, trans. and ed. (London: Messrs Luzac and Company, 1954) p. vii.

strative proof that the soul is a spiritual substance.

19.   Refutation of the philosophers' proof for the immortality of the soul.

20.   Concerning the philosophers' denial of bodily resurrection.[104]

Al-Ghazzāliyy declared these philosophers blasphemous on three counts: "their saying that all substances (jawāhir) are eternal, that Allah does not know particular accidents involving people and their denial of the resurrection of bodies." He held that these three issues" do not fit Islam in any fashion".[105]

In this vein, modern and contemporary scholars have questioned the nature of Islamic philosophy: exactly what is Islamic about it?[106] The only answer, I think, that could reconcile the various positions regarding this issue is the notion that this philosophy is Islamic as a product of the Islamic civilization. Thus, "Islamic" in the cultural sense could be applied to every contribution to knowledge that took place anywhere in the land of Islam during that era, including that of a Jew like Mūsā Ibn Maymūn (Maimonides) or a Christian like Yahiyā Ibn 'Adī.[107] It would be inappropriate to call it Arabic philosophy, since this would imply that those who contributed to it were Arabs;

104   Averroes, *Tahafut al-Tahafut*, pp. vii-viii. I have used Bergh's translation of these twenty issues with some modifications.
105   Al-Ghazzaliyy, *Tahafut*, pp. 307–309.
106   An example of this is Leaman's statement: "It is a shame that Islamic philosophy as a topic of interest is at present largely confined to orientalists (e.g. Goldziher, Muller, Munk, Noldeke, Renan and De Boer) rather than philosophers. The former often have concerns and interpretive methods which are not shared by the latter, and vice versa." See Oliver Leaman, *An Introduction to Medieval Islamic Philosophy* (Cambridge: Cambridge University Press, 1985) p. xi.
107   Yahia Ibn 'Adi, also known as the Logician (*Al-Mantiqiyy*), was a tenth century Jacobite theologian and philosopher. He translated Aristotle's *Poetica, Sophistica, Topica,* and possibly *Metaphysica.* He was credited with a translation of Plato's *Laws,* a commentary on *Topica* and parts of *Physica* VIII and *Metaphysica,* and the whole of *De Generatione.* In addition, he wrote a series of original philosophical treatises. Fakhry, *History,* p. 28.

it would be Arabic only in the sense that it was written in the Arabic language. As a matter of fact, those who used Arabic did so because it was *lingua franca*. Ibn Khaldūn (d. 808 A.H./1406 C.E.) stated in his *Muqaddimah* that in the majority of the sciences, most scholars were non-Arabs (*'Ajam*) except in very rare cases, and in some fields, they were all non-Arabs.[108]

Al-Ghazzāliyy sought to develop a philosophy that is Islamic in its very essence. He knew that in order to do that, he had to establish and verify the epistemology upon which this body of thought depends.

In addition to his criticism of the twenty questions that he listed in the introduction of *Tahāfut al-Falāsifah*, Al-Ghazzāliyy argued against the methodology and general acceptance of metaphysics by the philosophers in the Islamic world. This is of particular interest because of the original goal that he established for himself; he was still looking for a method that would lead to true knowledge.

His first argument was that the philosophers (i.e. Al-Fārabī and Ibn Sīnā) acquired their thought through habitually communicated conformism (*taqlīd samā'ī ilfī*). According to Al-Ghazzāliyy, they simply moved from one mode of conformism to another without verification. His second argument was psychological: they accepted Greek philosophy because of the fame of names like Socrates, Hippocrates, Plato and Aristotle.[109] The third was based upon Aristotle's criticism of all his predecessors including Plato, his own teacher, which Al-Ghazzāliyy thought was an indication of an incoherent metaphysical system. In his last argument, Al-Ghazzāliyy accused the philosophers of using the accuracy of logic and mathematics to create a false impression of a sound generalization which would encompass metaphysics because he held that metaphysics lacked precise proofs.[110]

Regarding the fairness of Al-Ghazzāliyy's position, I think that he was consistent in the first point which was directed at the Islamic Philosophers; he rejected confor-

---

108 Ibn Khaldun, *al-Muqaddimah* (Beirut: Dar al-Qalam, 1984) pp. 543–545.
109 Al-Ghazzaliyy, *Tahafut*, pp. 73–74.
110 *Ibid.*, pp. 76–77.

mism or uncritical acceptance of any set of thought including that of Sharī'ah. The originality of these philosophers is still a disputed issue. On the second point, I would reiterate the position of Dunya who defended, in his commentary on the *Tahāfut*,[111] the philosophers' order of subjects and thus there is no problem with beginning either with mathematics or logic. Yet, Dunya did not rule out the possibility that Al-Ghazzāliyy had a debate with some philosopher who gave him the impression that the philosophers were entrenching themselves behind a shield of logic and mathematics.[112] The third point is a clear case of a false *ad hominem* argument.

One issue in particular, the seventeenth in the *Tahāfut*, which is concerned with causality, is especially noteworthy. Long time before David Hume, Al-Ghazzāliyy said that, in his opinion, "the conjunction (*al-iqtirān*) between what is conceived, by way of habit (*fī al-'ādah*), as cause and effect is not necessary (*laysa darūriyyan*)".[113] He provided a list of pairs that were usually thought of as cause and effect by the philosophers (e.g., fire and burning, light and sunrise, diarrhea and laxatives). For him, the conjunction between them was a result of the sequence in which they were created by Allah, not because this conjunction was necessary in itself. Moreover, he thought that it was possible for either one of these pairs (eg. fire or burning) to exist without the other.[114] He did not see any logical contradiction since these pairs are the phenomena of nature and nature as such, according to the philosophers' own admission, does not belong to the realm of necessity but to that of possibility, which may or may not exist.[115]

Al-Ghazzāliyy criticized the philosophers' proof of causality because it was limited to observation (*mushāhadah*) which depends on the senses (eg. sight), a source of knowledge that he could not accept on its own merit. Thus Al-

111 Dunya, "Commentary", *Tahafut*, by Al-Ghazzaliyy, pp. 76–77.
112 Al-Ghazzaliyy, *Tahafut*, p. 77.
113 *Ibid.*, 239.
114 *Ibid.*
115 In *Tahafut al-Tahafut* Ibn Rushd (Averroes) considered Al-Ghazzaliyy's concept of causality a denial of the efficient cause, which led him to accuse Al-Ghazzaliyy of Sophistry. Sheikh, p. 98.

Ghazzāliyy's position regarding causality is consistent with his theory of knowledge. Using the example of fire and burning, he said that "observation could only prove that burning took place when there was fire, and not by fire". He held that inert and lifeless objects such as fire are incapable of action and thus cannot be the agent.[116] To prove his point that fire is not the agent (al-fā'ilah) that causes burning, Al-Ghazzāliyy used a proof, which is Neoplatonic in its tone, from the arguments of the philosophers. They held that accidents (a'rāḍ) and incidents (hawādith) emanate, at the time of contact between "bodies", from the provider of forms (wāḥib al-ṣuwar) whom they thought to be an angel.[117] Accordingly, one cannot claim that fire is the agent of burning. In addition, Al-Ghazzāliyy argued that the agent "creates" burning at the time of contact between a cotton ball and fire with his will (bi'irādatihi).[118] Al-Ghazzāliyy reduced the problem of causality to that of "will" which makes it rationally possible for the agent, whom he held to be Allah, not to create burning even though there is contact.[119]

Al-Ghazzāliyy presented this theory of causality in order to allow room for the existence of miracles (mu'jizāt) that were associated with prophets, without resorting to allegorical interpretations as the philosophers did.[120] One of the miracles that he chose as an example, was that of prophet Ibrāhīm [a.s.][121] The story was that the people

116· Al-Ghazzaliyy, *Tahafut*, p. 240.
117 *Ibid.*, 242.
118 This particular concept influenced Nicolaus of Autrecourt who

argued that "this consequence, namely, 'fire is close to flax and there is no impediment, hence the flax will be consumed', is not evident by an evidence deduced from the first principle." See, Harry A. Wolfson, "Nicolaus of Autrecourt and Ghazzaliyy's Argument Against Causality", *Speculum* (1969), pp. 234–238.
119 Al-Ghazzaliyy, *Tahafut*, pp. 242–243.
120 *Ibid.*, p. 236.
121 This miracle was wrongly disputed by Ilai Alon as the only miracle to be mentioned by Al-Ghazzaliyy in *Tahafut al-Falasifah* when he discussed causality. Ilai Alon, "Al-Ghazzaliyy on Causality", *Journal of the American Oriental Society* 100. 4 (1980) p. 402. Al-Ghazzaliyy mentioned three other miracles of Moses, Jesus and Muhammad in chronological order, although he only mentioned the name of Moses in addition to that of Ibrahim which disqualifies Alon's claim. Al-Ghazzaliyy, *Tahafut al-Falasifah*, p. 236.

of Ibrāhīm attempted to punish him for breaking their idols by throwing him into fire but no burning took place. In the Qur'an it was Allah's will that the fire would not harm Ibrāhīm.[122] Al-Ghazzāliyy maintained that Allah [S.W.T.] was the agent (*fa'il*) of every action, either directly or indirectly (i.e. by the angels).[123] This deprivation of lifeless objects (eg. fire) from being the agent can be interpreted as Al-Ghazzāliyy's defence of Allah's omnipotence and free will. Indeed, Ibn Sīnā held that Allah is the supreme essential efficient cause which indicates that the world is a necessary product of His essence (i.e. He cannot but create the world).[124]

The conclusion that Al-Ghazzāliyy reached after studying philosophy was that this science did not fulfill the aim of his search. In addition, he stated that "reason ('*aql*) is not capable of attaining all the goals nor can it solve all problems".[125] Al-Ghazzāliyy used reason in showing the limitations of reason in his criticism of philosophy, and as such he was paving the way for a source of kowledge other than that of reason. Al-Ghazzāliyy's position towards reason had resemblance to the course Kant took in showing the limitations of reason, although in a different way since Kant attempted to reconcile the position of the rationalists and the empiricists (i.e. Descartes and Hume).[126] Eventually, as it will be shown below in the section on Sufism, Al-Ghazzāliyy wanted to establish a faculty higher than that of reason which drew on the same source of knowledge as prophets. This stance of Al-Ghazzāliyy was an attempt to place prophecy above reason, a position which was antogonistic to that of the Muslim philosophers who raised reason above prophecy.

122   Al-Qur'an Sura *al-Anbiya'* 21:69 . The verse reads, "*Qulna ya naru kuni bardan wa salaman 'ala Ibrahim*". The meaning of it is, "We (Allah) said, O Fire! Be cool and peace for Ibrahim."
123   Al-Ghazzaliyy, *Tahafut*, pp. 243–247.
124   Marmurah, p. 186.
125   Al-Ghazzaliyy, *Al-Munqidh*, pp. 117–118.
126   In addition to the above similarity between Kant and Al-Ghazzaliyy, although not identical there are other mutual interests of both thinkers. Kant states in the *Critique of Pure Reason* that he was seeking to provide room for faith and morality, a position that is celebrated in much of Al-Ghazzaliyy's writings.

It has been suggested that Al-Ghazzāliyy was affected in a more substantive way by his review and subsequent critique of philosophy. One of his students, Abū Bakr Ibn Al-'Arabiyy, asserted that his teacher "entered inside the philosophers and wanted to exit but couldn't".[127] In addition, among contemporaries, Badawi holds that Al-Ghazzāliyy was always faithful to philosophy and that he was an Aristotelian for some time before he ended up a neo-Platonist.[128] However, the findings of Hava Lazarus-Yafeh, who studied the works of Al-Ghazzāliyy from a philological point of view and used philosophical terms as a criterion of authenticity in his writings shed doubt upon these interpretations. She said that the common medieval philosophical terms (which were mostly Neoplatonic, but to a certain extent also Aristotelian) were entirely absent from those books by Al-Ghazzāliyy which scholars accepted as authentic books written by him. Only in those of his books which dealt with description or refutation of philosophical doctrines, such as his *Maqāṣid, Tahāfut, Mihak al-Naẓar, Mi'yār al-'Ilm* and to a lesser degree also *Mīzān al-'Amal,* did this terminology appear. Moreover, after stating that Al-Ghazzāliyy was well versed in philosophical doctrines and knew their technical terminology better than any Muslim theologian before him, she added:

> "Yet here is a most astonishing linguistic fact that in a large number of his books including his major works, there is nowhere any use of a single philosophical term, even when Al-Ghazzāliyy deals with typical metaphysical subjects and not in the usual orthodox way."[129]

It should be noted here that Lazarus-Yafeh excluded some books whose authenticity was disputed. She maintained that these books, which did include philosophical terms, could have been possibly written by one of three groups. First, admirers who wanted to expound Al-Ghazzāliyy's ideas while at the same time incorporating philo-

<hr>

127　Ibn Taymiyyah, *Naqd al-Manṭiq* (Cairo: Maktabat Al-Sunnah Al-Muhammadiyyah, 1951) p. 56.
128　Badawi, *Dawr al-'Arab fī Takwīn al-Fikr al-Awrubbiyy* (Al-Kuwait: Wakalat al-Matbu'at, 1979) pp. 203–205.
129　Lazarus-Yafeh, p. 249.

88

sophical notions from other sources that they admired as well; second, unknown authors who wanted their own books to survive by attributing them to famous scholars; third, enemies of Al-Ghazzāliyy who wanted to paint a distorted picture of him. Nevertheless, Lazarus-Yafeh admitted that the authenticity of books should not be based only on stylistic or linguistic criteria.[130]

3.7 AL-GHAZZĀLIYY'S SEARCH CONTINUES; THE CONFRONTATION WITH THE ESOTERICS (*AL-BĀṬINIYYAH*)

When he was done with the philosophers, Al-Ghazzāliyy turned to the *Bāṭiniyyah* who flourished during his life time. Not only was he interested in their methodology, but he also found himself confronting them politically. The Caliph requested that Al-Ghazzāliyy write a book about the veracity of their belief, showing that the Batinites were perceived as a threat to the central government in Baghdad. Upon this request from the Caliph, which Al-Ghazzāliyy considered a motivation from without added to the original one from within, he sought the Batinites's book and treatises. Moreover, he asserted that, during that time, he was already aware of some of their newly invented vocabulary and statements, which were different from those of their predecessors.[131]

In preparation for his research in this area. Al-Ghazzāliyy collected and organized the Batinite's statements and views. His presentation of these views prompted one of his contemporaries, whom Al-Ghazzāliyy referred to as "one of the people of truth" (*ba'd ahl al-ḥaq*), to denounce what he called an exaggeration (*mubālaghah*) in the extent Al-Ghazzāliyy took in reporting their belief. He held that Al-Ghazzāliyy helped the Batinites to a degree that they themselves could not match.[132] Al-Ghazzāliyy reacted to this

130   Lazarus-Yafeh, pp. 255–257.
131   Al-Ghazzaliyy, *al-Munqidh*, p. 118. For further information on this historical period see p. 22.
132   Al-Ghazzaliyy narrated that a similar criticism was directed by Ahmad Ibn Hanbal toward Al-Harith Al-Muhasibiyy when the latter responded to the *Mu'tazilah*. Al-Ghazzaliyy, *Al-Munqidh*, pp. 118–119.

criticism by saying that it could have been correct if the beliefs of the Batinites were not already known. However in this case their views had been previously disseminated.[133]

In addition, Al-Ghazzāliyy said that the Batinites claimed that no authors (*musannifūn*) at the time understood their arguments. Hence, Al-Ghazzāliyy found it appropriate to explain their arguments before criticizing them, an approach similar to his treatment of the philosophers. Al-Ghazzāliyy said that he did not want anyone to think that he criticized the Batinites without understanding them.[134]

According to the Batinites, there was a need for learning and a teacher, yet not every teacher was equipped to disseminate knowledge which could be acquired only through the inffalible (*ma'sūm*) teacher or Imam. Al-Ghazzāliyy maintained that the cause of the Batinites flourished because those who argued against the principles advocated by the Batinites were "ignorant". He thought that their premises were true but their conclusion was false. Al-Ghazzāliyy found that the problem was in arguing against the true premisses rather than the false conclusion.[135] He added that one should question the knowledge that they claim to have acquired, and he did. Not only they could not answer his questions, they did not understand them in the first place, and that was exactly why they would return to the notion that only the infallible Imam would know the answer. Al-Ghazzāliyy based his discourse with the Batinites upon numerous historical occurences.[136]

Al-Ghazzāliyy criticized the Batinites in several books written during the different stages of his life beginning with the first period of public teaching. He wrote the first, *Al-Mustazhiriyy*, at the request of the Caliph Al-Mustazhir, (after whom it was named).   This was followed by *Hujjat al-Haq* (The Proof of the Truth), which was written as a direct response to the arguments of Batinites which he encountered in Baghdad. After leaving his position at the Nizāmiyyah, he wrote *Mufassil al-Khilāf* (The Clarifier of the Dis-

<hr>

133 Al-Ghazzaliyy, *Al-Munqidh*, p. 118.
134 *Ibid.*, pp. 118–119.
135 *Ibid.*, p. 120.
136 Ibid., p. 127.

agreement) which was written in reaction to their statements in *Hamadhān* and *Al-Darj al-Marqūm bī al-Jadāwil* (The Annotated Scroll with Tabulars) which was written in answer to their allegations in Tus.[137] In addition, Al-Ghazzāliyy wrote *Al-Qistās al-Mustaqīm* (The Correct Balance) which was intended as an indirect response to the Batinites by presenting an alternative source of knowledge other than their Infallible Imam. Al-Ghazzāliyy's last written expose of the Batinites, which took place during the second period of public teaching, was in *Al-Munqidh min al-Dalāl* where he devoted a chapter to criticizing them for the last time.[138]

There is an account in *Al-Munqidh* where Al-Ghazzāliyy characterized the position of the Batinites as part of the philosophy of Pythagoras. Al-Ghazzāliyy probably held Aristotle in high regard because he criticized Pythagoras. Al-Ghazzāliyy learned of this account of Aristotle from the writings of a secretive philosophical group called *Ikhwān al-Safā'* (the Brethren of Purity).[139] It appears that Al-Ghazzāliyy did not see the strong relationship between the Batinites and *Ikhwān al-Safā'*. However, the first four chapters of the forty-fourth letter reveal that both of them had the same strategy for disseminating their belief.[140] In fact, it was argued that the Brethren were connected with the Batinite propaganda against the Abbasid caliphate.[141] Once he recognized the truth about the Batinites, Al-Ghazzāliyy

137   Many scholars, have had a problem translating the title of this book. I think that the problem arose from their reading the stressed 'd' of *Al-Darj*, which means a scroll, with a *dummah* and thus it became *al-Durj* which means a small cabinet. 'Scroll' makes more sense than 'cabinet'.

138   Al-Ghazzaliyy, *Al-Munqidh*, p. 127.

139   *Ikhwan al-Safa'* was a secret association of philosophers. It was established at Basrah in 373 A.H./983 C.E. with a branch in Baghdad. They wrote fifty two treatises which were presented as an Encyclopedia. These covered mathematics, logic, metaphysics, mysticism, astrology, magic and the natural sciences. The Brethren of Purity were eclectic in their philosophy with borrowings from Greek, Indian, Persian, Jewish and Christian sources. Sheikh, *Islamic Philosophy*, pp. 32–41.

140   *Rasa'il Ikhwan al-Safa wa Khillan al-Wafa* (Dar Beirut: Beirut, 1983) Vol. IV, pp. 14–40.

141   Sheikh, *Islamic Philosophy*, p. 33.

cleared them from his path and continued his march in pursuit of truth.[142]

3.8 AL-GHAZZĀLIYY BECOMING A SUFI

Sufism, or Islamic mysticism as it is sometimes referred to, was the last class of seekers that Al-Ghazzāliyy considered in his quest for true knowledge. He said that after his completion of the study of the other sciences, he came to study *ṭuruq al-ṣūfiyyah* (the ways of the Sufis). He knew that their way could only be realized through knowledge and activity together. By knowledge, Al-Ghazzāliyy meant the theoretical aspect of the Sufi way and by activity its application.[143] Concerning the relationship between theory and practice, Al-Ghazzāliyy offered an example in which he said that there is a great difference between knowing the definition of health and being healthy. Analogous to this is the gap between knowing what the reality of *zuhd* (asceticism)[144] is and being an ascetic.[145]

Soon Al-Ghazzāliyy realized that the theoretical part of Sufism was much easier than its application. He started acquiring knowledge of the Sufi 'way' through reading the books of Sufis such as *Qūt al-Qulūb*) (The Food of the Hearts) by Abū Ṭālib Al-Makkiyy (d. 388 A.H./998 C.E.) and the books of Al-Hārith Al-Muhāsibiyy (d. 243 A.H./857 C.E.). He also studied the known fragments of al-Junayd (d. 297 A.H./ 909 C.E.), Al-Shibliyy (d. 334 A.H./945 C.E.) and Abū Yazīd Al-Bustāmiyy (d. 264 A.H./877 C.E.0 among others.[146]

None of Al-Ghazzāliyy's books ever mentioned the names of his Sufi mentors. In the references to his direct

---

142 Al-Ghazzaliyy, *Al-Munqidh*, pp. 128–129.

143 *Ibid.*, p. 130.

144 Acccording to Al-Wakil, there was only one verse in the Qur'an where

a noun participated in the same root of the word *zuhd*. In Qur'an 12:20, it was the word *zahidin* which Al-Wakil thought it to be negative because it meant making little of things which are the bounty of Allah, and thus *zuhd* could not be associated with something positive. 'Abd al-Rahman Al-Wakil, *Hadhihi Hia Al-Suffiyyah* (This is Sufism). (Beirut: Dar al-Kutub al-'Ilmiyyah, 1984) p. 136.

145 Al-Ghazzaliyy, *Al-Munqidh*, p. 132.

146 *Ibid.*, pp. 130–132.

contact with the Sufis, he only referred to them by means of general terms such as the *arbāb al-qulūb wa al-mushāhadat* (men of hearts and vision) whom he consulted about his return to teaching later on in Nishapur.[147] Specific references to the names of his Sufi mentors can be found in books of Sufis as Ibn 'Ajibah who stated in his commentary on *Fuṣūṣ al-Ḥikam* of Ibn 'Atā' Al-Sakandary, that Al-Kharrāz was Al-Ghazzāliyy's mentor.[148] In addition, Al-Subkiyy reported that Al-Fāramdhiyy influenced Al-Ghazzāliyy's Sufism.[149] It should be noted that Al-Fāramdhiyy was placed in a *silsilah* (a chain of Sufi mentors) after Abū Al-Qāsim Al-Jurjaniyy[150] under whom Al-Ghazzāliyy studied jurisprudence and wrote *Al-Ta'līqah*.[151]

Al-Ghazzāliyy attained whatever could be acquired about the 'way' of the Sufis through learning and listening (*bi al-ta'allum wa al-sama*). He realized that they possessed special knowledge that could only be achieved through what the Sufis call *dhawq* (tasting),[152] *ḥāl* (state, as in "ecstatic state")[153] and the changing of one's character (i.e. becoming moral).

At this stage and before proceeding to show the impact of studying Sufism on his life, Al-Ghazzāliyy asserted that

---

147 Al-Ghazzaliyy, *Al-Munqidh*, p. 159.
148 Ahmad Ibn Muhammad Ibn 'Ajibah Al-Hasaniyy, *Iqaz al-Himam fi Sharh al-Hikam* (Cairo: Abd al-Hamid Ahmad Hanafi, No Date) p. 28.
149 Al-Subkiyy, Vol. VI, p. 209.
150 J. Trimingham, *The Sufi Orders in Islam* (London: Oxford University Press, 1971) p. 262.
151 Al-Subkiyy, Vol. VI, p. 195.
152 Sufis use the word *dhawq*, literally tasting, metaphorically to indicate that there is a kind of knowledge that transcends the physical reality and which is available only through immediate experience. Al-Ghazzaliyy maintained that this kind of knowledge cannot be expressed linguistically. In *The Varieties of Religious Experiences*, William James used "ineffability" to express the inadequacy of language to express the knowledge involved in mystical experiences. Ralph W. Clark, *Introduction to Philosophical Thinking* (St. Paul: West Publishing Co., 1987) p. 67.
153 *Hal* is the ecstatic state which is achieved by the Sufi through constant *dhikr* (recollection of the name and attributes of Allah). It is in this state that a Sufi starts receiving transcendental knowledge. If the Sufi can maintain such a *hal*, which denotes a sense of temporality, it evolves to become a *maqam* which indicates that the Sufi took a permanent metaphorical residence in transcendental noetic conditions.

he had acquired true belief (*īmān yaqīniyy*) in Allah, the prophecy and the day of judgment. He added that these three fundamentals of faith were firmly established in his soul, not because of any specific formulated proof, but because of numerous reasons, circumstances and experiences.[154]

In order to be on the right Sufi 'way' and to gain eternal happiness, Al-Ghazzāliyy concluded that he had to sever his ties with wordly things; he had to shun fame and money and to flee from distracting attachments. He scrutinized his conditions and found himself devoid of activities that could be useful in the hereafter. Not even the best of these activities, his teaching, was for the sake of Allah which he considered the criterion for success. He said his teaching had been motivated by fame. Al-Ghazzāliyy realized that he was about to fall into Hell fire if he did not act fast.[155]

Al-Ghazzāliyy spent six months, starting Rajab 488 A.H./1095 C.E., trying to abandon all things that were not for the sake of Allah. This included his position at the Nizāmiyyah which was to no avail. He was torn apart by worldliness on the one hand and the motivations for the hereafter on the other. Eventually, he developed an impediment of speech which prevented him from teaching. This impediment caused him sadness which, in turn, brought with it a new problem; Al-Ghazzāliyy could not digest food or drink. When he realized his weakness and inability to make a decision, he sought refuge in Allah [S.W.T.] who facilitated his abandonment of "fame, money, wife, children and friends".[156]

Al-Ghazzāliyy knew that neither the Caliph nor his friends would approve his plans to leave Baghdad and to settle in Al-Shām.[157] In addition, he was sure that none of the scholars of Iraq would understand the religious aspect of his plight. All of this led Al-Ghazzāliyy to plan his de-

---

154 Al-Ghazzaliyy, *Al-Munqidh*, pp. 133–134.
155 *Ibid.*, p. 134.

156 *Ibid.*, p. 136.
157 There are two places identified by the name, Al-Sham. One is the area covered by Jordan, Lebanon, Palestine and Syria. In the second instance, it is used as a synonym for Damascus. Al-Ghazzaliyy used it in the latter sense.

parture from Baghdad as if he were going to Makkah in order to perform pilgrimage. Al-Ghazzāliyy distributed his wealth, keeping only enough to sustain him and his children and left Baghdad with the intention never to see it again. Thus concluded Al-Ghazzāliyy's first period of public education.[158]

3.9 AL-GHAZZĀLIYY'S EPISTEMOLOGY IN HIS WRITINGS ON 'AQĪDAH (CREED)

According to Bouyges, Al-Ghazzāliyy wrote four books on 'aqīdah towards the end of his first period of teaching: *Al-Iqtiṣād fī al-I'tiqād* (The Median Course in Creed), *Al-Risālah al-Qudsiyyah fī Qawā'id al-'Aqā'id* (The Jerusalemite Treatise in the Fundamentals of Beliefs), *Qawā'id al-'Aqā'id* (The Fundamentals of Beliefs) and *al-Ma'ārif al-'Aqliyyah wa al-Asrār al-Ilāhiyyah* (Rational Knowledge and divine Secrets).[159] Thus, I cannot conclude this chapter without some mention of his thought regarding 'aqīdah. Indeed, his writings on 'aqīdah help to define Al-Ghazzāliyy's epistemology as he conceived of it just before he left Baghdad.

According to Badawi, *Al-Risālah al-Qudsiyyah fī Qawā'id al-'Aqā'id* and *Qawā'id al-'Aqā'id* are the same book and, as is indicated by the first title, this book must have been written originally as part of *Iḥyā' 'Ulūm al-Dīn* in Jerusalem after Al-Ghazzāliyy left Baghdad.[160] For this reason such a book belongs to the following chapter. As for the fourth book, *Al-Ma'ārif al-'Aqliyyah wa al-Asrār al-Ilāhiyyah*, it is still in manuscript form and we know of it only through secondary sources. It includes five chapters: on utterance (*nutq*), on *Kalam* and the *Mutakallim*, on speech (*al-qawl*), on writing and on the desired goal (*al-gharaḍ al-maṭlūb*).[161]

Unfortunately, therefore, I am confined to discussing only the first book, *Al-Iqtiṣād fī al-I'tiqād*, which has a

---

158 Al-Ghazzaliyy, *Al-Munqidh*, p. 137.
159 Badawi, *Mu'allafat*, p. xvi.
160 *Ibid.*, pp. 89–92.
161 Badawi, *Mu'allafat*, pp. 93-97. These chapter titles suggest this book might shed considerable light on Al-Ghazzaliyy's philosophical positions at this time in general and his philosophy of language in particular. A thorough study of this work of Al-Ghazzaliyy would be most desirable.

short, yet very important introduction in relation to the topic of Al-Ghazzāliyy's epistemology. The main themes of this book are the proof of the existence of Allah [S.W.T.] and his attributes (in which he followed the method of the Asha'irites),[162] the proof of the prophecy of Muhammad [S.A.A.S.], and discussion of other articles of faith.[163] In the penultimate section of this book, Al-Ghazzāliyy discussed the need of designating a ruler (*Imām*); he proved the necessity of having a ruler by reason as well as from the texts of the Shari'ah.[164] He ended this book with a section that sum-marized his position towards all other religions, sects and groups that were predominant at the time.[165]

In the introduction to *Al-Iqtisād*, Al-Ghazzāliyy asserted that there could be no contradiction between the Shari'ah and reason (*la mu'anadata bayna al-shar' al-manqūl wa al-ḥaq al-ma'qūl*). He classified all other positions into two categories: those who restricted themselves to conformism (*taqlīd*) which he described as a deficiency (*tafrīṭ*); and, the philosophers and the extremists among the Mu'tazilites who relied on reason only. The latter position he regarded as an excess (*ifrāṭ*). For Al-Ghazzāliyy, neither reason nor Shari'ah suffices on its own, for the right group is that which brings reason and Shari'ah together. Al-Ghazzāliyy explained his position by the following metaphor:

"Reason is similar to a healthy vision and the Qur'an is similar to the bright sun. The one who seeks guidance in one of them without the other is certainly among the stupid. If he thinks that the light of the Qur'an suffices him without reason, then he is comparable to the one who exposes himself to the light of the sun with his eyelids shut, then there is no difference between him and the blind, for (the existence of) reason with Shari'ah is like light upon light."[166]

Thus, one can say that it was Al-Ghazzāliyy's intention

162 For more details on Al-Ghazzaliyy's relationship to the Asha'irites see page 32.
163 Al-Ghazzaliyy, *Al-Iqtisad*, p. 13.
164 *Ibid.*, pp. 195–201.
165 *Ibid.*, pp. 205–213.
166 *Ibid.*, pp. 7–8.

96

in *Al-Iqtiṣād* to present a "median" account of Islamic creed, which is the meaning of the title of this book, with the help of reason.

In *Al-Iqtisād*, Al-Ghazzāliyy restricted himself to the use of six sources of premises. These sources were listed as follow:

1. The sensibles (*al-ḥissiyyāt*): Al-Ghazzāliyy here defined the sensibles as that which is perceived through external and internal "witnessing" (*mushāhadah*). Examples of external are accidents (*a'rāḍ*) like sounds and colors, and internal like the presence of pain and joy.

2. Pure Reason (*al-'aql al-maḥḍ*): an example of this kind of knowledge is reaching the conclusion that there could be no third predicate to those in the premise, "the world is either eternal or accidental".

3. Knowledge related by several sources (*al-tawātur*): such as the testimony of the existence of certain prophets (eg. Moses [a.s.]).

4. Premises that comprise other premises that are dependent upon the above three sources.

5. The Shari'ah (*al-sam'iyyāt*).

6. Premises derived from the beliefs of opponents in arguments against them because they cannot deny them, even if there is no proof of its validity.[167]

It should be noted that Al-Ghazzāliyy criticized the *Mutakallimūn* for their usage of arguments that resemble the sixth category above which he considered conformism (*taqlīd*).[168] In addition, the fact that he "restricted" himself to the use of these six sources is a clear indication that a complete list is available in a previous book. In fact *Mi'yār*

167 Al-Ghazzāliyy, *Al-Iqtisad*, pp. 25–27.
168 *Ibid.*, p. 92.

al-'Ilm is the last book during the first period of public teaching to include a comprehensive list of the sources of knowledge; subsequent books (i.e. *Mihak al-Nazar* and *Al-Iqtisād fī al-I'tiqād*) included partial lists only. *Mihak al-Nazar* included seven sources of "knowledge and belief"; primary knowledge, internal "vision" (*al-mushāhadāt al-bātinah*), external sensibles, experimentals, knowledge related by many groups (*tawātur*), imagination and famous premises.[169]

Al-Ghazzaliyy listed in *Mi'yar al-'Ilm* four sources that yield indubitable knowledge; pure rational logical necessities (*al-uwwaliyyāt al-'aqliyyah al-mahdah*), the sensible, the experimentals and intuition (*hads*). His list differed from that of the philosophers in *Maqāsid Al-Falāsifah* only in the addition of intuition as a source of indubitable knowledge. He held that the knowledge acquired through intuition cannot be proved, cannot be denied, and cannot be taught. It must be for this reason that he did not include intuition in the sources of premises in *Al-Iqtisād*. Al-Ghazzāliyy stated that the only thing that can be done to the student who is seeking intuitive knowledge is to direct him to the same path which led those before him to intuitive knowledge. This guidance does not gurantee intuitive knowledge; the student's mind should be perfect in terms of strength and clarity in order to be able to have intuition. Although he held intuition to be a source of indubitable knowledge, Al-Ghazzāliyy said that one cannot use arguments from intuition in debates; one should share the experience. For him, this concept of sharing is similar to "tasting".[170] The latter analogy is a clear indication of Al-Ghazzāliyy's use of the Sūfī language which is a mark of the new direction that he chose to follow.

3.10 CONCLUSION

Al-Ghazzāliyy's writings during this period, which lasted for a decade, reflect one of the most important stages in his intellectual development. He broke with conformism which dominated his work as a student, and began a systematic

169   Al-Ghazzaliyy, *Mihak*, pp. 57–65.
170   *Ibid.*, pp. 178–182.

98

inquiry of the schools of thought that were available at the time in search for true knowledge and its sources.

Al-Ghazzāliyy encountered many schools of thought in his quest for true knowledge. Eventually, he restricted the possibility of finding such knowledge to four "classes of seekers": the dialectical theologians, the Bātinites, the philosophers and the Sūfīs whose methodology he finally accepted. A careful study of the language that Al-Ghazzāliyy used to describe these four group reveals that he narrowed them to two only; the Bātinites and the philosophers in one group, and the *Mutakallimūn* and the Sūfīs in the other. The choice of words reflects a subtle approval of the latter group.

When Al-Ghazzāliyy became a teacher at the Niẓā-miyyah of Baghdad, he started studying philosophy as part of a systematic approach in which he was attempting to study all sects, religions and schools of thought in search for true knowledge. According to him, he could not find such knowledge in all the traditional subjects of philosophy; the only two exceptions were logic and mathematics. Although he was critical of philosophy, we shall see in the following chapter that he adopted many positions from the works of the philosophers (e.g., Al-Fārābī).

One of the most important contributions of Al-Ghazzāliyy during this period is his position on logic. He wrote several books which he intended as a criterion for science. He held in *Mi'yār al-'Ilm* that every person has three judges: a judge of sensibles, a judge of imagination and a judge of reason. It is the addition of a "judge of imagination" here that contributes to the development of his genetic epistemology even though he would drop it later on in *Al-Munqidh.*

Another contribution was in the subject of debate. In what seems to be a reaction to a trend of public debates between the various schools of jurisprudence at the time, Al-Ghazzāliyy wrote four books in which he outlined the etiquette of debate (*adab al-munāẓarah*) without which an unhealthy atmosphere of animosity and hatred would arise. He realized that these debates, in which he participated at the Camp of Niẓām Al-Mulk, were motivated by material gains and therefore, he made a pledge later on never to engage in such activity again.

Al-Ghazzāliyy's search for indubitable knowledge led him to reject all knowledge that was based on authority (e.g., parents, teachers) which he blamed for the differences among people. He defined this knowledge in terms of mathematical certitude. He scrutinized all his cognition in search for knowledge that would meet the previous description; he thought for a while that the sensibles and the self evident truths are conforming to the level of certitude that he was looking for. Nevertheless, meditating upon such knowledge he found that he could doubt them, and thus he found himself devoid of any indubitable knowledge. As a result, he found himself doubting all sources of knowledge including reason which was based upon the possiblity of the existence of a higher faculty which he defined in terms of its relation to reason (i.e. the faculty above reason [*malakah fawqa al-'aql*]). In fact, he underwent the most genuine and dramatic experience of skepticism in the history of thought. This state of doubt continued for the duration of two months and eventually ended by divine illumination.

The first thing that Al-Ghazzāliyy regained after he emerged from his state of doubt was his trust in logical necessities. According to him, this would not have been possible without divine illumination which he considered a source of knowledge that he called *kashf* and which he described as acquiring knowledge directly (i.e. from Allah). Evidently, this latter source of knowledge forms the backbone of Sūfi epistemology; he would expand on this concept during his first period of withdrawal from public life which I will deal with in the following chapter.

Chapter FOUR

AL-GHAZZALIYY'S QUEST FOR KNOWLEDGE: THE YEARS OF SECLUSION (488–499 A.H./1095–1106 C.E.)

This chapter deals with the works Al-Ghazzāliyy wrote following his first withdrawal from public life, a period which extended from the time he brought his first teaching career to an end at the Niẓāmiyyah of Baghdad in 488 A.H./1095 C.E. and until his return to public teaching at the Niẓāmiyyah of Nishapur in 499 A.H./1106 C.E. This period of seclusion was marked by a long journey in which Al-Ghazzāliyy left Baghdad for Damascus from which he went to Jerusalem, then to Hebron for a short visit and eventually to Makkah and Madīnah before he decided to return to his homeland.[1]

During this time, Al-Ghazzāliyy wrote 28 books, letters and treatises[2] of which four were written in Farsi: *Kīmyā*

1 Al-Ghazzaliyy, *Al-Munqidh*, pp. 137–138.
2 These are: 1. *Ihya' 'Ulum al-Din*, 2. *Kitab fi Mas'alat Kul Mujtahid Musib*, 3. *Jawab Ila Mu'ayyad Al-Mulk Hinama Da'ahu Limu'awadati al-Tadris Bil Nizamiyyah*, 4. *Mufassil al-Khilaf*, 5. *Jawab al-Masa'il al-Arba' al-Lati Sa'alaha al-Batiniyyah Bihamadhan*, 6. *Al-Maqsad al-Asna Sharh Asma' Allah al-Husna*, 7. *Risalah fi Ruju' Asma' Allah Ila Dhat Wahidah 'Ala Ra'y al-Mu'tazilah wa al-Falasifsah*, 8. *Bidayat al-Hidayah*, 9. *Al-Wajiz*, 10. *Jawahir al-Qur'an*, 11. *Al-Arba'in fi Usul al-Din*, 12. *Al-Madnun 'bihi 'ala Ghayri Ahlihi*, 13. *Al-Madnun bihi ala Ahlihi*, 14. *Al-Darj al-Marqum bi al Jadawil*, 15. *Al-Qistas al-Mustaqim*, 16. *Faisal al-Tafriqah bayn al-Islam wa al-Zandaqah*, 17. *Al-Qanun al-Kulli fi al-Ta'wil*, 18. *Kimya Sa'adat*, 19. *Ayyuha al-Walad*, 20. *Nasihat al-Muluk*, 21. *Zad Akhrat*, 22. *Risalah Ila Abi al-Fath Ahmad Ibn Salamah al-Dimamiyy bi al Musil*, 23. *Al-Risalah al-Ladunniyyah*, 24. *Risalah Ila Ba'd Ahl 'Asrih*, 25. *Mishkat al-Anwar*, 26. *Tafsir Yaqut al-Ta'wil*, 27. *Al-Kashf wa al-Tabyin fi Ghurur al-Khalq Ajma'in*, 28. *Talbis Iblis*.

Sa'adat (The Alchemy of Happiness),[3] *Zad Akhrat* (The Pack for the Hereafter, which Al-Ghazzaliyy wrote as a simplified version of the preceding book to make it more accessible to the general public), *Ayyuha al-Walad* (O Child) and *Al-Tibr al-Masbuk fi Nasihat al-Muluk* (The Golden Ingot for Advising Kings). The latter two are translated into Arabic.[4] Of these twenty eight books, two are in manuscript form,[5] five lost[6] and another two of disputed authenticity.[7] In addition, two works that are usually listed separately were originally sections of other books: *Risalah fi Ruju' Asma' Allah Ila Dhat Wahidah 'ala Ra'y al-Mu'tazilah wa al-Falasifah* (A Treatise Concerning Allah's names Indicating One Essence According to the Opinion of the Mu'tazilites and the Philo-

sophers) which is the third chapter of *Al-Maqsad al-Asna Sharh Asma' Allah al-Husna* (The Sublime Aim in the Interpretation of Allah's Beautiful Names)[8] and *Al-Arba'in fi Usul al-Din* (The Forty in the Fundamentals of Religion) which is the third section of *Jawahir al-Qur'an* (The Jewels of the Qur'an).[9]

3   This book is different from the Arabic one which has the same title: *Kimya' al-Sa'adah*. Badawi stated that Bouyges doubted the *authenticity* of the section designated for books that their authenticity could not be verified. Medieval historians like Al-Murtada Al-Zubaydiyy listed the Arabic book seperetely. The original book in Farsi is believed to be the equivalent of *Ihya' 'Ulum al-Din* (The Revival of Islamic Sciences) which was written in Arabic. For further information, see Badawi, *Mu'allafat*, pp. 172–178 and 275–276.
4   Badawi, *Mu'allafat*, pp. 188–189.
5   These are *Zad Akhrat* and *Al-Wajiz*.
6   These are *Fi Mas'alat Kul Mujtahid Musib, Mufassil al-Khilaf, Al-Darj al-Marqum bi al-Jadawil, Tafsir Yaqut al-Ta'wil* and *Talbis Iblis*. It should be noted that Ibn Al-Jawziyy (d. 597 A.H./1200 C.E., who studied at the hands of Judge Ibn Al-'Arabiyy, one of Al-Ghazzaliyy's students, wrote a book with the same title as the latter book: *Talbis Iblis* (The Devil's Concealment of Truth). In this book, which I believe it be influenced by the original *Talbis Iblis*, one could see that Ibn Al-Jawziyy used the same example in the introduction that was used previously by Al-Ghazzaliyy in the introduction of *Al-Iqtisad*. Nevertheless, Ibn Al-Jawziyy followed the method of the scholars of Hadith which is different from the approach of Al-Ghazzaliyy. For further information see Abu Al-Faraj 'Abd Al-Rahman Ibn Al-Jawziyy Al-Baghdadiyy, *Talbis Iblis*, Muhammad Munir Al-Dimashqiyy Al-Azhariyy, ed. (Cairo: Maktabat Al-Mutanabbiyy, No Date) p. 1.
7   These are *Nasihat al-Muluk* and *al-Madnun bihi 'ala Ghayri Ahlih*.
8   Badawi, *Mu'allafat*, p. 137.
9   *Ibid.*, p. 149.

In addition to the traditional subjects that he used to cover in his writings, Al-Ghazzāliyy started expressing his deep conviction in the Sufi way. His writings were either direct representations of this new line of thought, or indirect as in the texts (e.g., exegesis of the Qur'an) he wrote with the spirit of Sufism during his years of seclusion. It is the aim of this chapter to discuss the impact of his acceptance of Sufism on his epistemology. Of the many books that he wrote during this period, only about seven of them can be related directly to the development in his theory of knowledge. These are: *Ihyā' 'Ulūm al-Dīn* (The Revival of Islamic Sciences), *Al-Maqsad al-Asnā fi Sharh Asmā' Allah al-Husnā, Bidāyat Al-Hidāyah* (The Beginning of Guidance) *Jawāhir al-Qur'an* and *Al-Qistas al-Mustaqim* (The Just Balance), *Al-Risālah al-Ladunniah* and *Mishkāt al-Anwār* (The Niche for Lights).

These books form a consistent unified whole with "unveiling" (*kashf*) forming the highest source of knowledge. We shall see that "unveiling" takes more than one form (e.g., vision) but always aiming at peremptory transcendental knowledge. Thus, the following discussion of these books aims at showing Al-Ghazzāliyy's consistency during this period.

4.1 *IHYA' 'ULUM AL-DIN*

The first book that was written in seclusion was *Ihyā' 'Ulūm al-Dīn* (The Revival of Islamic Sciences), a voluminous encyclopedic work.[10] In this book, Al-Ghazzāliyy held that the highest forms of knowledge are found in Sufism and that all other forms are subordinate. He argued for the priority of Sufi knowledge along several different fronts, namely the science of action (*'ilm al-mu'āmalah*), sociology of knowledge, the division of the sciences, the intellect, dialectical theology (*kalām*), philosophy, creed (*'aqīdah*) and dreams. However, as we shall see, his newly attained vision produced an

10 The edition of *Dar al-Ma'rifah*, without the indexes or appendixes, has 1,700 pages.

enthusiasm which led him to set forth several flawed arguments and claims in support of his position. Some of these flaws were overcome in his later writings.

4.1.1 On the Science of Action (*'Ilm al-Mu'āmalah*)

As the title of this book indicates, Al-Ghazzāliyy wanted to revive the Islamic Sciences, an intention which he clearly states in the first few lines of the introduction.[11] The concept of "revivification" should be understood as an act directed towards something which is dead or dying. In this case, he was referring to the Islamic sciences which became distanced from the original aims of the Shari'ah (*maqāṣid al-shari'ah*). He saw that Muslim scholars, especially in Jurisprudence, preoccupied themselves with trivial and useless details, forgetting the spirit of the Shari'ah. The *Iḥyā'* represents an attempt to reconnect *Fiqh* with the aims of the Shari'ah.

In the introduction to the *Iḥyā'*, which is considered Al-Ghazzāliyy's most important work, he stated that the necessary knowledge for attaining happiness in the hereafter (*'ilm al-ākhirah*) is divided into two sections: the science of action (*'ilm al-mu'āmalah*) and the science of "unveiling" divine knowledge (*'ilm al-mukāshafah*). He restricted the subject matter of *Iḥya' 'Ulūm al-Dīn* to the science of action because, as he put it, he had no permission to disclose *'ilm al-mukāshafah* in any books, even though it is the goal to which seekers aspire. He said that his position had to resemble that of the prophets[12] who related this science using metaphoric language because people are not equipped to understand this subject. He added that the science of action is the guide (i.e. a prerequisite) to *'ilm al-mukāshafah*.[13]

Al-Ghazzāliyy divided the science of action into two

11 Al-Ghazzaliyy, *Ihya' 'Ulum al-Din* (Beirut: Dar al-Ma'rifah, No Date) Vol. I, p.1.
12 Al-Ghazzaliyy based his position upon a Hadith that was narrated by Abu Al-Darda' in which prophet Muhammad [S.A.A.S.] said, "Scholars are the heirs of prophets" (*Al-'ulama' warathat al-anbiya'*). This Hadith bwas verified by Abu Dawud, Al-Tirmidhiyy, Ibn Majah and Ibn Hayyan in his *Sahih.*
13 Al-Ghazzaliyy, *Ihya'*, Vol. I, pp. 3–4.

104

sections: exoteric science (*'ilm zāhir*) and esoteric science (*'ilm bātin*). Furthermore, he divided each of these two sections into two subdivisions. These four sections formed the basis for the format of *Ihyā' 'Ulūm al-Dīn* which comprises, in his words, four quarters: the Acts of Worship (*'ibādat*), the Social Ethics (*'ādāt*), the Matters that are Dangerous (*muhlikāt*) and finally the Things that are Conducive to Salvation (*munjiyāt*).[14] Each of these four quarters includes ten chapters. A general overview of this book can be obtained from a list of the headings of the chapters:

The quarter on the Acts of Worship:

1. The Book of Knowledge (*Kitāb al-'Ilm*)

2. The Articles of Faith (*Qawā'id al-'Aqā'id*)

3. The Mysteries of Purity

4. The Mysteries of Prayer

5. The Mysteries of Alms giving

6. The Mysteries of Fasting

7. The Mysteries of Pilgrimage

8. The Rules of Reading the Qur'an

9. On the Invocations and Supplications

10. On the Arrangement of *Awrād*[15] According to the Different Times.

The quarter on Social Ethics:

1. The Ethics of Eating

2. The Ethics of Marriage

---

14   Al-Ghazzaliyy, *Ihya'*, Vol. I, pp. 2–3.
15   *Wird* (plural *awrad*) is one or more form of recollection of Allah (*dhikr*). In a Sufi order, the novice (*murid*) is assigned certain *wird* to perform by his own Sufi master. Nabih Amin Faris translated the title of the tenth chapter of the first quarter as "On the Office of portions", a translation which does not reflect the subject matter of this chapter. Al-Ghazzaliyy, The Book of Knowledge (of *Ihya' 'Ulum al-Din*), Nabih Amin Faris, ed. and trans. (Lahore, Sh. Muhammad Ashraf, 1962) p. 3.

3. The Ethics of Earning a Livelihood

4. On the Lawful and the Forbidden

5. The Ethics of Companionship and Fellowship with the Various Types of Men

6. On Seclusion (*al-'uzlah*)

7. The Ethics of Travel

8. On Audition (*samā'*) and passion (*wajd*)[16]

9. On Enjoining Good and Forbidding Evil

10. The Ethics of Living as Exemplified in the Virtues of the Prophet

The quarter on the Matters that are Dangerous:

1. On the Wonders of the Heart

2. On the Discipline of the Soul

3. On the Curse of the Two Appetites - the Appetites of the Stomach and the Genitals

4. The Curse of the Tongue

5. The Curse of Anger, Rancour and Envy

6. The Evil of the World

7. The Evil of Wealth and Niggardliness[17]

8. The Evil of Pomp and Hypocrisy

9. The Evil of Pride and Conceit

10. The Evils of Vanity

16 Faris translated *wajd* as "grief". See Al-Ghazzaliyy, *The Book of Knowledge*, p. 4. I think that *wajd* is an ecstatic expression of the psychological "state" (*hal*) of a Sufi, which is the outcome of listening to poetry or singing. This "state" could be either that of grief or joy depending on the theme in the song or poetry. In addition, a Sufi can induce such a "state" but in this case it is called *tawajud*.

17 Faris translated *bukhl* as avarice. See Al-Ghazzali, *The Book of Knowledge*, p. 5.

106

The quarter on Those Things That are Conducive to Salvation:

1. On Repentance

2. On Patience and Gratitude

3. On Fear and Hope

4. On Poverty and Asceticism

5. On Divine Unity and Dependence

6. On Love, Longing, Intimacy and Contentment

7. On Intentions, Truthfulness and Sincerity

8. On Self-Examination and Self-Accounting

9. On Meditation

10. On Death.

After listing the contents of the *Ihyā'*, Al-Ghazzāliyy outlined the specific aims of each of the four quarters. More important than the aims themselves is the language that Al-Ghazzāliyy used to describe these aims. More than once, he mentioned the "mysteries", "secrets" and the "hidden" elements that were neglected in previous studies and which he now intends to resolve or clarify.[18] It is clear that this language which is different from previous works of Al-Ghazzāliyy, can be attributed to his new intellectual "state"!

The first quarter, on the acts of worshipping, began with the book of knowledge (*Kitāb al-'Ilm*) as its first chapter. It is rather peculiar to include such a chapter, let alone assign it priority, among other chapters on subjects such as prayer, alms giving and pilgrimage. The use of Jurisprudence (e.g. the details of prayer) is not essential to the aim of the *Ihyā'*; knowing that students at the time were interested in jurisprudence, Al-Ghazzāliyy included it in his book to attract them.[19] Evidently he was aiming at presenting his newly "acquired" understanding of knowledge and the method or "way" to acheive it. He was convinced that people at the

18   Al-Ghazzali, *The Book of Knowledge*, p. 5.
19   Al-Ghazzaliyy, *Ihya'*, Vol. I, p. 4.

time were inclined to accept as science what he described metaphorically as the "peels" instead of the pulp".[20] One can
interpret these "peels" as the useless or   harmful sciences,
and the "pulp" as the peremptory knowledge (*yaqīn*) that is unveiled to the Sufi.

The aim of discussing knowledge at the beginning of the *Iḥyā'* is intended to show the knowledge that is required of everyone. It is obvious that Al-Ghazzāliyy is referring to a hidden knowledge that cannot be derived from conventional sources of knowledge (e.g. the senses, reason). He wanted the seeker to transcend worldly affairs which construct a barrier that prevents one from achieving the knowledge that Sufis claim to have acquired. He asserted that attainment of this knowledge can be promoted by "self-mortification, discipline, and through purifying the heart by freeing it from the affairs of this world, as well as through emulating the prophets and very virtuous people (*awliyā'*) so that it may be revealed to every seeker in proportion to what Allah has allocated (*rizq*) for him, rather than in proportion to the seeker's efforts and labours (*jahd*). yet diligence in it is indispensable for self-mortification which is the sole key to guidance."[21]

The book of knowledge (*Kitāb al-'Ilm*) comprises seven sections: 1. On the value of knowledge, instruction and learning. 2. On the branches of knowedge which are *farḍ 'ayn*;[22] on the branches of knowledge that are *farḍ kifāyah*;[23] on the definition of jurisprudence and dialectical theology (as disciplines) in the science of religion; and on the science of the hereafter and that of this world. 3. On what is popularly but erroneously considered to be part of the science of religion, including a discussion of the nature of blameworthy knowledge. 4. On the defects of debate and the reasons why people have engaged in dissension and

20   Al-Ghazzaliyy. *Ihya'*, Vol. I, p. 2.
21   Al-Ghazzali. *The Book of Knowledge*, p. 100.
22   Divinely ordained, and binding for every individual Muslim.
23   Divinely ordained, and binding for the Muslim community as a

    whole. Therefore this collective obligation can be discharged, for the community by the actions of one or more persons, and is not necessarily binding for each individual member.

disputation. 5. On the qualities of the teacher and the student. 6. On the deficiency of knowledge, the (drawbacks) of the learned, and the characteristics distinguishing the scholars of the science of the hereafter from those of the science of this world. 7. On reason, its value, categories, and what has been said concerning it (in tradition).[24] Of these seven, sections one, two and seven are of special importance in the development of Al-Ghazzāliyy's epistemology.

4.1.2 The Sociology of Knowledge

In the first section of the book of knowledge, Al-Ghazzāliyy discussed the importance of knowledge and ranked the scholars, after the prophets, who were second to none.[25] The implication of this hierarchy can be explained as an attempt by him to place revelation as the first source of knowledge and reason second. This position was his response to the philosophers who placed reason above prophecy in their epistemological hierarchy.

Moreover, he raised the question of the definition of man whom he distinguished from animals by virtue of having the faculty of reason. In addition, he stated that the human being was created only for the sake of acquiring knowledge (*lam yukhlaq illa lil 'ilm*).[26]

Al-Ghazzāliyy discussed the knowledge of science that could be rendered *fard 'ayn* and he found that there were twenty different positions regarding this issue. He mentioned only four groups along with their positions regarding *fard 'ayn*. The *Mutakkalimūn* said that this science must be dialectical theology, the jurists maintained that fiqh was the *fard 'ayn*, the scholars of Hadith stated that it was the knowledge of the Qur'an and the Sunnah, and the fourth group was the Sufis who while being different from the other three positions, did not comprise one single position in their understanding of *fard 'ayn*. One group of Sufis stated that it is the knowledge of one's "state" (*hal*) and position (*maqām*) in relation to Allah [S.W.T.]. Other Sufis thought it to be the knowledge of sincerity between the

---

24 Al-Ghazzali, *The Book of Knowledge*, p. 9.
25 Al-Ghazzaliyy, *Ihya'*, Vol. I, p. 5.
26 *Ibid.*, p. 7.

followers of Allah [S.W.T.] and the followers of Satan.[27] A third group of Sufis said that it was the esoteric science whose acquisition is required only of the qualified, select few, who accordingly did not accept the exoteric meaning of *fard 'ayn* which would have made it imperative upon everyone to learn this particular science.[28] The last Sufi position was that

of Abū Ṭālib Al-Makkiyy who understood it in terms of what later on became known as the five pillars of Islam.[29]

In principle, Al-Ghazzāliyy accepted Al-Makkiyy's view but he stressed the idea that this *fard 'ayn* is what he called earlier *'ilm al-mu'āmalah* (the science of action). Moreover, while Al-Ghazzāliyy maintained the same notion as the basis for his science of action, it must be said that he devised a timetable for the acquisition and application of the science that is *fard 'ayn* taking into consideration the conditions surrounding the person who was on the path of acquiring such knowledge.[30] I found that his accounts in this paragraph are copied almost *ad verbum* from Al-Makkiyy's *Qūt al-Qulūb*.[31] In fact, one can see the influence of this book on a wide range of topics in the *Ihyā'*.

4.1.3 On the Division of the Sciences

In the second section of the book of knowledge, Al-Ghazzāliyy divided knowledge into two sections; *'ulūm shar'iyyah* (sciences of the Shari'ah) and the *ghayr-shar'iyyah* (non-Shari'ah) such as medicine and mathematics. According to him, the latter sciences are *fard kifāyah*. Nevertheless, he criticized unnecessary studies in these sciences such as the branches of mathematics that do not have practical applications. As for the sciences of the Shari'ah, he held

27 Al-Ghazzaliyy, *Ihya'*, Vol. I, p. 14.
28 Al-Ghazzali, *The Book of Knowledge*, pp. 30–31.
29 These are: bearing witness that there is no God but Allah and that Muhammad is His prophet, prayer, regular alms giving, fasting the month of Ramadan and pilgrimage to the House of Abraham (Al-Ka'bah) in Makkah. These five pillars were part of a Hadith that was narrated on the authority of Ibn 'Umar by both Al-Bukhariyy and Muslim. Thus, this Hadith is rendered *muttafaq 'alayh* (agreed upon) which is the highest level of certitude of a sound Hadith.
30 Al-Ghazzaliyy, *Ihya'*, Vol. I, p. 14.
31 Abu Talib Al-Makkiyy, *Qut Al-Qulub* (Cairo: dar Sadir, 1892) pp. 129–130.

110

that they were concerned with two subjects; the first pertains to life in this world which is covered by jurisprudence, and the second addresses issues related to the hereafter. He described the second as the science of the states of the heart (*'ilm aḥwāl al-qalb*) which forms the subject matter of the *Iḥyā'*.[32]

Al-Ghazzāliyy stated that jurisprudence cannot extend its jurisdiction to the affairs of the heart, and whenever the knowledge that leads to the hereafter is compared with jurisprudence, the superiority of the former is evident. He divided the science that leads to the hereafter into two parts: the science of unveiling[33] (*'ilm al-mukāshafah*) and the science of action (*'ilm al-mu'āmalah*). According to him, *'ilm al-mukāshafah* is the science of esoteric knowledge (*'ilm al-bāṭin*) which is the aim of all sciences. Furthermore, *'ilm al-mukāshafah* is the science concerned with those who are favoured by Allah [S.W.T.]. It stands for a light which shines in the heart when it is cleansed and purified of its blameworthy qualities (e.g. pride, the love of this world) which prevent the attainment of such light. Al-Ghazzaliyy provided a long list of the truths that are attained through this light. He said:

> "Through this light is revealed the truth of several things, whose names were known, and to which illusions were attached. Through it, these truths are clarified until the true knowledge of the essence of Allah [S.W.T.] is attained together with that of His eternal and perfect attributes, His works and wisdom in the creation of this world and the hereafter as well as the reason for His exalting the latterover the former. Through it also is attained the knowledge of the meaning of prophecy and prophet, and the importance of revelation. Through it is obtained the truth about Satan, the meaning of the words angels and devils, and the cause of the enmity between Satan and man. Through it is known how the Angel appeared to prophets and how they received the [divine] revelation. Through it is achieved the knowledge of the kingdom of heaven and earth, as well as the

---

32   Al-Ghazzaliyy, *Iḥya'*, Vol. 1, pp. 16–17.
33   Revelation (*kashf*) here means unveiling knowledge that is usually withheld from human beings. This concept is different from (*waḥy*) which is restricted to prophetic revelation.

knowledge of the heart and how the angelic hosts have confronted the devils. Through it is gained the knowledge of how to distinguish between the company of heaven and the company of the Devil, a knowledge of the hereafter, Paradise, and hell, the punishment of the grave, the bridge (al-ṣirāṭ) across the infernal fire, the balance of the judgement day, and knowledge (of the day) or reckoning."[34]

Al-Ghazzāliyy argued that those who attain such knowledge, in addition to others, take different positions regarding their significance. Some consider all the kinds of knowledge mentioned above as mere examples; others hold that some of these kinds of knowledge are mere patterns while the rest of these kinds are identical with the realities indicated by their names. Others hold that the limit to which our knowledge of Allah can reach is knowledge of the inability to know Him. In addition, there are those who claim great things on the subject of knowing Allah [S.W.T.] while others maintain that we cannot go beyond what all the common people (al-'awām) have reached, namely, that Allah exists (mawjūd), that He is omniscient and omnipotent, that He hears and sees, and that He speaks.[35] I find it rather hard to believe that the latter position corresponds to that of common people since the language is clearly Ash'arite.

Furthermore, Al-Ghazzāliyy explained 'ilm al-mukāshafah as that science whereby the veil is removed so that the truth regarding these things becomes as clear as if it were seen by the eye, leaving no room for any doubt. Man would be capable of such a thing had not "rust and rot resulting from the filth of this world accumulated over the surface of the mirror of his heart".[36] He asserted that the science of the road of the hereafter is the knowledge of how to cleanse the surface of this mirror from the filth that prevents the knowing of Allah, His attributes, and His works. Such cleansing is possible through desisting from lust and emulating the prophets in all their states. Thus, to the extent the heart is cleansed and made to face the truth, to that same extent will it reflect His reality. To reach this

34 Al-Ghazzali, *The Book of Knowledge*, pp. 46–47.
35 *Ibid.*, p. 48.
36 *Ibid.*

level of knowledge, one should go through discipline (*riyā-dah*), learning and instruction. These sciences are not re-corded in books and are not discussed by the one who is blessed with this grace except among his own circle of intimates who along with him partake of them through discourses and secret communication.[38] Moreover, he be-lieved that *'ilm al-mukāshafah* is an occult science (*'ilm khāfī*) and that there were references to it in a Hadith that was judged by Al-'Iraqiyy to be *da'īf*.[38]

The second part, namely, the science of action (*'ilm al-mu'āmalah*), is the science of the states of the heart. Al-Ghazzāliyy provided two lists of states: the first is a list of praiseworthy states such as that of sincerity (*al-ikhlāṣ*), and the second is a list of blameworthy states as the fear of poverty. He stated that the knowledge of these states (i.e. of morals) comprises the way to the hereafter which is a must (*fard 'ayn*) for every one. He argued that such knowledge is more important than jurisprudence which he called the exoteric science (*'ilm al-ẓāhir*). To support his argument, he stated that the scholars of fiqh, including Al-Shāfi'iyy and Ibn Ḥanbal, used to study the science of the hereafter (*'ilm al-ākhirah*) at the hands of the scholars of esoteric know-ledge (*'ulamā' al-bāṭin*) whom he also described as the people of the hearts, namely, the Sufis.[39]

The relationship between the studies of the Shari'ah and Sufism according to Al-Ghazzāliyy can be understood from an account of Al-Junayd and Al-Sari,[40] his Sufi teacher. Al-Junayd said:

> "Once upon a time my teacher Al-Sari asked me saying, "When you leave my place whose company do you keep?" I said, "Al-Muḥāsibiyy's." To which he replied, "Well have you chosen! Follow his learning and culture, but avoid his affectation in speech and his refutation of the theologians." Upon leaving I overheard him say, "May Allah make you first a scholar of Hadith and then a Sufi rather than a Sufi first and then a scholar of Hadith".[41]

37 Al-Ghazzali, *The Book of Knowledge*, pp. 48–49.
38 Al-Ghazzaliyy, *Ihya'*, Vol. I, p. 20.
39 *Ibid.*, p. 21.
40 Abu Hasan Ibn Al-Mughallis Al-Saqatiyy (256 A.H./870 A.D.)
41 Al-Ghazzali, *The Book of Knowledge*, p. 52.

Al-Ghazzāliyy asserted that he who studies the science of hadith and the Shari'ah before he turns to Sufism comes off well; he who takes to Sufism before learning the Shari'ah exposes himself to danger.[42] This position can be interpreted as an attempt by Al-Ghazzāliyy to weigh Sufism with the balance of the Shari'ah. Apparently, his adherence to such criterion was not without loopholes. Ibn Al-Jawziyy critized him for breaking the laws of jurisprudence more than once to accommodate Sufi doctrines and actions.[43]

4.1.4 On the Intellect (Al-'Aql)

The seventh section in the book of knowledge is concerned with the intellect (al-'aql); its noble nature, its definition, and its division. Al-Ghazzāliyy said that it is superfluous to show the noble nature of the intellect because it is the source and fountainhead of knowledge as well as its foundation. He described the relationship between knowledge and the intellect, using a Neoplatonic theme, as that between light and the sun. He found sufficient evidence for the nobility of the intellect in the fact that it is the means of happiness in this world and the hereafter. In addition, he maintained that the nobility of the intellect is something known by instinct.[44]

Moreover, Al-Ghazzāliyy attempted to support his argument regarding the nobility of the intellect by citing verses from the Qur'an and reports from the Sunnah, as was his practice. The first of these is a verse that in literal translation reads "Allah is the Light (Nūr) of the Heavens and Earth. His Light is like a niche in which there is a lamp – the lamp encased in glass - the glass, as it were, a glistering star".[45] He interpreted the word, light, as intellect so that the nobility of intellect was established by its likeness to the divine light.

In addition, he related a Hadith, which is considered da'if, that the intellect was the first thing that was created by Allah. This creation, however, proved to be problematic

42 Al-Ghazzali, *The Book of Knowledge*, p. 52.
43 Ibn Al-Jawziyy, *Talbis Iblis*, p. 166.
44 Al-Ghazzali, *The Book of Knowledge*, p. 221.
45 Al-Qur'an, Sura *al-Nur* 24:35.

114

in Al-Ghazzāliyy's view. He questioned the nature of the intellect according to this Hadith. Because it is the first thing to be created, he held that the intellect must be either an accident (*'araḍ*) or an essence (*jawhar*). But how could an accident be created before bodies? Again, if it is an essence, how could it have pure existence which is spaceless (*min ghayri taḥayyuz*)?[46] Al-Ghazzāliyy did not provide an answer to these questions here; he argued that the answer belongs to the science of "unveiling" (*'ilm al-mukāshafah*)[47] The meaning is that one has to follow the Sufi path in order to achieve such knowledge.

Al-Ghazzāliyy provided answers to these questions in *Faiṣal al-Tafriqah bayn al-Islām wa al-Zandaqah* (The Decisive Marker between Islam and Disbelief) which was written at a later stage, though during the same period. In this book, Al-Ghazzāliyy held that the first creation (i.e. intellect, *'aql*) cannot be an accident; he thought that it must be an angle that is called intellect. Moreover, in a language that reflects Al-Fārābī's influence, he argued that this noun (i.e. intellect) is given to the angel because it is his essence (*jawhar*) to conceive himself and other things without the need of a teacher.[48] It is lamentable that he had to resort to this Fārābian idea in order to solve a problem which resulted from his inappropriate knowledge of the Hadith.

Another influence of Al-Fārābī can be seen in the following argument. Al-Ghazzāliyy's interpretation of this Qur'anic verse, namely, that light in "Allah is the light" is interpreted as intellect which means that Allah is the intellect of the Heaven and the Earth (i.e. the universe). Not only is this a clear departure from the Sunni approach to the attributes of Allah [S.W.T.] and, thus, the interpretation of such verses,[49] if combined with the Hadith about the

---

46   This idea is similar to Descartes' regarding the mind which "does not need space nor is dependent on any material thing." Descartes, Discourse on the Method and the Meditations, John Veitch, tr. (Buffalo: Prometheus Books, 1989), p. 31.

47   Al-Ghazzaliyy, *Ihya'*. Vol. I, p.83.

48   Al-Ghazzaliyy, "*Faisal al-Tafriqah Bayn al-Islam wa al-Zandaqah*", *Majmu'at Rasa'il al-Imam al-Ghazzaliyy* (Beirut: Dar al-Kutub al-'Ilmiyyah, 1986), Vol. III, p. 125.

49   Ibn Kathir related in his *Tafsir* the interpretation of several prominent scholars from among the first generation (*al-Salaf*) of Muslims and the

intellect being the first creation, becomes that the Intellect created another intellect. This idea, although reconstructed, is reminiscent of Al-Fārābī's cosmology which is Neoplatonic in its essence.

In addition, Al-Ghazzāliyy held that the term 'intellect' is applied to several things; he found that there are four distinct meanings to this term that are related to knowledge. The first is the quality which distinguishes man from animals and enables him to understand the theoretical sciences (*naẓariyyah*), and to learn the abstract (*fikriyyah*) disciplines. He held that the intellect is an instinct whereby, as a natural disposition, some animals are capable of grasping the theoretical sciences, except that Allah [S.W.T.], as a matter of fact, imbued man alone with these sciences. He added that "the relationship of this instinct, (namely, the intellect), to the sciences is similar to that of the eye to vision; while the relationship of the Shari'ah to the intellect, in so far as it leads to the unfolding of the sciences, is like that of the light of the sun to seeing".[50]

The second meaning of intellect (*'aql*) is explained in terms of its application to logical necessities. Al-Ghazzāliyy maintained that this kind of knowledge "is present even in the infant who discerns[51] the possibility of possible things (*jā'izāt*) and the impossibility of impossible things (*mustaḥilāt*), such as the knowledge that two is greater than one and that one individual cannot be in two different places at the same time".[52]

In the third place the word intellect is applied to empirical knowledge. Al-Ghazzāliyy said that this know-

subsequent generation (*al-Khalaf*), including Ibn 'Abbas, Mujahid, Anas Ibn Malik, Ubayy Ibn Ka'b and al-Sadi. The meaning of the term "light" in this verse revolves around the notion of guidance (i.e. Allah is the guide of the inhabitants of the Heavens and Earth). See, Ibn Kathir, Tafsir (Beirut: Dar al-Jil, 1988), Vol. III, p. 280.

50 Al-Ghazzali, *The Book of Knowledge*, pp. 226–227.
51 It should be noted that at a later stage in *Al-Munqidh*, Al-Ghazzaliyy considered "discernment" the second level in the epistemological development of man; this level is higher than the sensibles and is possible to children who are seven years old. The knowlededge of the *"ja'izat"* and the *"mustahilat"* belong to a higher level, namely, that of reason. See Al-Ghazzaliyy, *Al-Munqidh*, p. 145.
52 Al-Ghazzali, *The Book of Knowledge*, p. 227.

116

ledge "is acquired through experience, in the course of events". To explain the relationship between empirical knowledge and the intellect he said that he who is taught by experience is called intelligent (*'āqil*).[53]

In the fourth place the term intellect is used when "the power of the instinct develops to such an extent that its possessor will be able to tell what the end will be, and, consequently, he will conquer and subdue his appetite which hankers for immediate pleasures". Al-Ghazzāliyy maintained that this is another quality that distinguishes man from animals.[54]

Al-Ghazzāliyy concluded that "these forms of knowledge are inherent in the intellect by nature, and come to light when some cause which will bring them out takes place". According to him, this knowledge is latent in the instinct and later appears as if there is no external influence. He illustrated this notion by comparing it to "water in the earth: it appears up on digging and accumulates at the bottom of the well (in this process)".[55] In addition, he cited verses in the Qur'an which indicate that every human being is born with an inherent knowledge of reality. He held that belief is instilled by nature in the human soul, but because of passing time, some people forgot all about it, others forgot it for a while, but finally remembered it. Moreover, he cited another group of verses which include an invitation for recalling and remembering the understanding that the human being was endued with. He stated that "there are two kinds of remembrance: the one is to recall a picture which once existed in one's mind but has since disappeared, while the other is to recall a picture which is inherent in one's mind by nature (*fiṭrah*)". In addition, he argued that "these facts are evident to him who exercises his insight, but are abstruse to him who is given to blind imitation and conformism".[56]

Al-Ghazzāliyy held that people differ in their intellectual capabilities only in regard to the second field of know-

---

53 Al-Ghazzali, *The Book of Knowledge*, p. 227.
54 *Ibid.*, p. 228.
55 *Ibid.*, pp. 229–230.
56 *Ibid.*, pp. 230–231.

ledge, namely, knowing logical necessities such as what is possible or impossible. As far as the intellect is concerned, it follows a course of development that begins at the age of discernment (*tamyīz*) and reaches its completion at age forty.[57] It might not be just a coincidence that he was about forty years old himself when he wrote these words. It is quite possible that he believed that he reached the prime of his intellectual capabilities as manifested in the *Ihyā'*.

4.1.5 On Dialectical Theology ('Ilm al-Kalām)

Al-Ghazzaliyy's position regarding *Kalām* and philosophy in the *Ihyā'* seems to be stricter than any other book, even those that were written later on (i.e. *Al-Munqidh*). For him, "whatever *Kalām* offers by way of useful evidence is contained in the Qur'an and the Sunnah; anything else is either reprehensible argumentation which, as will be seen, is an innovation (*bid'āh*), or mere wrangling by dwelling or distinctions or amplification through the array of different opinions, most of which are drivel and nonsense". Nevertheless, he stated that although *Kalām* would be considered heresy at the time of the prophet [S.A.A.S.], circumstances changed and it became *fard kifāyah.*[58]

4.1.6 On Philosophy

Regarding philosophy, Al-Ghazzāliyy held that it is not a science in itself but comprises four parts: the first includes geometry and arithmetic which are permissible, unless there is reason to fear that they might lead a person to blameworthy sciences.[59] He did not discuss the reasons that led him to take such a position, and thus I find no justification for his position. Perhaps he was carried off by a fervour of Sufi attitude that rendered many things irrelevant to the way of the hereafter. It should be noted

57 Al-Ghazzaliyy, *Ihya'*, Vol. I, p. 88.
58 Al-Ghazzali, *The Book of Knowledge*, p. 53.
59 Al-Ghazzaliyy, *Ihya'*, Vol. I, p. 22.

that this remark is not normal for Al-Ghazzāliyy and does not reflect his general position regarding arithmetic, geometry and the exact sciences and the Shari'ah. Rather, he described their relation in neutral language.

The second part of philosophy is logic, which Al-Ghazzāliyy defined as the study of proofs, definitions and their conditions. He maintained that both are included in *Kalām*.[60] Moreover, he cited a Hadith which indicates that those who deal with logic will be unable to perform good deeds. Al-'Iraqiyy held that this Hadith is fabricated and that it has no origin (*la asla lah*) in the Sunnah.[61] Such a narration is an indication that there were people who circulated fabricated Hadith in order to prove a point or to defend a position. This Hadith proved to be problematic for someone like Al-Ghazzāliyy; his position towards logic in his earlier and later works shows an acceptance that is different from the one in the *Ihyā'*.

The third part of philosophy is metaphysics which Al-Ghazzāliyy regarded as the science that addresses the existence of Allah and his attributes. He held that this science is also contained in *Kalām*. He compared the position of the philosophers with respect to this science to that of the Mu'tazilites who represented a branch of *Kalām*. He described the contribution of the philosophers in this field either as blasphemous or innovation. On the other hand he described the contribution of the Mu'tazilites as invalid (*bāṭil*).[62]

Physics is the fourth part of philosophy, some parts of which contradict the Shari'ah, religion and truth, and are, therefore, folly. These are not sciences and may be classified as such. The other parts of physics are concerned with the different substances: their properties, transmutation, and change. Al-Ghazzāliyy compared the contribution of the philosophers in physics to medicine but failed to see any practical application for this study and thus declared it useless.[63]

In this classification, Al-Ghazzāliyy elevated the know-

---

60 Al-Ghazzaliyy, *Ihya'*, Vol. I, p. 22.
61 *Ibid.*, p. 41.
62 *Ibid.*, p. 22.
63 Al-Ghazzali, *The Book of Knowledge*, p. 54.

ledge of the esoteric (*'ilm al-bāṭin*), which is the domain of the Sufi, to the highest possible rank compared to the other sciences. He intentionally restricted the importance and role of the jurists to this world and advised many of them to seek a profession that would benefit the Muslims instead of wasting their time in studying minute details in jurisprudence that are of no benefit. In addition, he undermined the contribution of the dialectical theologians and declared *Kalām* as a veil that prevents the *Mutakallim* from achieving peremptory knowledge since they do not have recourse to *'ilm al-mukāshafah*.[64] If this was his attitude towards jurisprudence and *Kalām*, it should come as no surprise that his position towards the philosophers was that of rejection. It seems that Al-Ghazzāliyy was caught at this stage with an enthusiasm for the Sufi path which dwarfed the importance of other sciences.

Al-Ghazzāliyy's aim in discussing knowledge at the beginning of the *Iḥyā'* is to identify the science that is required of everyone. Clearly, he is referring to a science that is hidden and which cannot be attained through sources of knowledge such as reason. He wanted the seeker to realize that worldly affairs constitute a barrier that prevents one from achieving the knowledge that Sufis claim to have acquired, and, therefore, he needs to look with disdain at worldly things. Al-Ghazzāliyy asserted that attainment of this knowledge can be promoted by "self-mortification, discipline, and through purifying the heart by freeing it from the affairs of this world, as well as through emulating the prophets and very virtuous people (*awliyā'*) so that it may be revealed to every seeker in proportion to what Allah [S.W.T.] has allocated (*rizq*) for him, rather than

in proportion to the seeker's efforts and labours (*jahd*). Yet diligence in it is indispensable for self-mortification which is the sole key to guidance".[65]

Like all Sufis, Al-Ghazzāliyy believed that one needs a Sufi guide to help prepare him to receive divine illumination.

Nevertheless, the *Iḥyā'* was intended as a manual that

64 Al-Ghazzāliyy, *Iḥya'*, Vol. I, pp.22–23.
65 Al-Ghazzali, *The Book of Knowledge*, p. 100.

120

describes what the novice needs to achieve such knowledge. He concluded the Book of Knowledge by defending the position of the Sufis who were accused of disparaging the intellect and reason as well as the rational and the reasonable. He said that the reason for such accusations is that "men have transformed the term intellect or reason (*'aql*) and the term rational or reasonable (*ma'qūl*) to indicate argumentation and debate over contradictions and requisites, things that have to do with dialectical theology (*Kalām*). Consequently, the Sufis could not tell that men have used this epistemology in ways different than the original meanings; it has not been possible to remove that from their minds in view of its current and well-established usage. As a result, they disparaged reason and rationalism."[66] The later position of the Sufis can be interpreted as a reaction to what might be described as a wave of rationalism that prevailed during the golden age of Islamic civilization which is manifested in the writings of the philosophers, the *Mutakallimūn* and the *Mu'tazilah* in addition to others.

4.1.7 On Creed ('Aqĭdah)

Al-Ghazzāliyy reiterated his position on the acquisition of knowledge throughout the *Ihyā'*. In the chapter on *Qawā'id al-'Aqā'id* (The Fundamentals of Belief) he said that one is not required to do research or to arrange proofs in order to achieve knowledge; the only thing that he has to do is to follow the path of the hereafter and to preoccupy himself with discipline and self-mortification. Only then will "the doors of guidance open and reveal the truths of this creed through divine light which strikes the hearts". He added that this knowledge is possible because there is a verse in the Qur'an in which Allah promises guidance for those who strive to act virtuosly.[67] Therefore, he interpreted the possibility of knowledge through divine illumination as a fulfillment of the latter promise.[68]

---

66 . Al-Ghazzali, *The Book of Knowledge*, p. 235.
67 Al-Qur'an, Surah *al-'Ankabut* 29:69.
68 Al-Ghazzaliyy, *Ihya'*, Vol. I, p. 94.

4.1.8 On Dreams

In the chapter on the reality of poverty and mysticism
(*zuhd*) where he advocated that intentional poverty is a condition that enables the ascetic, who embraces poverty (*al-
faqīr al-zāhid*),[69] to know things that are not permitted for
those who are preoccupied with money whether rich or
poor. One of the most important issues here is that he
adopted dreams as another source of knowledge. He related
a Hadith of the prophet [S.A.A.S.] in which he said, "True
vision is a part of forty six parts of prophecy".[70] He commented on this ratio and said that it is not possible to know
the reason behind it; he held that any attempt to do so will be
nothing more than guessing.[71] In another section in the
Ihya', he discussed other conditions that pertain to such
vision (e.g. purification). In this section, Al-Ghazzāliyy maintained that he could only talk about the nature of dreams
through the use of examples because this subject belongs to
'ulum al-mukāshafah which should not be discussed.[72]

It seems that Al-Ghazzāliyy's position on the possibility
of attaining peremptory knowledge through dreams is
substanstiated   by sound traditions, which is not the case
with those on poverty. His arguments regarding poverty are
filled with traditions that are "weak" and several others that
are fabricated (*mawdū'*). I think that he failed to cite sources
in the Shari'ah to support his position regarding intentional
poverty. In addition, Ibn Al-Jawziyy criticized him for
adopting this position which he considered contradictory
to both the Shari'ah and reason.[73] Thus, if intentional
poverty, which is supposed to be an action that brings one

69   The term *faqir* (poor) was used as a synonym for "Sufi" in Sufi literature.
70   This Hadith, "*Al-Ru'ya al-salihah juz' min sittah wa'arba'in juz' min al-

nubuwwah*", was related by Al-Bukhariyy from the narration of Abu
Sa'id. There is another version of this Hadith in which the prophet says,
"The vision of the believer is a part of forty six parts of the prophecy."
This latter version was related by both Al-Bukhariyy and Muslim in
their collections of Sahih from the narrations of Abu Hurayrah, 'Ubadah
Ibn Al-Samit and Anas Ibn Malik. It is apparent that this Hadith
is ranked *muttafaq' alayh*, the highest rank among the narrations
that are considered correct.
71   Al-Ghazzaliyy, *Ihya'*, Vol. IV, p. 194
72   *Ibid.*, p. 504.
73   Ibn Al-Jawziyy, *Talbis*, pp. 176–178.

122

closer to the possibility of acquiring peremptory knowledge, is against the Shari'ah, how could someone claim that he has a true vision?

4.1.9 Conclusion

Al-Ghazzāliyy had to rethink his position regarding all fields of knowledge upon his acceptance of the Sufi path as the only way that leads to the attainment of peremptory knowledge. He used this Sufi knowledge as the criterion to be used when considering the various subjects that he used; the variety of these subjects made it rather difficult to reconcile all of them within the framework of his epistemology.

Al-Ghazzāliyy held that there exists a faculty higher than reason in which knowledge is "unveiled" to the Sufi. Through this faculty one can achieve knowledge directly from divine sources. He did not discuss the nature of this knowledge, claiming that he had no permission to reveal it, and that language is not suitable to express such experience. Yet, in order to qualify for this divine knowledge, one should lead a disciplined and an immaterial life leading to self-mortification. The *Ihyā'* is written primarily as a guide that contains the science of action which is a prerequisite to the attainment of divine knowledge.

The positions Al-Ghazzāliyy took in the *Ihyā'* show that he was carried away by Sufism. His positions regarding many subjects (e.g., logic, *kalām*) contain flaws. In some cases in his later works, these flaws were overcome by corrected arguments.

4.2 *AL-MAQSAD AL-ASNA FĪ SHARH ASMĀ' ALLĀH AL-HUSNĀ*

The writings that followed the *Ihyā'* continued to reflect Al-Ghazzāliyy's position towards reason and other sources of knowledge. In the introduction of *Al-Maqsad al-Asnā fī Sharh Asmā' Allāh Al-Husnā* (The Sublime Aim in the Interpretation of Allah's Beautiful Names) he emphasized the inability of reason to attain transcendental knowledge,

namely, knowledge of Allah and the reality of his attributes.
He added that such knowledge, which he acquired through
"unveiling" (*mukāshafah*), does not conform to the ideas,
on this subject, that were presented by the scholars before
him. He knew that it is rather a difficult task to change the
customs and beliefs that people are accustomed to. Nevertheless, he believed that whoever has "seen" the Truth and
knows Allah, cannot but convey such knowledge.[74]

4.3 *BIDĀYAT AL-HIDĀYAH*

In *Bidāyat al-Hidāyah* (The Beginning of Guidance), Al-
Ghazzāliyy wrote a chapter on the gradual introduction of
guidance. The introduction of this chapter[75] is an exact
repetition of a similar text in his *Qawā'id al-'Aqā'id* which
stresses discipline and self-mortification as prerequisites for
the attainment of peremptory knowledge. This introduction
is another proof of the consistency during this period regarding the method or the "path" that Al-Ghazzāliyy advocated for the attainment of knowledge.

4.4 *JAWĀHIR AL-QUR'ĀN*

In another book, *Jawāhir al-Qur'ān* (The Jewels of the
Qur'an), Al-Ghazzāliyy asserted the position that one could
have a true vision, as a source of knowledge, while asleep.
He argued, similar to his position in the *Ihyā'*, that this
form of knowledge is the equivalent of one forty-sixth of
prophecy.[76] Moreover, he held that such knowledge is always
revealed in metaphorical language that represents transcendental knowledge. Since not everyone knows the meaning
of these metaphors only those who possess knowledge of the
hidden relationship between this world and the other
one

---

74 Al-Ghazzaliyy, *Al-Maqsad al-Asna Sharh Asma' Allah Al-Husna*,
Muhammad Mustafa Abu Al-'Ula, ed. (Cairo: Maktabat al-Jindi, 1968)
pp. 5–6.

75 Al-Ghazzaliyy, *Bidayat al-Hidayah*, Muhammad Al-Hajjar, ed. (Damascus: dar al-Sabuni, 1986), pp. 27–29.

76 Al-Ghazzaliyy, *Jawahir al-Qur'an*, Muhammad Mustafa Abu Al-'Ula,

ed. (Cairo: Maktabat al-Jindi, 1964) p. 31.

124

can interpret them. Once again, he asserted that to unveil the secrets of the other world one should resort to discipline and self-mortification.[77]

In another section in *Jawāhir al-Qur'ān*, Al-Ghazzāliyy pointed to insight (*baṣīrah*) as a source of knowledge. He said, "It appeared to me through clear insight and beyond doubt, that man is capable of acquiring several sciences that are still latent and not existent."[78] The meaning of this statement is that he perceived sciences other than those existing at the time. These sciences are latent, yet they are within reach of human beings. Though the concept of latent sciences which are not discovered yet is an interseting idea in itself, the emphasis here is on his use of insight as a source of knowledge which is consistent with his position in the *Ihyā'*.[79]

There is yet another book of considerable importance to the problem of knowledge, namely, *Al-Qistās al-Mustaqīm* (The Just Balance). Although this book could be considered primarily as polemic against the Batinites, Al-Ghazzāliyy also shows his ability to criticize the arguments commonly used in *Kalām* and jurisprudence. In the course of pursuing this critique, he presents strong arguments on the role of reason in Islam and defines the limits of personal opinion (*ra'y*) and analogy (*qiyās*). [80]

In his argument against opinion, Al-Ghazzāliyy provided an example from the doctrines of the Mu'tazilites in which they argued that, "Allah is obliged to order the best for His servants". He said that if they are asked to establish this, they have recourse only to opinion that they judge to be good by means of their intellects by analogy between the Creator and His creation and by likening His wisdom to theirs. Al-Ghazzāliyy assessed their opinion and found it to be false according to the rule of concomitance (*mīzān al-talāzum*) which he derived from the Qur'an, saying:

77 Al-Ghazzaliyy, *Jawahir*, pp. 33–34.
78 *Ibid.*, p. 28.
79 Al-Ghazzali, *The Book of Knowledge*, p. 231.
80 D.P. Brewster, trans. and ed., *Al-Qistas al-Mustaqim*, by Al-Ghazzaliyy (Lahore: Sh. Muhammad Ashraf, 1978), p. xx.

"If the best was obligatory for Allah, He would have done it.
It is known that He has not done it.
This demonstrates that it is not obligatory, For He does not neglect that which is obligatory."[81]

He added that if the Mu'tazilites do not admit that "Allah has not done it", he would reply that if He had done that which was best He would have created them in Paradise and would have left them there.[82] One of the most important aspects that can be derived from such arguments, is Al-Ghazzāliyy's ability to paint Aristotelian logic with Islamic color.

In his criticism of analogy Al-Ghazzāliyy used an example from the Mujassimah who believe that Allah has a body. They said, "He (Allah) is an agent and an artisan and by analogy with other agents and artisans (who have bodies). He has a body". Al-Ghazzāliyy considered this analogy false. He held that it is called the Great Rule (*al-mīzān al-akbar*) and that it runs like this:

"Every agent has a body.

The Creator is an agent.

Hence He has a body."

According to him, the problem in this analogy is not with the second premise which he accepted; it is the validity of the first premise that he questioned. He said that the Mujassimah derived the first premise from two sources: induction (*istiqrā'*) and the extended categories (*al-qismah al-muntashirah*). He stated that induction, in this case, consists of examining all the classes of agents (e.g., the shoemaker, the tailor, the carpenter) and finding that they all have bodies. Al-Ghazzāliyy found this generalization to be incomplete, since they did not examine every agent including Allah [S.W.T.] In addition, he asserted that induction cannot provide a certain conclusion.[83]

With regard to the use of extended categories, Al-

<hr>

81   Al-Ghazzaliyy, *Al-Qistas*, pp. 97–98.
82   *Ibid.*, p. 98.
83   *Ibid.*, pp. 101–102.

126

Ghazzaliyy provided an example where one of the Mujassimah says:

> "I have examined the attributes of agents and found
> them to possess bodies. This is because of their exist-
> ence as agents or, alternatively, because of their very
> existence, or for some other reason."[84]

Then he sets aside all categories (*aqsām*)[85] and states
that they possess bodies because of their existence as
agents. Al-Ghazzāliyy described this position as an extended
category and considered it to form a false analogy. It is
based on the method of induction, which Al-Ghazzāliyy
previously criticized, because in the example, it begins with
a premise that is derived from examining the attributes of
agents and finding them to possess bodies. It then sets aside
all categories (*aqsām*) and states that they possess bodies
because of their existence as agents. Therefore, I find the
position of assigning a special category for the extended
category is rather ambiguous.[86]

The spirit of *Al-Qistas al-Mustaqīm* and Al-Ghazzāliyy's
stance on the syllogism prompted Brewster to compare
him to Bernard Lonergan:

> "The function of the syllogistic expression is not to
> eliminate but to facilitate the occurence of the reflective
> act of understanding... . Inversely, when a man pro-
> nounces a judgement on the value of deciding to believe,
> it is not because of a syllogism but only because the
> syllogism has to grasp the virtually unconditioned in his
> acceptance of the premises."[87]

---

84 Al-Ghazzaliyy, *Al-Qistas*, p. 103.
85 Dar al-Kutub al-'Ilmiyyah published an Arabic edition of *Al-Qistas al-
Mustaqīm* in which the word *aqsam* (categories) was substituted with
ajsam (bodies). I find Brewster's translation to be more accurate for two
reasons. First, it does not make sense to "set aside all bodies and to state
that they possess bodies." The second reason is that Brewster cited the
source (i.e. Chelhot's printed text of 1959, which was based on the
printed text of Cairo, 1900, revised according to the readings of the
manuscripts of the Euscurial and Kastamonu dated 544 A.H.) that he
used for his translation, while the Arabic edition does not cite any
manuscripts and thus resembles the many uncritical editions that
flood the market. See Brewster, Introduction, *Al-Qistas al-Mustaqīm* by
Al-Ghazzaliyy, p. xxii.
86 Al-Ghazzaliyy, *Al-Qistas*, p. 103.
87 Brewster, Appendix III, *Al-Qistas*, by Al-Ghazzaliyy, p. 124.

He concluded *Al-Qistās* by asserting his position regarding the relationship between reason and revelation. He said that what is intelligible (*al-ma'qūl*) should be measured against that which is transmitted (*al-manqūl*, i.e. the Qur'an and the Sunnah). This statement is a clear indication of the supremacy of the Shari'ah over reason in the eyes of Al-Ghazzāliyy.[88]

4.5 *AL-RISĀLAH AL-LADŪNNIYYAH*

In *Al-Risālah al-Ladūnniyyah*,[89] Al-Ghazzāliyy appeared to be defending "metaphysical transcendental knowledge (*al 'ilm al-ghaybiyy al-ladūnniyy*) upon which elite Sufis depend (for knowledge)". In terms of certitude, he ranked this kind of knowledge higher than that which is acquired through conventional education.[90] This position was based upon the source of knowledge (i.e., Allah) and not its mode (e.g. rational vs. Shar'iyy). Regarding the relationship between the rational sciences and those of the Shari'ah, he stated that he who really *knows* both fields finds that the distinction that divides them into two fields disappears in many cases. He considered many rational sciences to be part of the Shari'ah and many of the sciences in the field of the Shari'ah to be part of the rational sciences.[91]

Nevertheless, he held that all sciences are important because science indicates the existence of knowledge, and ignorance is the absence of it. Moreover, he maintained that knowledge corresponds to the soul and ignorance to the body. He said that bodies are finite and not equipped to

88 Al-Ghazzaliyy, *Al-Qistas*, p. 111.
89 Literally, *Ladun* means "at the place or hands of". In the title of this and

every Sufi treatise it is used in relation to a verse mentioned in the Qur'an (18:65) the meaning of which is: "So they (prophet Moses and his attendant) found one of Our servants, on whom We had bestowed mercy from Ourselves and whom We had taught knowledge from Our own presence (*ladunna*). Thus, Sufis are striving to acquire this kind of knowledge which Al-Ghazzaliyy calls *al-'ilm al-ghaybiyy al-ladunniyy*, directly from Allah. It is apparent that an accurate concise translation is not possible. For a translation of the meaning of this particular verse in the Qur'an, see Abdullah Yusuf Ali's *Ma'ani al-Qur'an al-Karim* (Lahore: Sheikh Muhammad Ashraf, 1934).
90 Al-Ghazzaliyy, *"Al-Risalah al-Ladunniyyah"*, *Majmu'at Rasa'il al-Imam Al-Ghazzaliyy*, (Beirut: Dar Al-Kutub al-'Ilmiyyah, 1986), Vol. III, p. 87.
91 Al-Ghazzaliyy, *Al-Risalah al-Ladunniyyah*, p. 96.

hold the many sciences unlike the soul which accepts all knowledge without any obstacle.[92]

Al-Ghazzāliyy elaborated on the sources of human knowledge which he limited to two: human and divine (*rabbani*). He considered the first as a known path which all intelligent people accept. Knowledge in this source is achieved in two ways: from without which is formal learning, and from within which is thinking. He held that knowledge exists in potentiality inside the souls and defined learning as the process which brings knowledge out of potentiality into actuality. To explain his idea he used an analogy, writing:

> "The sciences are concentrated in the souls in potentiality, similar to the seeds in earth... . Learning is seeking to bring out that thing from potentiality to actuality, while teaching *is* bringing it out. The learner's soul imitates that of the teacher and tries to get close to it because the scholar is similar to the peasant in benefiting others, and the learner is similar to the earth in gaining benefit. The science in potentiality is similar to the seed, while in actuality is the plant. Once the learner's soul is perfected (through education) it becomes similar to a fruitful tree."[93]

Moreover, once the basics of any science are learned, the soul uses intuition (*ḥads*) to reach that which is required. At this stage an insight brings out the knowledge that exists in his soul from potentiality to actuality.[94] The idea that what is in potentiality comes to actuality by some agency, is Aristotelian. Aristotle said, "For from the potentially existing the actually existing is always produced by an actually existing thing, e.g. man from man". In addition, two words that Al-Ghazzāliyy used in his analogy, namely, "seed" and "earth" were used by Aristotle in his analogy in the *Metaphysics* which corresponds to the same notion.[95] These similarities indicate the possibility that Al-Ghazzāliyy was aware of this particular concept in Aristotle's *Metaphysics*.

---

92   Al-Ghazzaliyy, *Al-Risalah al-Ladunniyyah*, p. 90.
93   *Ibid.*, p. 102.
94   *Ibid.*, p. 103.
95   Aristotle, *"Metaphysics"*, *The Basic Works of Aristotle*, Richard McKeon, ed. (New York: Random Haouse, 1941) 1049 al–1049b35/pp. 827–829.

The second source of knowledge (i.e. divine) was also divided into two kinds: revelation (*wahy*) and inspiration (*ilham*). Concerning revelation, Al-Ghazzaliyy believed that it is restricted to prophets and that it is no longer available after the death of prophet Muhammad [S.A.A.S.] Regarding inspiration, he stated that unlike revelation where knowledge is presented in clear terms, inspiration constitutes hints of the same kind of knowledge which is called prophetic (*nabawiyy*) in the first case and *ladunni* in the second. Another major difference between these two forms of knowledge is that revelation is known through Allah [S.W.T.], while inspiration is known through the emanation of the universal intellect (*al-'aql al-kulliyy*). Al-Ghazzaliyy held that the *ladunniyy* knowledge is a condition for the attainment of wisdom which is sufficient; one does not have to go through formal education in order to achieve knowledge.[96] This latter position, which was common among the Sufis, was criticized by Ibn Al-Jawziyy.[97] Moreover, in *Ayyuha al-Walad* (O Child), Al-Ghazzaliyy considered learning or reading subjects such as poetry, *Kalam*, grammer and medicine, unless it is done for the sake of Allah [S.W.T.], a waste of time that will be regretted.[98]

4.6 *MISHKAT AL-ANWAR*

Al-Ghazzaliyy wrote *Mishkat al-Anwar* (The Niche for Lights) towards the end of this period of seclusion. The *Mishkah* was written as a reply to someone who asked him to disseminate the secrets of divine illumination, along with the interpretation of the verses of light (e.g. Allah is the light of Heaven and Earth). His answer to this request was that such knowledge is restricted to the few. In addition, he related the position of some Sufis who held that disclosing the divine secret is blasphemous (*Ifsha' sir al-rububiyyah kufr*). Nevertheless, he was willing to reveal some of this knowledge metaphorically through hints, signs and symbols.

96 Al-Ghazzaliyy, *Al-Risalah al-Ladunniyyah*, pp. 105–107.
97 Ibn Al-Jawziyy, *Talbis*, p. 150.
98 Al-Ghazzaliyy, *"Ayyuha al-Walad"*, *Majmu'at Rasa'il al-Imam Al-*

Ghazzaliyy, (Beirut: Dar al-Kutub al-'Ilmiyyah, 1986), Vol. III, pp. 154–155.

Moreover, he held that it is in Allah's hands to allow the hearts to understand the meaning of these metaphors.[99] The latter idea indicates that he considered the heart (al-qalb), which he distinguishes from the physical one, as a source of knowledge. According to him, the heart has an "eye" for knowledge which is sometimes referred to as intellect, soul and human spirit. He defined it as that "which differentiates the intelligent (human being) from the nursing infant, the animal and the insane".[100]

Al-Ghazzāliyy argued that the intellect moves from being insightful in potentiality (bi al-quwwah) to that of actuality (bi al-fi'l) when the light of wisdom shines. It is this kind of illumination that allows the "eye" of the heart to perceive the realities of the other world ('alam al-malakūt) in a fashion analogous to the function of the physical eye in the sensible world ('alam al-shahādah). He went as far as to describe those who settle for knowledge of the latter world as merely beasts (bahīmah).[101]

In relation to this neotic illumination, Al-Ghazzāliyy distinguish five levels of spirits with each corresponding to a level of knowledge. The first of these is the sensible spirit (al-rūh al-hassās) which is responsible for receiving whatever comes through the five senses. This spirit is possible for both animals and infants. The second spirit is the imaginative (al-rūh al-khayāliyy) which is responsible for storing the sensibles and presenting them to the intellect whenever there is need. He maintained that this one is possible for children and some animals. An example of this is a dog which is hit with a stick, it runs away upon seeing the same stick again. This is an example of conditioned learning, the subject of which is sensible objects. The third is the intellectual spirit (al-rūh al-'aqliyy) with which subjects other than the sensibles and imagination are perceived [e.g., generalizations). This spirit is the essence of adult human beings; it is not possible for children or animals, neither any other level beyond this one. The fourth one is the

99   Al-Ghazzāliyy, *Mishkat al-Anwar*, 'Abd Al-'Aziz 'Izz al-Din Al-Siyarawan, ed. (Beirut: 'Alam al-Kutub, 1986), pp. 115–118.
100   Al-Ghazzāliyy, *Mishkah*, p. 122.
101   *Ibid.*, pp. 129–131.

thinking spirit (*al-rūḥ al-fikriyy*) which is responsible for generating knowledge from pure intellectual sciences. The fifth is the holy prophetic spirit (*al-rūḥ al-qudsiyy al-nabawiyy*) which is restricted to prophets and some pious people (*awliyā'*). Al-Ghazzāliyy argued that it is through this spirit that divine knowledge is acquired. Most importantly, he held that the lower levels (e.g. intellectual) are not equipped to attain such knowledge.[102]

Towards the end of the *Mishkah*, he addressed those who sought retreat in the world of reason. He argued that the possibility of having a faculty higher than that of reason is similar to the possibility of reason being a faculty higher than the level of discernment and senses.[103] The meaning of this is that reason does exist regardless whether someone does not possess it (i.e. his/her faculties are on the level of the sense or discernment); by the same token, a noetic faculty which is higher than reason (i.e. prophetic) also exists.

In addition, he believed that through the faculty which ranks higher than reason, elite Sufis are capable of acquiring ultimate knowledge from the same source as the prophets, and therefore, they do not need assistance from them.[104]

As a devout Sufi, Al-Ghazzāliyy concluded *Mishkāt al-Anwār*, by an invitation to strive for divine knowledge which could only be hampered by waves of lust and worldliness.[105] As a matter of fact, his last surviving book to be written during this period, namely, *Al-Kashf wa al-Tabyīn fī Ghurūr al-Khalq Ajma'īn* (Unveiling and Explanation of the Deception of all Creation), was an attempt to detail the areas where people need to change their worldly behavior.[106] In addition, when he brought his seclusion to an end by returning to public teaching, the declared motives indicate that it was consistent with the principles that led him to abandon public teaching in the first place; he asserted that both were for the sake of Allah [S.W.T.]

102   Al-Ghazzāliyy. *Mishkah*, pp. 165–166.
103   *Ibid.*, pp. 166–167.
104   *Ibid.*, pp. 170–171.
105   *Ibid.*, pp. 172–173.
106   See Al-Ghazzāliyy, *Al-Kashf wa al-Tabyīn fī Ghurur al-Khalq Ajma'īn* (Cairo: Matba'at Mustafa Muhammad, No Date). This book is printed in the margin of *Tanbīh al-Mughtarrīn* by 'Abd Al-Wahhab Al-Sha'raniyy.

4.7 CONCLUSION

Al-Ghazzāliyy emphasized in his writings the limited capability of reason and that "unveiling" (*kashf*) is the only source of knowledge that is absolutely capable of attaining indubitable transcendental knowledge. In the *Iḥyā' 'Ulūm al-Dīn* (The Revival of Islamic Sciences), he stressed the superiority of Sufi knowledge over that which is attained by conventional sources of knowledge. This Sufi knowledge which he referred to as *'ilm al-mukāshafah* is the aim of intellectual activity, yet he stated that such knowledge should not be revealed to the public. Therefore, the subject of the *Iḥyā'* is that knowledge which leads to "unveiling" (*kashf*), namely the science of action (*'ilm al-mu'āmalah*). By action, he means self-mortification and discipline which form a prerequisite for attaining peremptory transcendental knowledge. In addition, he held that "unveiling" (*kashf*) is possible through the faculty higher than reason. The aim of this position is to show the limitations of reason which cannot achieve peremptory knowledge. This position is reinforced by listing prophecy as the highest level in relation to the attainment of knowledge which is followed by the scholars in what might be considered Al-Ghazzāliyy's response to the Muslim philosophers who ranked reason as the highest faculty. Finally, he added in the *Iḥyā'* another form for the attainment of peremptory knowledge, namely, vision.

Similar to his position in the *Iḥyā'*, Al-Ghazzāliyy continued in *Al-Maqsad al-Asnā Sharḥ Asmā' Allāh Al-Ḥusnā* (The Sublime Aim in the Interpretation of Allah's Beautiful Names) to stress the limitations of reason and its incapability to attain peremptory transcendental knowledge. The only way to achieve such knowledge is through "unveiling" (*kashf*). It is obvious that these two notions are consistent with Al-Ghazzāliyy's epistemology in the *Iḥyā'*.

As to *Bidāyat al-Hidāyah* (The Beginning of Guidance), there are whole sections which are identical with *Qawā'id al-'Aqā'id* which is considered a part of the *Iḥyā'* and therefore it adds to the consistency of Al-Ghazzāliyy's epistemology

during this period.   In these sections he asserted the notion
of discipline and self-mortification as prerequisites to the
attainment of peremptory knowledge.

In *Jawāhir al-Qur'ān* (The Jewels of the Qur'an) which
corresponds to his position in the *Ihyā'* and *Bidāyat Al-
Hidāyah*, Al-Ghazzāliyy maintained the notion of discipline
and self-mortification as conditions for the attainment of
transcendental knowledge. He held that transcendental
knowledge can be revealed through true vision in metaphorical language.

In *Al-Risālah al-Ladūnniyyah*, Al-Ghazzāliyy discussed
the notion of "metaphysical transcendental knowledge" (*al-
'ilm al-ghaybiyy al-ladūnniyy*) which is acccessible to elite
Sufis only.   This kind of knowledge can be attained through
inspiration (*ilhām*).

The last book dealing with the epistemology of Al-
Ghazzāliyy during the first period of seclusion is *Mishkat
al-Anwār* (The Niche for Lights). He reiterated his position
regarding the existence of a faculty higher than reason.
According to him, elite Sufis are capable of attaining knowledge directly from the same source, similar to prophets.

Although Al-Ghazzāliyy introduces different sources
(e.g., inspiration, insight) for the attainment of knowledge,
these six books emphasize Sufism as the common theme
and, therefore, this period of seclusion reflects a unified
epistemology.

Chapter FIVE

AL-GHAZZALIYY'S QUEST FOR KNOWLEDGE: THE SECOND PERIOD OF PUBLIC TEACHING (499–503 A.H./1106–1110 C.E.)

This chapter deals with Al-Ghazzāliyy's writings during the second period of public teaching at the Niẓāmiyyah of Nishapur which lasted for about four years. After spending more than a decade in seclusion, he realized that there was nothing that could justify his withdrawal from public life, especially when he could see that the society at large was astraying from the straight path, and was, therefore, in desperate need for reformation. He knew that by attempting to play the role of a reformer, he would win the animosity of many people if not all. Nevertheless, realizing that this return to public life was taking place at the turn of the sixth century A.H. (Dhu al-Qi'dah, 499 A.H.), he was convinced that he was going to be the expected reformer (*mujaddid*) in accordance with a Hadith of the Prophet [S.A.A.S.] in which he said that Allah [S.W.T.] will send a reformer to the Muslim nation (*ummah*) at the turn of each century to revive its religion.[1] Al-Ghazzāliyy's decision to leave his seclusion was made in consultation with prominent Sufis; it was also supported, he argued, by many visions of good people.[2] In addition, he received an official request from vizier Fakhr al-Mulk in which he asked him to teach at the Niẓāmiyyah of Nishapur.[3]

---

1 This Hadith (*Inna Allaha Ta'ala yab'athu lihadhihi al-ummah 'ala ra'si kulli mi'ati sanatin man yujaddidu laha dinaha*) was verified by Abu Dawud, Al-Hakim and Al-Bayhaqiyy. See Al-Ghazzaliyy, *Al-Munqidh*, p. 159.

2 Al-Ghazzaliyy, *Al-Munqidh*, p. 159.

3 Al-Qarah Daghi, Vol. I, p. 123.

During these years, he wrote four books[4]: his auto-
biographic work *al-Munqidh min al-Dalāl* (Deliverance from
Error), a ruling (*fatwā*) on divorce *Ghāyat al-Ghawr fī
Dirāyat al-Dawr, al-Mustaṣfā min 'Ilm al-Uṣūl* (The Chosen
from the Science of the Fundamentals of Jurisprudence),
and a defence of the *Iḥyā'* which he called *al-Imlā' fī Ishkālāt
al-Iḥyā'* (The Dictation on the Problems of the Revival).[5] It is
the aim of this chapter to continue tracing Al-Ghazzāliyy's
theory of knowledge in these books with the exception of
Ghayāt al-Ghawr fī Dirāyat al-Dawr which is not related
to the subject matter of this chapter.

5.1 *AL-MUNQIDH MIN AL-DALĀL*

The first book to be written during this period is *al-Munqidh
min al-Dalāl* (The Deliverance from Error). This book was
written in response ·to a brother in religion who wanted
Al-Ghazzāliyy to communicate to him "the aim and secrets
of the science and the dangerous and intricate depths of
the different doctrines and views".[6] It is not now possible
to determine whether this request actually took place; it
is likely that this question-answer is nothing but the
writing style of Al-Ghazzāliyy. It is possible that he picked
up this style from Platonic dialogues.[7]

Al-Ghazzāliyy gave an account of his "trail in dis-
engaging the truth from amid the welter of the sects, despite
the polarity of their means and methods". In addition, he
discussed why and how he moved from conformism to
independent investigation.[8] He next deliberately took the

4 Bouyges listed two other books, the first is *'Aja'ib al-Khawas* (The

Wonders of the Qualities [of Chemicals and Magic]); the authenticity
of this book was disputed by many scholars. The second book is *Sir
al-'Alamyn wakashf ma fi al-Darayn* (The Secret of the Two Worlds); the
authenticity of this book was disputed by many scholars including
Bouyges himself. See Badawi, *Mu'allafat*, p. 205 and p. 271.

5 Badawi, *Mu'allafat*, p. xvii.

6 Al-Ghazali, *Freedom and Fulfillment*, p. 61.

7 In addition to *Al-Munqidh min al-Dalal*, examples of this style can be
found in *Al-Maqsad al-Asna Sharh Asma' Allah Al-Husna, Al-Qistas al-
Mustaqim, al-Risalah al-Ladunniyyah, Faisal al-Tafriqah*, and *Ayyuha
al-Walad.*

8 Al-Ghazzaliyy, *Freedom and Fulfillment*, p. 61.

136

reader on an intelectual tour that has Sufism as the last station. This station was not intended as a layover, where the reader would take a rest before returning to his first station; *Al-Munqidh* was designed to take the reader on a one-way journey that has Sufism as the last station. As a matter of fact, he wanted the reader to avoid the other stations because he tried them and found them not suitable for the aim of this tour which is the attainment of true knowledge.

In the introduction of *Al-Munqidh*, Al-Ghazzāliyy described his quest for knowledge, his attemp to examine creed and every sect or group, as an on going process that began when he was less than twenty years old. According to him, this process continued on; he said that it was still the case with him at the time he was more than fifty years old.[9] This statement supports the idea that he maintained his inquisitive nature throughout his life. Moreover, he declared that his "thirst to perceive the reality of things" was an instinct (*gharīzah*) that was placed in his nature by Allah [S.W.T.] and, therefore, he had no choice but to seek true knowledge.[10]

Al-Ghazzāliyy described the history of his search for true knowledge. The first change in his epistemology was to break away from conformism (*taqlīd*) which he defined as uncritical acceptance of knowledge, presented by parents or teachers, as true. As a result, he rejected all inherited creed (*al-'aqā'id al-mawrūthah*). According to him, the inherited creed is nothing but dictated knowledge (*talqīniyyāt*) which is received by way of imitation. He held that this source of knowledge (i.e. *taqlīd*) is responsible for the differences between people.[11] He emphasized the neccessity to reject conformism as an essential step in any search for true knowledge.

Al-Ghazzāliyy realized the necessity of defining the nature of knowledge as part of his search for the reality of things. He reached the conclusion that peremptory knowledge (*al-'ilm al-yaqīniyy*) is that knowledge which is indubitable and devoid of mistake or illusion regardless of

9 Al-Ghazzaliyy, *Al-Munqidh*, p. 79.
10 *Ibid.*, p. 81.
11 *Ibid.*, pp. 81–82.

the circumstances.
It is here that he compared the certitude
that he was seeking with that which is generated in mathematics (e.g. as the certitude that results from knowing that ten is greater than three).[12]

Al-Ghazzāliyy used his concept of peremptory knowledge as a criterion to verify the sciences that he acquired previously. He fond that the sensibles (*al-ḥissiyat*) and logical necessities (*al-darūriyyāt*) which he believed to be trustworthy for a while, proved to be subject to doubt and, therefore, he categorized them in terms of certitude along with the knowledge acquired through conformism.[13]

Al-Ghazzāliyy's language in *Al-Munqidh* is different from that of previous works, where he used to present his discussions regarding the sources of knowledge in independent sentences or clauses. There was a transition between defining peremptory knowledge and its application to the sensibles and logical necessities: he used the term "next" (*thumma*) at the beginning of a new chapter (i.e. The Avenues to Sophistry and Agnosticism)[14] in addition to other places.[15] The use of this conjunction in Arabic (i.e. *thumma*) creates a sense of continuity that portrays the whole process as a systematic approach to epistemology.

Al-Ghazzāliyy's doubt of the senses was based upon his examination of sight (*basar*) which he considered the strongest sense; if he could doubt sight then he could doubt the rest of the senses as well. He provided several accounts where sight is deceived. In one of these examples he said:

> "The strongest of the senses is the sense of sight. Now this looks at a shadow and sees it standing still and motionless and judges that motion must be denied.

---

12 Al-Ghazzaliyy, *Al-Munqidh,* p. 82.
13 *Ibid.,* p. 83.
14 R.J. McCarthy translated the title of this chapter *Madakhil al-Safsata wa Jahd al-'Ulum,* as "The Avenues of Sophistry and Skepticism." I think that Al-Ghazzaliyy did not intend "*Jahd al-'Ulum*" as skepticism here, a translation which cannot be justified linquistically. The literal translation is "denial of the sciences" which the context renders it closer to the concept of agnosticism rather than skepticism or doubt. Al-Ghazzaliyy, *Freedom,* p. 64.
15 Al-Ghazzaliyy, *Al-Munqidh,* pp. 82–83.

Then, due to experience and observation, an hour later
it knows that the shadow is moving, and that it did not
move in a sudden spurt, but so gradually and imperceptibly that it was never completely at rest."[16]

Al-Ghazzāliyy realized that while the judge of the
senses finds the sensibles acceptable, the reason judge
refutes the latter judgement. At this stage, he trusted
the knowledge that comes through reason and which
belongs to "the category of primary truths (al-awwaliy-
yāt), such as asserting that 'Ten is greater than three', and
'One and the same cannot be simultaneously affirmed
and denied', and 'One and the same cannot be incipient
and eternal, existent and nonexistent, necessary and
impossible'.[17]

Soon Al-Ghazzāliyy found that his trust in reason
was also challenged. He was presented with another
problem; it was the personified senses that asked him
the following question, "What assurance have you that
your rational knowledge is not like your reliance on sense
judge?"[18] The basic argument is that the existence of a
higher faculty makes the lower one doubtful and if it
was not for the reason judge, he would have trusted the
sense. How then can he be sure that there is not a higher
judge than that of reason which once reveals itself, it
gives the lie to the judgement of reason? Moreover, the
fact that there is no appearance of this higher faculty does
not indicate the impossibility of its existence.[19]

Furthermore, this problem was reinforced by Al-
Ghazzāliyy's soul, which hesitated about the answer, by
appealing to dreaming[20] saying:

16 Al-Ghazzaliyy, *Freedom and Fulfillment*, p. 64.
17 *Ibid.*, p. 65.
18 *Ibid.*
19 Al-Ghazzaliyy, *Al-Munqidh*, pp. 84–85.
20 R.J. McCarthy mistakenly thought that it is the sense judge which
    reinforced its position by appealing to dreaming. In Arabic, the term
    "judge" (hakim) is masculine while both the "soul" (al-nafs) and
    "reinforced" (ayyadat): the verb reinforced has to be in the masculine
    form *ayyada* in order for McCarthy's translation to be correct. In
    addition, the suffixed pronoun *ha* in *ishkalaha* (its problem) is feminine
    and, therefore, refers to the soul and not the judge. Al-Ghazzaliyy,
    Freedom, p. 65 and al-Ghazzaliyy, *Al-Munqidh*, p. 85.

"Don't you see that when you are asleep you believe
certain things and imagine circumstances and believe
they are fixed and lasting and entertain no doubts about
that being their status? Then you wake up and know that
all your imaginings and beliefs were groundless and
unsubstantial. So while everything you believe through
sensation or intellection in your waking state may be
true in relation to that state, what assurance have you
that you may not suddenly experience a state which
would have the same relation to your waking state as
the latter has to your dreaming, and your waking state
would be dreaming in relation to that new and further
state? If you found yourself in such a state, you would be
sure that all your rational beliefs were unsubstantial
fancies."[21]

Al-Ghazzāliyy thought this state beyond reason might
be either that which the Sufis claim is theirs, or death. In
the first case, the Sufis allege in their states that when
they concentrate inwardly and suspend their sensation,
they see phenomena which are not in accord with reason.
The other possibility is death, where he derived this notion
from what he falsely believed to be a Hadith in which
the Prophet [S.A.A.S.] said, "People are asleep: then after
they die they awake".[22] In addition, he held that this notion
corresponds to a verse in the Qur'an which says, "But
we have removed from you your veil and today your sight
is keen".[23]

Al-Ghazzāliyy explained that he could not find a way
out of these thoughts, because to arrange any proof
he needed to combine primary truths, which was in-
admissible at the time. Hence, he was left in the condition
of rejecting as false all kinds of knowledge, which lasted
for two months. He regarded this condition as practically
equivalent to sophistry (safsaṭa),[24] but his condition did
not extend to utterance or doctrine.[25]

21 Al-Ghazzaliyy, *Freedom and Fulfillment*, p. 65.
22 This narration is not a Hadith: Muhammad Al-Hut related in *Asna
    al-Matalib fi Ahadith Mukhtalifat al-Maratib* that this is a saying of
    Ali Ibn Abi Talib, the fourth Caliph. See Al-Ghazzaliyy, *Al-Munqidh*,
    pp. 85–86.
23 Al-Qur'an, Sura *al-Mu'minun* 50:22.
24 *Safsatah* is an Arabicized form of Greek *sophos*.
25 Al-Ghazzaliyy, *Freedom and Fulfillment*, p. 66.

Al-Ghazzāliyy considered this condition as a sickness which was "healed" by a light (nūr) that Allah has [S.W.T.] caste into his chest. He came to regard this light as the key to most knowledge. From it, he regained his trust in necessary rational knowledge (al-ḍarūriyyāt al-'aqliyyah). He asserted that one should not restrict the possibility of unveiling truth (al-kashf) to precisely formulated proofs.[26]

Al-Ghazzāliyy reflected on this experience in terms of the concept of "dilation" (al-sharḥ).[27] In the Qur'an there is a verse which reads, "So he whom Allah wishes to guide aright, He dilates[28] his breast for submission to Himself (i.e. to embrace Islam)".[29] In a Hadith, the Prophet [S.A.A.S.] interpreted this verse as follows, "It is a light which Allah casts into the heart." Then someone said, "And what is the sign of it?" He replied, "Withdrawal from the mansion of delusion and turning to the mansion of immortality".[30] Al-Ghazzāliyy also adverted to other Hadiths on the same subject, concluding that one should seek to unveil truth through that light which gushes forth from the divine generosity, and one must be on the watch for it. He added that these narrations are intended so one should seek truth in areas other than primary truths which are given.[31]

After his trust in primary truths was reinstated at the end of this period of doubt, Al-Ghazzāliyy returned to searching for true knowledge in the teachings of every sect and school of thought. Eventually he narrowed the list of the "classes of seekers" to the Batinites, the dialectical theologians (al-Mutakallimūn), the philosophers and the Sufis. His aim was to show that only the Sufis possessed the methodology (i.e. "tasting" or dhawq) that lead to true knowledge.[32]

26 Al-Ghazzaliyy, *Al-Munqidh*, p. 86.
27 *Sharh* is a metaphorical expansion of the breast in order to indicate an acceptance of or to accommodate truth.
28 'Ali translated the meaning of *yashrah* as "*openeth*". See Yusuf 'Ali, *Tarjamat Ma'ani al-Qur'an al-Karim*, p. 326.
29 Al-Qur'an, Surah *al-An'am* 6:125.
30 Al-Ghazzaliyy, *Freedom and Fulfillment*, p. 66.
31 Al-Ghazzaliyy, *Al-Munqidh*, pp. 87–88.
32 This stage was discussed at length in chapter three. See p. 93.

5.1.1 The Influence of *al-Munqidh* on Descartes

'Uthmān *Ka'āk* related that he found a translated copy of *al-Munqidh* in Descartes' library in Paris with his comments in the margin.[33] Although there is no account of the nature of these comments, I think a comparison of Descartes' epistemology with that of Al-Ghazzāliyy is in order, because of the remarkable similarities.

Like Al-Ghazzāliyy, Descartes expressed his dissatisfaction with authoritative instruction which he considered deceptive.Therefore, as soon as his age permitted him to pass from under the control of his instructors, he abandoned formal studying: he began travelling and holding intercourse with men of different disposition by way of studying what he described as the great book of the world.[34] This position is similar to that of al-Ghazzāliyy regarding conformism. Descartes described his delight in the certitude of mathematic.[35] Likewise, Al-Ghazzāliyy made the certitude of mathematics as the criteria he aspired to reach in all knowledge. [36] Again, Descartes considered the revealed truths to be beyond the scope of reason's comprehension, and that there was a need of "some special help from heaven" in order to understand them.[37] This is comparable to Al-Ghazzāliyy's assertion that *sharḥ* is some special help from heaven. In addition, like Descartes he held that reason is impotent to verify revealed truths.

The most important comparison between the two is in the steps each one took forward verification of knowledge. Descartes doubted the sense and reason, and then followed with a comparison of knowledge in dreaming to that of being awake. He said:

> "When I considered that the very same thoughts (presentations) which we experience when awake may also be experienced when we are asleep, while there is at

---

33   Al-Qardawiyy, *Al-Ghazzaliyy*, p. 115.
34   Descartes, *Discourse on Method and the Meditations*. John Veitch, trans. (Bufalo: Prometheus Books, 1989) p. 15.
35   Descartes, p. 14.
36   Al-Ghazzaliyy, *Al-Munqidh*, p. 82.
37   Descartes, p. 14.

142

that time not one of them true, I supposed that all the objects (presentations) that had ever entered into my mind when awake, had in them no more truth than the illusions of my dreams."[38]

He went on to ask:

"How do we know the thoughts which occur in dreaming are false rather than those other which we experience when awake, since the former are often not less vivid and distinct than the latter?"[39]

All these steps made Descartes consider every idea that he had as false, except that he who thinks must exist, and therefore established the first principle of his philosophy.[40] Al-Ghazzāliyy followed the same steps: he doubted the senses, reason and presented a similar account regarding the relationship between knowledge in dreaming and that of being awake, saying:

"Don't you see that when you are asleep you believe certain things and imagine certain circumstances and believe they are fixed and lasting and entertain no doubts about that being their status? Then you wake up and know that all your imaginings and beliefs were groundless and unsubstantial. So while everything you believe through sensation or intellection in your waking state may be true in relation to that state, what assurance have you that you may not suddenly experience a state which would have the same relation to your waking state as the latter has to your dreaming, and your waking state would be dreaming in relation to that new and further state?"[41]

It is apparent that there are numerous similarities between *Al-Munqidh* and *Discourse on Method*, which seem to support *Ka'āk*'s observations. Thus it seem that an investigation of Al-Ghazzāliyy's influence upon Descartes might be a profitable line of research. Such an investigation is,

38 Descartes, pp. 30.
39 *Ibid.*, pp. 33–34.
40 *Ibid.*, p. 30.
41 Al-Ghazzaliyy, *Freedom and Fulfillment*, p. 65.

however, beyond the scope of this book.

5.1.2. The Stages of Epistemological Development in Human Beings

Al-Ghazzāliyy outlined the epistemological develoment in human beings in his chapter, "The True Nature of Prophecy and the Need All Men Have for It" in *Al-Munqidh*. He began with the essence of man in his original condition at the time of his creation and held that man is born devoid of any knowledge of the existing things. Each category of the existing things is known through a perception (*idrāk*) that is created.[42]

In the first stage of development, the sense are created in the human being. The first thing to be created in this stage is the sense of touch (*ḥāssat al-lams*). The category perceived with it includes the knowledge of heat and cold, wetness and dryness, and softness and harshness in addition to others. Next, sight is created for him with which he perceives colors and shapes. Al-Ghazzāliyy considered this category the largest of the "world" of the sensibles. Next, hearing is created in him with which he hears sounds and tones. Next, tasting is created for him, and so on until he passes the "world" of the sensibles.[43]

The second stage comes after all the senses are completed. The only thing to be created in the human being at this stage is discernment (*tamyīz*) and it is created at the age of seven.[44] With discernment, the human being perceives things other than the sensibles.[45] Al-Ghazzāliyy did not provide examples of the things perceived on this level.

Following discernment, the human being ascends to the third level where reason is created. With reason he

42 Al-Ghazzaliyy, *al-Munqidh*, p 144.
43 *Ibid.*, pp. 144–145.
44 It might be that Al-Ghazzaliyy chose age seven for the beginning of new stage from a Hadith, part of which indicates that children need to be taught prayer, at age seven though it does not become obligatory (*Muru Awladakum Bi al-Salati Idha Balaghu Sab'ah...*) This Hadith was verified by Ahmad Ibn Hanbal, Abu Dawud and al-Hakim who held that it is sound (sahih) according to the criterion of Muslim.
45 Al-Ghazzaliyy, *al-Munqidh*, p. 145.

144

perceives the necessary, the possible and the impossible in addition to matters that are not perceived in the stages before.[46]

The fourth stage is that which comes after reason, something which Al-Ghazzāliyy does not give a specific name. It is always described in terms of its order relative to reason. He held that another "eye" is opened at this stage, and that it is used to "see" metaphysical things. The knowledge that is acquired through this faculty is the one usually attained by the prophets; only part of it can be acheived through "tasting" (dhawq) by following the Sufis way.[47] Al-Ghazzāliyy's argument in support of the existence of this faculty is based upon the relationship between the different stages, he said:

> "Just as the intellect is one of man's stages in which he receives an "eye" by which he "sees" various species of intelligibles from which the senses are far removed, the prophetic pore is an expression signifying a stage in which man receives an "eye" possessed of a light, and in its light the unknown and other phenomena not normally perceived by the intellect become visible."[48]

The importance of Al-Ghazzāliyy's account of what might be described as the post-intellect faculty, can be seen as a response to the Muslim philosophers who placed reason as the highest faculty of knowledge and, therefore, denied prophecy. In addition, it can be considered a response to those who equated the Shari'ah with wisdom (ḥikmah) and, thus, prophecy would appear subservient to the intellect.[49]

5.2 AL-MUSTAṢFĀ MIN 'ILM AL-UṢŪL

Al-Ghazzāliyy wrote Al-Mustaṣfā min 'Ilm al-Uṣūl (The Filtered in the Fundamentals of Jurisprudence) at the request of some students of jurisprudence at the Niẓāmiyyah of Nishapur. They wanted a book which would be median in its

46 Al-Ghazzaliyy, *Al-Munqidh*, p. 145.
47 *Ibid.*, pp. 145–148.
48 Al-Ghazzaliyy, *Freedom and Fulfillment*, p. 98.
49 Al-Ghazzaliyy, *Al-Munqidh*, p. 161

size relative to *Tahdhīb al-Uṣūl* which they have considered very long and *Al-Mankhūl* which does not have enough details.[50]

In this section on *Al-Mustaṣfā*, I will inquire into whether Al-Ghazzāliyy remained faithful to the epistemology contained in Sufism and whether it had any impact on the fundamentals of jurisprudence. His basic epistemological position is included in both the preface and the introduction.

Unlike the introduction of *Al-Mankhūl* which addressed the relationship of jurisprudence to the fundamentals of jurisprudence,[51] the preface to *Al-Mustaṣfā* began with a criticism of this world for being deceptive and for not being a place of happiness. Al-Ghazzāliyy was calling people to consider this world as a passage to the next one. According to him, both reason and the Shari'ah agree to this latter position.[52] Certainly, the tone of the latter is that of a Sufi rather than that of a jurist.

In this preface, he also provided two classifications of the sciences. In the first classification, he divided the sciences into three categories according to their relations with reason and the Shari'ah. In the second, he divided the scienced into two categories only: rational (*'aqliyyah*) and religious (*dīniyyah*).The first category comprises purely rational (*'aqliyy maḥḍ*) sciences such as mathematics, geometry and astronomy. These subjects are based on either false opinions, or true knowledge that is not useful. Al-Ghazzāliyy admits that these sciences do yield benefit, but they are worldly and, therefore, do not help in attaining real happiness in the hereafter. This language indicates the continuity of his Sufi vision of the world. In addition, he held that the Shari'ah is neutral regarding the study of these sciences; it neither encourages nor discourages it.[53]

The second category is what he considered purely textual (*naqliyy maḥḍ*). It comprises sciences of the Shari'ah such as Hadith and exegesis (i.e. of the Qur'an). He argued

---

50 Al-Ghazzaliyy, *Al-Mustasfa min 'ilm al-Usul* (Cairo: al-Matba'ah al-Amiriyyah, 1904) Vol. 1, p. 6.
51 Al-Ghazzaliyy, *Al-Mankhul*, p. 3.
52 Al-Ghazzaliyy, *Al-Mustasfa*, Vol. 1, p. 3.
53 *Ibid.*, Vol. 1. p.3.

146

that these sciences depend on memory and that reason plays no role in them.

The third category comprises the sciences, such as the fundamentals of jurisprudence, that draw on both the Sharī'ah and reason. According to Al-Ghazzāliyy, this category is the most honorable. It is better than the sciences that are based on pure reason and do not enjoy the acceptance of the Sharī'ah, and it is also better than the sciences of the Sharī'ah that are based on pure conformism (*mahd al-taqlīd*) that is not supported by reason.[54]

Turning to his second classificaton, Al-Ghazzāliyy intended this classification to show the relationship between the fundamentals of jurisprudence and the rest of sciences. The rational includes sciences such as medicine, arithmetic and geometry; these sciences are of no concern to the fundamentals of jurisprudence. The religious sciences comprise dialectical theology, jurisprudence, the fundamentals of jurisprudences, Hadith, exegesis and the science of esoteric knowledge (*'ilm al-bātin*) or the science of the heart (i.e. the one that cleans it).[55]

The rational and the religious categories include some sciences that are concerned with universals and others that are concerned with particulars; the science which is concerned with universals is superior to one concerned with particulars. Among the religious sciences, *kalām* addresses universals, while all other religious sciences are concerned with particulars. The latter include jurisprudence, fundamentals of jurisprudence, Hadith and exegesis.[56]

Al-Ghazzāliyy elevated *kalām* to the highest of the religious sciences because all others are dependent on it. He maintained that not everyone has to study it; only those who wish to be considered an absolute scholar (*'alīm mutlaq*) and knowledgeable in all the religious sciences, should acquire *kalām*.[57] This position regarding *kalam* is totally different from that presented in the *Ihya'* in which Al-Ghazzāliyy, newly under the influence of Sufism, under-

54 Al-Ghazzaliyy, *Al-Mustasfa*, Vol. I, p.3
55 *Ibid.*, Vol. I, p. 5.
56 *Ibid.*
57 *Ibid.*, Vol. I, pp. 5–7.

mined *kalām* and regarded it as a veil that prevents the attainment of peremptory knowledge.[58]

The role of *kalām* is restricted to studying existence by using reason. It establishes the necessity of a Creator and that it is possible for Him to send messengers, and that the possible became reality. The last thing to verify is the truthfulness of the Prophet [S.A.A.S.] and after that, reason receives from the Prophet [S.A.A.S.] knowledge that it can neither reach by itself, nor render impossible.[59] The other religious sciences address parts of the message of the Prophet [S.A.A.S.], "Exegesis is concerned with the meaning of the Qur'an, the science of Hadith verifies the soundness of the Hadith, jurisprudence covers the rulings that are concerned with the actions of the *mukallaf*,[60] and the fundamentals of jurisprudence pertains to the sources of the latter rulings".[61]

Of these particular religious sciences, the fundamentals of jurisprudence is especially important. Al-Ghazzāliyy listed the Qur'an, Sunnah and consensus (*al-ijmā*)[62] as the only sources of this sciences.[63] He used reason to derive knowledge (e.g. by analogy, *qiyās*) from these three sources.[64] Al-Ghazzāliyy emphasized his restriction of the sources of the Shari'ah to these three whenever he mentioned them together by adding "only" (*faqaṭ*).[65] This position is consistent with *al-Mankhūl*, his first book on the fundamentals of jurisprudence written as a student, in which he also held the Qur'an, Sunnah and consensus as the only three sources of the Shari'ah.[66] The question is whether this restriction of the sources of the Shari'ah marks a new stage in the development of Al-Ghazzāliyy's epistemology, in which he returned to traditional positions? This

58 Al-Ghazzaliyy, *Ihya'*, Vol. 1, pp. 22–23.
59 Al-Ghazzaliyy, *Al-Mustasfa*, Vol. 1, p. 6.
60 *Mukallaf* is the adult [i.e. who reached puberty] and sane Muslim. 61 Al-Ghazzaliyy, *Al-Mustasfa*, Vol. 1, p.5.
62 Al-Ghazzaliyy defined consenses (*ijma*) as the common agreement of all

acknowledged Muslim scholars (*ahl al-hal wa al-'aqd*) on any one issue in religion. See al-Ghazzaliyy, *al-Mustasfa*, Vol. 1, pp. 173–174.
63 Al-Ghazzaliyy, *Al-Mustasfa*, p. 6.
64 *Ibid.*, Vol. 1. p. 7.
65 *Ibid.*, Vol. 1, pp.6–7.
66 Al-Ghazzaliyy, *Al-Mankhul*, pp. 4–6.

question can be answered by reference to the theory that I presented in Chapter II,[67] where I argued that Al-Ghazzāliyy maintained two independent lines of thought. In the first, he pursued peremptory knowledge (*'ilm yaqīn*); this line of thought, I believe, constitutes his search for universal truths. In the second, he sought particular truths in sciences such as the fundamentals of jurisprudence.

The last book that Al-Ghazzāliyy wrote during this period, *Al-Imlā' fī Mushkil al-Iḥya'*,[68] includes harsh criticism of those who were critical of the *Iḥyā'*, and very strong arguments in defense of Sufism and the possibility of attaining metaphysical knowledge by the post-reason faculty. This defense asserts beyond any doubt that he maintained his Sufi beliefs, at least till the end of the second period of public teaching.

The introduction to *al-Mustaṣfā* is for all practical purposes an introduction to logic, which he considered a concise form of what he presented in *Miḥak al-Naẓar fī al-Manṭiq* (The Touch-Stone of Reasoning in Logic) and *Mi'yār al-'Ilm fī al-Manṭiq* (The Criterion of Knowledge in Logic). Although Al-Ghazzāliyy included this introduction to logic at the beginning of *al-Mustaṣfā*, he did not consider it a part of the fundamentals of jurisprudence. Nevertheless, he held that logic is the prerequisite of all the sciences, and that whoever does not acquire logic cannot expect to have his knowledge trusted.[69]

5.3 *AL-IMLĀ' FĪ ISHKĀLĀT AL-IḤYĀ'*

This book, *Al-Imlā' fī Ishkālāt al-Iḥyā'* (The Dictation on the Problems of *al-Iḥyā'*), was written in response to the criticism that the *Iḥyā'* had endured at the hands of traditionalists whom Al-Ghazzāliyy did no mention by name. According to Al-Ghazzāliyy, they held that his book contradicts the Shari'ah in advocating "unveiling" (*mukāshafah*) as a source

---

67 See p. 55.
68 This book, *al-Imla' fī Mushkil al-Iḥya'*, is published as an appendix to *Iḥya' 'Ulum al-Din*. See al-Ghazzaliyy, *Iḥya'*, Appendix (*al-Mulhaq*), pp. 13-41. Subsequently, I will refer to it as *Al-Imla'*.
69 Al-Ghazzaliyy, *al-Mustasfa*, Vol. I, p. 10.

of knowledge and, therefore, they tried to censure it.[70]

The importance of this book is based on two elements; its subject matter and timing. In *al-Imlā'*, Al-Ghazzāliyy defends Sufism and the knowledge that can be derived from it. Chronologically, it was written at the end of the second period of public teaching at the Niẓamiyyah of Nishapur. It is clear, therefore that, contrary to the many voices which argue that he began to change his Sufi method towards the end of his life, and that he adopted the method of the traditionalists who stated that "unveiling" (*mukāshafah*) as a source of knowledge cannot be justified from the point of view of the Shari'ah, that Al-Ghazzāliyy made no such changes in his thought during this period. Rather, in his reply to those who were critical of Sufism, Al-Ghazzāliyy defended the existence of divine knowledge al-'ilm al-ilāhiyy).[71] It is certain that this work supports the notion that he remained faithful to his Sufi method until the end of this period; whether he maintained the same epistemology during the final period of his life is something that we shall be considering next.

70 Al-Ghazzaliyy, *Al-Imla'*, p. 10.
71 *Ibid.*, p. 16.

Chapter SIX

AL-GHAZZĀLIYY'S QUEST FOR KNOWLEDGE: THE SECOND WITHDRAWAL FROM PUBLIC TEACHING (503–505 A.H./1110–1111C.E.)

This chapter deals with the last stage in Al-Ghazzāliyy's life which extended from his withdrawal[1] from public teaching at the Nizāmiyyah of Nishapur until his death in 505 A.H./ 1111 C.E. During this period, he wrote three books: *Al-Durrah al-Fākhirah fī Kashf 'Ulūm al-Ākhirah* (The Precious Pearl in Unveiling the Sciences of the Hereafter), *Iljām al-'Awām 'an 'Ilm al-Kalām* (Preventing the Common People from Engaging in the Science of Kalām) and *Minhāj al-'Ābidīn* (The Course of the Worshippers).[2]

The aim of this chapter is to trace the last developments in his epistemology and to question the claim that he abandoned Sufism and adopted the method of the traditionalists who consider the Qur'an and the Sunnah as the two major sources of knowledge. According to al-Ḥāfiz Abū al-Qāsim Ibn 'Asākir, Al-Ghazzāliyy studied Al-Bukhāriyy's *Ṣaḥīḥ* at the hands of Abū Sahl Muḥammad Ibn 'Ubayd Allāh Al-Ḥafsiyy.[3] Nevertheless, it seems that 'Abd al-Ghāfir Al-Fārisiyy, Al-Ghazzāliyy's student and

---

1 According to Badawi, there are no primary sources that contain the exact date of his withdrawal from the Nizāmiyyah. He suggests that Al-Ghazzāliyy might have withdrawn some time after the assassination of vizier Fakhr al-Mulk in 500 A.H./1106 C.E. Badawi's opinion is based on the idea that Fakhr al-Mulk pressured Al-Ghazzāliyy to teach at the Nizāmiyyah of Nishapur, and that when Fakhr al-Mulk was assassinated, he did not feel obligated to continue teaching. See Badawi, *Mu'allafat*, p. xxv.

2 Badawi, *Mu'allafat*, p. xvii.

3 Al-Subkiyy, Vol. IV, p. 200.

the Khatib[4] of Nishapur, was the first one to relate his strong interest in studying Hadith. He said:

> "He (Al-Ghazzāliyy) concluded (the last years of his life) by studying the Hadith of Prophet Muhammad [S.A.A.S.] and by interacting with the scholars of Hadith. He began reading the two books of sound Hadith: Al-Bukhāriyy's *Sahīh* and Muslim's *Sahīh*.[5] Had he lived longer, he would have, in short time, excelled in this art more than everybody else. In addition, he studied Abū Dawūd Al-Sijistaniyy's *Sunan*[6] at the hands of Abū al-Fath Al-Hākimi Al-Tūsiyy."[7]

One cannot deny that Al-Fārisiyy's statement indicates a serious attempt by Al-Ghazzāliyy to study Hadith. This does not prove, however, as Dimashqiyyah attempts to show that Al-Ghazzāliyy returned to the method of the traditionalists (al-Salaf).[8] The statement is quoted by Dimashqiyyah from a page in Al-Subkiyy's *Tabāqat al-Shāfi'iyyah al-Kubrā* in which Al-Fārisiyy held that Al-Ghazzāliyy, upon his return to Tus, established his own school and built a lodge for the Sufis (khānaqāh li al-Sūfiyyah). Moreover, he devoted part of his time for the Sufis who were described as the people of the hearts (ahl al-qulūb).[9] It is obvious that this historical account of building a lodge for the Sufis and attending to them is an indication of a continued interest in Sufism. It remains that a study of his last three books is essential in determining Al-Ghazzāliyy's precise stand regarding Sufism.

6.1 *AL-DURRAH AL-FĀKHIRAH FĪ KASHF 'ULŪM AL-ĀKHIRAH*

This book *Al-Durrah al-Fākhirah fī Kashf 'Ulūm al-Ākhirah*

---

4 *Khatib* is the Imam who leads the Friday prayer which includes a *Khutbah* (speech). This *Khutbah* is considered part of the prayer.
5 According to Al-Hafiz Abu Sa'd Ibn al-Sam'aniyy, Al-Ghazzaliyy studied the two books of *Sahih* at the hands of Abu al-Fityan 'Umar Ibn Abu al-Hasan al-Rawasiyy al-Hafiz al-Tusiyy. See al-Subkiyy, Vol. IV, p. 215.
6 This is another collection of Hadith which is considered below the level of the *Sahih.*
7 Al-Subkiyy, Vol. IV, pp. 210–212.
8 Dimashqiyyah, *Abu Hamid al-Ghazali wa al-Tasawwuf,* p. 366.
9 Al-Subkiyy, Vol. IV, p. 210.

152

(The Precious Pearl in Unveiling the Sciences of the Hereafter) is less theoretical than the other two books. It is concerned primarily with Islamic eschatology; it describes in great details themes such as death, the Heavens and Hell. Nevertheless, there are scattered statements which indicate his high esteem for the Sufis whom he described as the Gnostics (al-'ārifūn). He said that some of those who die proceed through the seven Heavens until they reach the Throne (i.e. of Allah) . Some of them are denied access to Allah; only the Gnostics who know Him ('ārifūn) will reach Him.[10]

In another place in the Durrah, he relates the story of Prophet Muhammad's intercession (shafā'ah) on behalf of his own people on the day of judgement. This intercession begins with praising Allah [S.W.T.] in a fashion that was not used before. As to the nature of this praise, Al-Ghazzāliyy quoted some Gnostics (ba'd al-'ārifīn) who argued that it was originally "Allah's glorification of Himself at the time He completed His creation (i.e., of the world)."[11]

The term "Gnostic" is also used in a third context. Al-Ghazzāliyy listed the categories of those who are saved on the day of judgement. They are: the believers (al-mu'minūn), the Muslims (al-muslimūn), the doers of good works (al-muhsinūn), the Gnostics (al-'ārifūn), the believers in revelation (al-siddiqūn), the martyrs (al-shuhadā'), the righteous (al-sālihūn) and the messengers (al-mursalūn).[12] It should be noted that all of these categories are mentioned in the Qur'an, with the exception of the "Gnostics".

All of these three instances involving the Gnostics, namely, reaching the presence of Allah, acceptance of their argument regarding the exaltation of Allah [S.W.T.], and creating a special category for them along with the messengers on the day of resurrection are clear indications of Al-Ghazzāliyy continued acceptance of Sufis.

---

10 Al-Ghazzaliyy, *Al-Durrah al-Fakhirah fi Kashf 'Ulum al-Akhirah,* Muhammad Mustafa Abu al-'Ula, ed. (Cairo: Maktabat al-Gindi, 1968) p. 126. This book was printed as an appendix to Sir al-'Alamin, a book that was ascribed to Al-Ghazzaliyy.

11 Al-Ghazzaliyy, *Al-Durrah,* p. 151.

12 *Ibid.*

6.2 *ILJĀM AL-'AWĀM 'AN 'ILM AL-KALĀM*

Al-Ghazzāliyy wrote *Iljām al-'Awām 'an 'Ilm al-Kalām* (Preventing the Common People from Engaging in the Science of *Kalām*) in order to explain the creed of the first generation of Muslims (i.e. *al-Salaf*) regarding divine attributes, and to prove that their position is right and that any other position is an innovation (*bid'ah*). He held that this is necessary to avoid questions of anthropomorphism.[13]

This book was understood as a criticism of *kalām* and metaphorical interpretation (*ta'wil*) of divine attributes which forms the essential stand of the later generation of Ash'arites including Al-Ghazzāliyy. This position was misunderstood by many scholars including Dimashqiyyah, who said:

> "He experimented with Sufism: its illusion, self-mortification, "tasting", emotion, circle of *dhikr* (*hadrah*) and seclusion, believing the claim of its master that what is right is not received from written revelation, but rather from the hidden esoteric (source), and that Allah the Exalted did not provide guidance for the people in whatever verses He sent down for them, but rather in what He hid for the possessors of the stations (*maqāmat*) and supernatural powers (who know through) expositions, unveilings and emanations. He remained like this until it became clear to him when the train of life passed by and the sun of his lifetime dwindled that he had wasted his life in (seeking) a false illusion and the erroneous impossible, while the infallible peremptory source (of knowledge) was within the reach of his hands, rather close to his lips and he died, may Allah be merciful to him, with the *Sahih* on his chest,[14] as if he were resisting death so that he might drink from it (the *Sahih*) whatever sips to cleans his inside which was stuffed with (knowledge of) the Batinites, philosophy, *kalām* and Sufism."[15]

Dimashqiyyah held that "unveiling", the sufi source of knowledge, is a rival of the science of Hadith; he interpreted

13 Al-Ghazzāliyy, Iljam al-'Awam 'an 'Ilm al-Kalam, Muhammad al-Mu'tasim billah al-Baghdadiyy, ed. (Beirut: Dar al-Kitab al-'Arabi, 1985) pp. 51–52.
14 This anecdote about Al-Ghazzāliyy's death was mentioned originally by Ibn Taymiyyah. See Dimashqiyyah, p. 367.
15 Dimashqiyyah, p. 369.

Al-Ghazzāliyy's position as deserting the Sufi path in favour of the *Salafiyyah* methodology which is based on the Qur'an and the Sunnah.[16] Dimashqiyyah misinterpreted the meaning of "common people" (*'awām*) in *Iljam al-'Awām*. Regarding the definition of common people, Al-Ghazzāliyy said:

> "The category of common people (*al-'Awām*) includes the man of letters (*al-adīb*), the grammarian (*al-nahawī*), the scholar of Hadith (*al-muhaddith*), the interpreter (i.e. of the Qur'an), the jurist and the *Mutakallim.*"[17]

In fact, the Sufis were the only people who were not considered among the *'Awam* and, therefore, they were the only ones qualified to achieve divine knowledge. He held that only one in ten Sufis will reach what he described as the kept secret (*al-sir al-makhzūn*). Al-Ghazzāliyy wanted to prevent all those included in the definition of "common people" from engaging in *Kalām* and to accept the position of the *Salaf* regarding the interpretation of divine attributes.[18] Thus, the passage Dimashqiyyah refers to provides no basis for the claim that Al-Ghazzāliyy abandoned Sufism.

Instead, Al-Ghazzāliyy maintained the highest rank for the Sufi, as can be seen in the following analogy in which he compared divine presence to that of the Sultan, he said:

> "The Sultan has in his kingdom a private palace which is surrounded by a courtyard that has a gate where all the subjects gather without being permitted to enter through the gate; they are not permitted to the edge of the courtyard. Then the elites of the kingdom are permitted to enter through the gate and into the courtyard where they can sit according to their positions (i.e. the higher the rank, the closer one gets to the palace). It could be that only the vizier is permitted to the private palace where the king reveals to the vizier whatever he wishes of the secrets of his kingdom, and he (the king) keeps to himself matters that he would not reveal to him. It is the same regarding how close one can get to the divine presence. The gate is where all the *'Awām* (com-

16 Dimashqiyyah, p. 368.
17 Al-Ghazzāliyy, *Iljam*, p. 67.
18 *Ibid.*, pp. 67–68.

mon people) stop and if any one of them trespasses, he should be reprimanded. As for the Gnostics (*al-'ārifūn*), they enter through the gate into the courtyard where they spread according to their ranks without being able to get close, or even look at the sacred place (*haẓirat al-qudus*) in the center of the court."[19]

This analogy is a clear indication of Al-Ghazzāliyy's classification of the Sufis higher than "common people" which include scholars of Hadith, the very science that he was supposed to accept as the source of knowledge instead of "unveiling" according to the many claims in this respect. To avoid any misunderstandings, I should say that he accepted Hadith as a source of knowledge throughout his life, yet this acceptance on its own should not lead to any conclusion regarding his position towards other sources of knowledge (e.g., "unveiling", *kashf*).

Another indication that he did not change his position concerning Sufism is his assertion regarding the existence of a faculty higher than reason. He reiterated his argument in respect to the inability of reason to perceive things such as the harm that results from sinning or the benefit that results from obedience (i.e. to the Shari'ah) in relationship to after death. He added that all those who are rational agree that reason cannot lead to specific knowledge similar to that in the Shari'ah, and that only a post-reason faculty can perceive metaphysical knowledge.[20] It is obvious that Al-Ghazzāliyy maintained his idea on the limitations of reason which he used to support his argument on the existence of a faculty higher than reason, which is accessible to the Sufis.

6.3 *MINHĀJ AL-'ĀBIDĪN*

This book, *Minhāj al-'Ābidīn* (The Course for the Worshippers), is the last work known to be written by Al-Ghazzāliyy at the end of his life; 'Abd al-Malik Ibn 'Abdullāh, one of his students, said:

19 Al-Ghazzaliyy, *Iljam*, pp. 85–86.
20 *Ibid.*, p. 87.

156

> "My honorable Sheikh, the successful and happy mys-
> tical Imam, Proof of Islam and Ornament of religion,
> the honor of the nation, Abū Ḥāmid Muḥammad Ibn
> Muḥammad Ibn Muḥammad Al-Ghazzāliyy Al-Ṭūsiyy,
> may Allah sanctify his soul and may Allah raise his
> rank in Heavens, dictated this concise[21] book which was
> the last book to be written by him, and only copied by
> his very close companions (*khawāṣ aṣḥābih*).[22]

Ibn 'Abdullāh's preface to his own copy of *Minhāj al-'Ābidīn* is important not only because it indicates that this is the last book to be written by Al-Ghazzāliyy, but also because it comes from one of the close companions, or what might be described as a member of the inner circle, a fact that adds to the certitude of his statement.

According to Al-Ghazzāliyy, this book was written in the same spirit of the *Iḥyā'*, except that he was hoping that *Minhāj al-'Ābidīn* would not draw criticism similar to the *Iḥyā'* which he blamed on the inability of the "common people" to understand it. He found consolation in the fact that the Qur'an which is the perfect word of Allah [S.W.T.], was described, by non-Muslims, of being "stories of past nations" (i.e., not revealed).[23]

Moreover, he kept referring the reader throughout *Minhāj al-'Ābidīn*, because it is a concise book, to read the corresponding chapters in the *Iḥyā'*. Al-Ghazzāliyy gives no indication that he has retracted the basic positions expressed in the *Iḥyā'*, which of course includes his views on the superiority of Sufism as a source of knowledge over all other forms. Yet it is clear that he did not mention every thing he knew regarding Sufism for fear of misunder-standing. He cited four lines of a poem by Zayn al-'Ābidīn[24] in which he held that he kept as a secret the jewels of his knowledge fearing an ignorant person who would accuse him of being an idolator or worse, he might get killed if he reveals

---

21 *Minhāj al-'Ābidīn* which has more than 240 pages is considered a
concise book here relative to books like *Iḥya'*.
22 Al-Ghazzāliyy, *Minhāj al-'Ābidīn*, Muhammad Mustafa Abu al-'Ula, ed.
(Cairo: Maktabat al-Gindi, 1972), p. 13.
23 Al-Ghazzāliyy, *Minhāj*, p. 14.
24 Zayn al-'Abidin, 'Ali Ibn al-Husayn Ibn 'Ali Ibn Abu Talib, the grandson
of the fourth Caliph.

his knowledge.[25] This poem represents the outlook of Al-Ghazzāliyy when he wrote this book; it shows that he was not at ease in expressing all that he wanted to say. Nevertheless, we shall see direct statements that he made in favour of Sufism.

Like the *Ihyā'*, *Minhāj al-'Ābidīn* was written to explain the path to the hereafter.[26] Al-Ghazzāliyy described seven obstacles[27] that face the person who treads this path. According to him, the arrangement of the contents of this book was an inspiration (*ilhām*) from Allah [S.W.T.].[28] I will analyze the language that he used in discussing some of these obstacles where he explicitly uses Sufi terms and themes in order to determine whether there were any changes in his epistemology.

The first of these is the obstacle of science and knowledge (*'aqabat al-'ilm wa al-ma'rifah*). In order to worship, one needs to know what it is that one is worshipping and to be certain about it. To overcome this obstacle, he held that one should seek help "from the scholars of the hereafter (*'ulamā' al-ākhirah*) who are the guides of this path, the saddle of this nation and the leaders of the Imams. One should benefit from them and should ask them for their good supplication (*du'ā'*) so he can cross this path with the help of Allah, praise be to him, in order to attain peremptory knowledge (*'ilm al-yaqīn*)."[29] Al-Ghazzāliyy maintained, since he accepted the Sufi path as the only way to acheive peremptory knowledge. Thus, I understand the solution that Al-Ghazzāliyy provided to this obstacle as an invitation for people to seek a Sufi Sheikh among those whom he dscribed as "the scholars of the hereafter" who would guide the novice (*al-murīd*) on this path.

Furthermore, he stated that while studying at the hands of a teacher facilitates knowledge and makes it easier

25 Al-Ghazzaliyy, *Minhaj*, p. 15.
26 *Ibid.*, p. 255.
27 These are: *'aqabat al-'ilm wa al-ma'rifah* (the obstacle of knowledge),

   'aqabat al-tawbah (the obstacle of repentance), *'aqabat al-'awa'iq* (the obstacle of obstructions), *'aqabat al-'awarid* (the obstacle of crises), *'aqabat al-bawa'ith* (the obstacle of motivations), *'aqabat al-qawadih* (the obstacle of impunities) and *'aqabat al-hamd wa al-shukr* (the obstacle of gratitude and thankfulness).
28 Al-Ghazzaliyy, *Minhaj*, p. 20.
29 *Ibid.*, p. 16.

158

to achieve, Allah bestows his bounty on whomever He chooses from among His servants and becomes their direct Teacher.[30] The latter statement conforms to the Sufi notion of achieving knowledge directly from Allah which is known as *al-'ilm al-ladunniyy*.

In his discussion of another obstacle, that concerning worldly things, he considered the question of whether asceticism (*zuhd*) is an obligation (*farḍ*). Al-Ghazzāliyy held that asceticism is an obligation in regard to forbidden (*ḥaram*) things; it is voluntary (*nafl*) concerning what is lawful (*ḥalal*). That is to say, refraining from things which are forbidden is obligatory on all; but one may refrain, though one is not obliged to do so, in cases of things which are permitted by Islamic law. He maintained that there is a higher level than this where the lawful is considered forbidden and, therefore, asceticism becomes obligatory. This higher level is pertaining to the Sufis who become *Abdāl*.[31]

To explain this term *"abdāl"*, one needs to know the hierarchy of a Sufi order. The Sufi order has one Sheikh in the highest rank; he is described as *Qutub* (head).[32] The *Qutub* has three deputies (*Nuqabā'*, sing. *Naqīb*) who represent the second level. The third level comprises seven chiefs (*Awtād*, sing. *Watad*).[33] The fourth rank includes forty substitutes (*Abdāl*, sing. *Badal*).[34] It is the members of this latter rank that Al-Ghazzāliyy had in his mind when he made his comments that their asceticism is obligatory in both the lawful and the forbidden. The meaning of this is that once a Sufi reaches the fourth rank or higher, he regards lawful things as if they are dead animal.[35] According to Islamic jurisprudence, one can eat of a dead animal only in case where if he did not, he would die. For Al-Ghazzāliyy, the dead animal becomes a metaphor of this world, where the Sufi would use enough of it to subsist in order to be able to continue worshipping.

Moreover, he explained that asceticism should take

---

30 Al-Ghazzāliyy, *Minhaj*, p. 27.
31 *Ibid.*, p. 42.
32 Literally *qutub* means pole.
33 Literally *watad* means peg or stake.
34 Trimingham, J., The Sufi Orders in Islam (London: Oxford University Press, 1971) p. 262.
35 Al-Ghazzāliyy, *Minhaj*, p. 42.

place in regard to everything except for subsistence. He added that one might subsist with or without food and drink; if Allah wills the body to subsist without a cause (i.e., food and drink) it will do so, as do the angels. On the other hand, if He wills the body to subsist with something, it might be that you seek that thing, or that He would cause that thing to come to you without seeking it. To support his argument, Al-Ghazzāliyy cited a verse in the Qur'an which indicates that for one who fears Allah, He will find him a way out of his problems and that He will provide him with sustenance in ways that he did not expect.[36]

Another obstacle that al-Ghazzāliyy discussed is people. He held that people will keep one from worshipping, and if he does worship in their presence, he might change the way he worships (e.g., improve it), an act which renders him hypocrite. According to Al-Ghazzāliyy, the solution to this problem is seclusion (al-'uzlah). He related numerous Hadiths, poems and anecdotes of Sufis in support of this notion. In addition, he defended the existence of Sufi schools and lodges (ribātāt al-sūfiyyah) which fulfill the notion of seclusion, even though other people are present. He maintained that if problems arise in these special gatherings, then it is legitimate for the scholar to seek absolute isolation even if it leads to the "burial of knowledge". He emphasized that finding comfort in the presence of people without a need (e.g., for studying) is an indication of emptiness.[37]

Al-Ghazzāliyy discussed many other Sufi themes such as poverty and celibacy. He held that poverty is better than wealth and that celibacy is better than being preoccupied with the affairs of the wife and children. His position is based on the idea that the Sufi should be disentangled and independent from worldly affairs.[38]

Towards the end of this book, he described the nature of this path that the Sufi needs to follow, saying:

"This path in its length is unlike the existing distances that people cover by feet according to their strength and

36 Al-Qur'an, Sura *al-Talaq* 65:3. See Al-Ghazzaliyy, *Minhaj*, p.43.
37 Al-Ghazzaliyy, *Minhaj*, pp. 44-58.
38 *Ibid.*, p. 141.

160

weakness, it is rather a spiritual path that is tread by hearts which cover it with thought according to the faith and insight (of the seekers). Its origin is a Heavenly light (*nūr samāwiyy*) and a divine look (*naẓar ilāhiyy*) which descends on the heart of the servant who uses it to see the reality of both worlds."[39]

As to the length of time one spends in seeking this path, Al-Ghazzāliyy argued that someone might seek it for a hundred years without finding it due to mistakes in the way he seeks it or because he does not exert enough effort. On the other hand, someone else might find it in a moment with the care of the Lord, the Exalted, who is responsible for guidance.[40]

6.4 CONCLUSION

It is apparent, then, that *Al-Durrah al-Fākhirah, Iljām al-'Awām 'an 'Ilm al-Kalām* and *Minhāj al-'Ābidīn*, written during the last stage of Al-Ghazzāliyy's life, contain clear manifestations of his continued acceptance of Sufism as the path for true knowledge.

In *Al-Durrah al-Fākhirah*, he held that the Sufis, whom he describes as *'Ārifīn* (Gnostics), are the only people who upon their death could proceed through the seven Heavens to reach Allah. In *Iljām al-'Awām*, he employed the concept of "common people" to divide every other kind of scholar from the Sufis. He ranked the Sufis higher and he described them as the scholars of the hereafter. Finally, in *Minhāj al-'Ābidīn*, he defended Sufi schools and lodges. In addition, he described the knowledge of the Sufi in terms of a divine light which is typical of "unveiling" (*kashf*).

All of these Sufi themes, which were also using Sufi terminology, leave no room for any doubt or hesitation that Al-Ghazzāliyy's epistemology was Sufi in its essence. It should be noted that this is not a defence of Sufism against the *Salafiyyah* movement which tried to present Al-Ghazzāliyy in his final days as someone who abandoned Sufism. What

---

39 Al-Ghazzāliyy, *Minhaj*, p. 245.
40 *Ibid.*

I am trying to say is that they need a better argument for their position.

CONCLUSION

In this book, I have offered a comprehensive study of Al-Ghazzāliyy's epistemology in all his confirmed and available works. I have argued that his epistemology evolved through the various stages of his life. He began as a conformist (i.e, accepting knowledge on the authority of parents and teachers), but soon he broke away from conformism while still a child. He stressed the importance of this step for anyone seeking true knowledge. After releasing himself from the authority of conformism, he began a long intellectual journey in quest for truth which led him to question everything and eventually to experience one of the most original and dramatic cases of skepticism in he history of thought. The way out of his skepticism was divine illumination. After he regained his trust in logical necessities, he studied all the existing schools of thought including philosophy, dialectical theology and the Batinites; his search culminated in his acceptance of Sufism as the only path that leads to what he described as peremptory knowledge (*'ilm yaqīn*).

In Chapter One, I presented a sketch of Al-Ghazzāliyy's life as an aid to understanding the complexities and the controversies that surround this great Muslim thinker. Not only his writings (e.g., Al-Ghazzāliyy's books on knowledge), but also his life is a direct manifestation of his spiritual and intellectual development. This is especially true when the person is a Sufi whose everyday life is a manisfestation of the epistemological path he is using.

In the subsequent Chapters (2–6), I analyzed Al-

Ghazzāliyy's books in chronological order in order to portray the development in his epistemology.

As a student, Al-Ghazzāliyy wrote *Al-Mankhūl* on *uṣūl al-fiqh*. His basic epistemological interest in this book was mainly as a jurist. He concentrated on technical issues that were part of or related to *uṣūl al-fiqh*. As a student, Al-Ghazzāliyy imitated his teacher al-Juwainiyy, which he acknowledged at the end of this book. Although he differed in very few cases from his teacher in *Al-Mankhūl*, his originality in *uṣūl al-fiqh* was manifested in his later work *Al-Mustaṣfā*.

Although *Al-Mankhūl* shows Al-Ghazzāliyy as an imitating student, his bibliographic work *Al-Munqidh min al-Ḍalāl*, which was written towards the end of his life, projects a personality that is preoccupied with truth in itself. It was differences in belief that prompted him to search for truth. His awareness, during the early stages of his life , of the different creeds of people started him on his first stage of a long journey of systematic skepticism which lasted until the climax of his quest for knowledge during his last days as a teacher at the Niẓāmiyyah of Baghdad.

Al-Ghazzāliyy's critical thinking and regard for general questions of truth and knowledge, while apparent in *Al-Munqidh*, are absent from *Al-Mankhūl*. The fact that these two books reflected different areas of interest in Al-Ghazzāliyy's early life might appear contradictory. One question that might surface as a result of these two area is: how could someone like Al-Ghazzāliyy, who was investigating the general notions of knowledge and their sources as stated in *Al-Munqidh*, proceeded to verify the particular as the case in *Al-Mankhūl*:

"In the bloom of my life, from the time I reached puberty before I was twenty until now, when I am over fifty, I have constantly been diving daringly into the depth of this profound sea and wading into its deep water like a bold man, not like a cautious coward. I would penetrate far into every murky mystery, pounce upon every problem, and dash into every mazy difficulty. I would scrutinize the creed of every sect and seek to lay bare the secrets of each faction's teaching with the aim of discriminating between the proponent of truth and the advocate of

164

error, and between the faithful follower of tradition and the heterodox innovator."[1]

Al-Ghazzāliyy reaffirmed the early beginning of this search for truth and the source of this quest for knowledge in the same introduction. He said:

> "The thirst for grasping the real meaning of things was indeed my habit and wont from my early years and in the prime of my life. It was an instinctive, natural disposition placed in my makeup by God (Allah) Most High, not something due to my own choosing and contriving. As a result, the fetters of servile conformism (*taqlīd*) fell away from me, and inherited beliefs lost their hold on me, when I was still quite young."[2]

Although the above quotations showed the time frame of the first line of thought, which covered Al-Ghazzāliyy's life as a student, it remains that there were no books written by the student Al-Ghazzāliyy that reflected this independent approach to knowledge and truth. There were many works (e.g. *Al-Munqidh min al-Ḍalāl*) by the later Al-Ghazzāliyy that embodied this investigative course that he undertook in pursuit of knowledge and truth in what could be called the area of universals.

The second line of thought is represented in Al-Ghazzāliyy's works in fields like jurisprudence. Although the first line of thought must have influenced the way Al-Ghazzāliyy approached areas like *fiqh* by having that independent spirit which led him not to be a conformist to previous writings in such fields, one cannot claim that these works were reflecting the first line of thought because they were concerned with particulars. Unlike a reductionist, he addressed these areas of particulars as if there was no relationship between the general notions of knowledge, which he put under investigation, and these particular fields.

The fact that Al-Ghazzāliyy kept working in the particular fields of the Shari'ah indicate that he was never in doubt

---

1 Al-Ghazzaliyy, *Freedom and Fulfillment* (Al-Munqidh min al-Dalal), Richard Joseph McCarthy, tr. (Boston: Twayne Publishers, 1980) p. 62.
2 Al-Ghazzaliyy, *Freedom*, p. 63.

about the true validity of the premises which were derived from the Qur'an and the Sunnah. In fact, he continued lecturing on these subjects even at the Nizāmiyyah of Baghdad, when he was going through what I like to call the climax of his mental discourse regarding the first line of thought.[3]

Al-Ghazzāliyy's continuous inquiry into both universals and particulars is interesting because on the surface they seem incompatible. One could see that Al-Ghazzāliyy had an obvious, spontaneous interest in the first. It prompted a good deal of reflection throughout his life. The difficulty is in the question: why did he pursue the second? Part of the answer could be found in Al-Ghazzāliyy's formal education which started with training in the particulars (e.g. *fiqh*). Another partial answer comes from the fact that there was common interest in these particular sciences, especially in jurisprudence. In addition, Al-Ghazzāliyy pursued his interest in the particulars as a teacher who was expected, and thus there is a sense of duty, to lecture on such topics. All of these aspects and probably more provided the motivation for such pursuit of knowledge in the particulars. Moreover, one could think that once Al-Ghazzāliyy achieved universal knowledge, he found that his interest in the particulars was in line with his interest in the universals. In addition, there is a sociological element in this equation, where a scholar in the Islamic world is unlikely to be accepted without being deep rooted and having strong interests in the particulars.

The next stage in Al-Ghazzāliyy's epistemological development took place when he became the teacher of the Nizāmiyyah of Baghdad. His writings during this period, which lasted for a decade, reflect one of the most important stages in his intellectual development. He broke with conformism which dominated his work as a student, and began a systematic inquiry of the schools of thought that were available at the time in search for true knowledge.

Al-Ghazzāliyy encountered many schools of thought in his quest for true knowledge. Eventually, he restricted the possibility of finding such knowledge to four "classes of

3   Al-Ghazzaliyy, *Al-Munqidh*, p. 136.

seekers": *al-Mutakallimūn*, the Batinites, the philosophers and the Sufis whose methodology he finally accepted.

When Al-Ghazzāliyy became a teacher at the Niẓām-miyah of Baghdad, he started studying philosophy in his search for true knowledge as part of a systematic approach in which he was attempting to study all sects, religions and schools of thought in search of true knowledge. According to him, he could not find such knowledge in all the traditional subjects of philosophy; the only two exceptions were logic and mathematics. Although he was critical of philosophy, he adopted many positions from the works of the philosophers (e.g., Al-Fārābī).

One of the most important contributions of Al-Ghazzāliyy during this period is his position on logic. He wrote several books in which he intended to set forth a criterion for science. He held in *Mi'yār al-'Ilm* that every person has three judges: a judge of sensibles, a judge of imagination and a judge of reason. It is the addition of a "judge of imagination" here that contributes to the development of his genetic epistemology even though he would drop it later on in *Al-Munqidh*.

Al-Ghazzāliyy's search for indubitable knowledge led him to reject all knowledge that was based on authority which he blamed for the differences among people. He defined this knowledge in terms of mathematical certitude. He scrutinized all his cognition in search for knowledge that would meet the previous description; he thought for a while that the sensibles and the self evident truths conform to the level of certitude that he was looking for. Nevertheless, meditating upon such knowledge he found that he could doubt them, and thus he found himself devoid of any indubitable knowledge. As a result, he found himself doubting all sources of knowledge , including reason, which was based upon the possibility of the existence of a higher faculty and which he defined in terms of its relation to reason (*malakah fawqa al-'aql*). In fact, he underwent a most genuine and dramatic experience of skepticism. This state of doubt continued for the duration of two months and eventually ended by divine illumination.

The first thing that Al-Ghazzāliyy regained after he

emerged from his state of doubt was his trust in logical necessities. According to him, this would not have been possible without divine illumination which he considered a source of knowledge that he called *kashf* and which he described as acquiring knowledge directly (i.e. from Allah). This latter source of knowledge forms the backbone of Sufi epistemology; he would expand on this concept during his first period of withdrawal from public life which he believed to be a condition that he should fulfill in order to attain peremptory knowledge.

During the years of seclusion, Al-Ghazzāliyy emphasized in his writings the limited capability of reason and that "unveiling" (*kashf*) is the only source of knowledge that is absolutely capable of attaining indubitable transcendental knowledge. In the *Iḥyā' 'Ulūm al-Dīn*, he stressed the superiority of Sufi knowledge over that which is attained by conventional sources of knowledge. This Sufi knowledge which he referred to as *'ilm al-mukāshafah* is the aim of intellectual activity, yet he stated that such knowledge should not be revealed to the public. Therefore, the subject of the *Iḥyā'* is that knowledge which leads to *kashf*, namely the science of action (*'ilm al-mu'āmalah*). By action, he means self-mortification and discipline which form a prerequisite for attaining peremptory transcendental knowledge. In addition, he held that *kashf* is possible through the faculty higher than reason which forms one of the most important developments in his epistemology. The aim of this position is to show the limitations of reason which cannot achieve peremptory knowledge. This position is reinforced by listing prophecy as the highest level in relation to the attainment of knowledge which is followed by the scholars in what might be considered Al-Ghazzāliyy's response to the Muslim philosophers who ranked reason as the highest faculty. Finally, he added in the *Iḥyā'* another form for the attainment of peremptory knowledge, namely, vision.

Similar to his position in the *Iḥyā'*, Al-Ghazzāliyy continued in *Al-Maqsad al-Asnā Sharḥ Asmā' Allāh al-Ḥusnā* to stress the limitations of reason and its incapability to attain peremptory transcendental knowledge. The only way to achieve such knowledge is through *kashf*. It is obvious that

168

these two notions are consistent with Al-Ghazzaliyy's episte-mology in the *Ihya'*.

As to *Bidāyat al-Hidāyah*, there are whole sections which are identical with *Qawā'id al-'Aqā'id* which is considered a part of the *Ihya'* and therefore it adds to the consistency of Al-Ghazzaliyy's epistemology during this period. In these sections he asserted the notion of discipline and self-mortification as prerequisites to the attainment of peremptory knowledge.

In *Jawāhir Al-Qur'ān* which corresponds to his position in the *Ihya'* and *Bidāyat al-Hidāyah*, Al-Ghazzaliyy main-tained the notion of discipline and self-mortification as conditions for the attainment of transcendental knowledge. He held that transcendental knowledge can be revealed through true vision in metaphorical language.

In *Al-Risālah al-Ladunniyyah*, Al-Ghazzaliyy discussed the notion of "metaphysical transcendental knowledge" (*al-'ilm al-ghaybiyy al-ladūnniyy*) which is accessible to elite Sufis only. This kind of knowledge can be attained through inspiration (*ilhām*).

The last book dealing with the epistemology of Al-Ghazzaliyy during the first period of seclusion is *Mishkāt al-Anwār*. He reiterated his position regarding the existence of a faculty higher than reason. According to him, elite Sufis are capable of attaining know-ledge directly from the same source, similar to prophets.

Although Al-Ghazzaliyy introduces different sources (e.g., inspiration, insight) for the attainment of knowledge, the last six books emphasize Sufism as the common theme and, therefore, this period of seclusion reflects a unified epistemology.

After ending his seclusion and returning to teach at the Niẓāmiyyah of Nishapur, Al-Ghazzaliyy maintained his epistemology as a Sufi. His last book to be written during this period, *Al-Imlā' fī Ishkālāt al-Ihyā'*, was written in re-sponse to the criticism that the *Ihya'* had endured at the hands of traditionalists whom Al-Ghazzaliyy did not mention by name. According to Al-Ghazzaliyy, they held that his book contradicts the Shari'ah in advocating *mukāshafah* as a source of knowledge. His defence of the *Ihya'* is a sign of his commitment to Sufism as the only path for true knowledge.

After spending about four years at the Niẓāmiyyah of Nishapur, Al-Ghazzāliyy withdrew again from public life and settled in his hometown Tus. The most important task regarding the last period of his life in relation to epistemology is to question the claim that he abandoned Sufism and adopted the method of the traditionalists. It is apparent though, that *Al-Durrah al-Fākhirah, Iljām al-'Awām 'an 'Ilm al-Kalām* and *Minhāj al-'Ābidīn,* which were written during the last stage of his life, contain direct references to his continued acceptance of Sufism as the path for the true knowledge.

In *Al-Durrah al-Fākhirah,* he held that the Sufis, whom he described as *'Āriffīn,* are the only people who upon their death could proceed through the seven Heavens to reach Allah. In *Iljām al-'Awām,* he employed the term "common people" to distinguish every other kind of scholar from the Sufis. He ranked the Sufis higher and he described them as the scholars of the hereafter. Finally, in *Minhāj al-'Ābidīn,* he defended Sufi schools and lodges. In addition, he described the knowledge of the Sufi in terms of a divine light which is typical of *kashf.*

All of these themes, which were also written using Sufi terminology, leave no room for any doubt or hesitation that Al-Ghazzāliyy's final epistemology was Sufi in its essence. It should be noted that this is not a defence of Sufism against the traditionalists who tried to present Al-Ghazzāliyy in his final days as someone who abandoned Sufism. What I am trying to say is that they need to substantiate their claim.

BIBLIOGRAPHY

This bibliography is divided into four sections. The first is a chronological listing of Al-Ghazzaliyy's works in Arabic that were either cited or consulted for this book. The second section is a list of very few translated works of Al-Ghazzaliyy. The third is a list of medieval primary sources in Arabic and the fourth is a general list of books in Arabic and non-Arabic languages.

WORKS BY AL-GHAZZALIYY

_____ *Al-Mankhul min Ta'liqat al-Usul*, ed., Muhammad Hasan Hitu (Damascus: Dar al-Fikr, 1970)

_____ *Al-Wajiz* (Al-Ghuriyyah: Matba'at Hush, 1318 A.H. / 1901 C.E.)

_____ *Al-Wasit*, ed., Ali Muhyi al-Din al-Qarah Daghi, 2 vols. (Cairo: Dar al-Nasr li al-Tiba'ah al-Islamiyyah, 1984)

_____ "*Fatwa*", *Mu'allafat al-Ghazzaliyy*, ed., 'Abdurrahman Badawi, 2nd ed. (Kuwait: Wikalat al-Matbu'at, 1977)

_____ *Maqasid al-Falasifah*, ed., Sulaiman Dunya (Cairo: Dar al-Ma'arif bi-Misr, 1961)

_____ *Tahafut al-Falasifah*, ed., Suleiman Dunya, 7th ed. (Cairo: Dar al-Ma'arif, 1972)

_____ *Mi'yar al-'Ilm fi al-Mantiq*, ed., Ahmad Shams al-Din (Beirut: Dar al-Kutub al-'Ilmiyyah, 1990)

_____ *Mihak al-Nazar fi al-Mantiq*, ed., Muhammad Badr Ad-Din al-Na'saniyy (Beirut: Dar al-Nahdah al-Hadithah, 1966)

_____ *Mizan al-'Amal*, ed., Suleiman Dunya (Cairo: Dar al-Ma'arif bi-Misr, 1964)

_____ *Al-Iqtisad fi al-I'tiqad*, ed., Muhammad Mustafa Abu al-'Ula (Cairo: Maktabat al-Jindi, 1972)

_____ "*Qawa'id al-'Aqa'id fi al-Tawhid*", *Majmu'at Rasa'il al-Imam al-Ghazali*, Vol. II (Beirut: Dar al-Kutub al-'Ilmiyyah, 1986)

_____ *Ihya' 'Ulum al-Din*, 4 Vols. (Beirut: Dar al-Ma'rifah, n.d.)

_____ "*Jawab al-Masa'il al-Arba'* allati Sa'alaha al-Batiniyyah bi-

Hamadhan", al-Manar, XI (1908) pp. 601-608.

_____ *Al-Maqsad al-Asna Sharh Asma' Allah al-Husna*, ed., Muhammad Mustafa Abu Al-'Ula (Cairo: Maktabat al-Jindi, 1968)

_____ *Bidayat al-Hidayah*, ed., Muhammad al-Hajjar (Damascus: Dar al-Sabuni, 1986)

_____ *Jawahir al-Qur'an*, ed., Muhammad Mustafa Abu Al-'Ula (Cairo: Maktabat al-Jindi, 1964)

_____ *"Al-Madnun bihi ala Ghayri Ahlih"*, Majmu'at Rasa'il al-Imam al-Ghazali, Vol. IV (Beirut: Dar al-Kutub al-'Ilmiyyah, 1986)

_____ *"Al-Qistas al-Mustaqim"*, Majmu'at Rasa'il al-Imam al-Ghazali, Vol. III (Beirut: Dar al-Kutub al-'Ilmiyyah, 1986)

_____ *"Faisal al-Tafriqah Bayn al-Islam wa al-Zandaqah"*, Majmu'at Rasa'il al-Imam al-Ghazali, Vol. III (Beirut: Dar al-Kutb al-'Ilmiyyah, 1986)

_____ *Qanun al-Ta'wil.* Published with al-Ghazzaliyy's Ma'arij al-Quds, ed., Muhammad Mustafa Abu al-'Ula (Cairo: Maktabat al-Jindi, 1968)

_____ *"Ayyuha al-Walad"*, Majmu'at Rasa'il al-Imam al-Ghazali, Vol. III. (Beirut: Dar al-Kutub al-'Ilmiyyah, 1986)

_____ *Al-Tibr al-Masbuk fi Nasihat al-Muluk* (Cairo: Maktabat al-Kulliyat al-Azhariyyah, 1968)

_____ *"Al-Risalah al-Ladunniyyah"*, Majmu'at Rasa'il al-Imam al-Ghazali, Vol. III (Beirut: Dar al-Kutub al-'Ilmiyyah, 1986)

_____ *Mishkat al-Anwar*, ed., 'Abd Al-'Aziz 'Izz al-Din al-Siyarawan (Beirut: 'Alam al-Kutub, 1986)

_____ *Al-Kashf wa al-Tabyin fi Ghurur al-khalq Ajma'in* (Cairo: Matba'at Mustafa Muhammad, No date). Published with 'Abd al-Wahhab al-Sha'raniyy's *Tanbih al-Mughtarrin.*

_____ *Al-Munqidh min al-Dalal*, ed., Jamil Saliba and Kamil 'Aiyyad, 10th ed. (No city: Dar al-Andalus, 1981)

_____ *Al-Mustasfa min 'Ilm al-Usul*, 2 vols. (Bulaq: Al-Matba'ah al-Amiriyyah, 1322 A. H.)

_____ *Al-Imla' fi Mushkilat al-Ihya'*, Appendix, *Ihya' 'Ulum al-Din* (Beirut: Dar al-Ma'rifah, n.d.)

_____ *Al-Durrah al-Fakhirah fi Kashf 'Ulum al-Akhirah.* Published with al-Ghazzaliyy's *Sir al-'Alamin.*, ed., Muhammad Mustafa Abu al-'Ula (Cairo: Maktabat al-Jindi, 1968)

_____ *Sir al-'Alamin wa Kashf ma fi al-Darayn*, ed., Muhammad Mustafa Abu Al-'Ula (Cairo: Maktabat al-Jindi, 1968)

_____ *Iljam al-'Awam 'an 'Ilm al-Kalam*, ed., Muhammad al-Mu'tasim Billah al-Baghdadiyy (Beirut: Dar al-Kitab al-'Arabi, 1985)

_____ *Minhaj al-'Abidin*, ed., Muhammad Mustafa Abu al-'Ula (Cairo: Maktabat al-Jindi, 1972)

_____ *Ma'arij al-Quds fi Ma'rifat al-Nafs* (Cairo: Maktabat al-Jindi, 1968)

TRANSLATED WORKS OF AL-GHAZZALIYY

Al-Ghazzali, *The Book Of Knowledge* (*Kitab al-'Ilm* of *Ihya' 'Ulum al-Din*), Nabih Amin Faris, ed. and trans. (Lahore: Sh. Muhammad Ashraf, 1962)

Al-Ghazali, *"Fada'ih al-Batiniyyah wa Fada'il al-Mustazhiriyyah"*. Published with al-Ghazzaliyy's *Freedom and Fulfillment*, ed. and trans., Richard J. McCarthy (Boston: Twayne Publishers, 1980)

Al-Ghazali, *Freedom and Fulfillment* (*Al-Munqidh min al-Dalal*), Richard Joseph McCarthy, tr. (Boston: Twayne Publishers, 1980)

Al-Ghazzali, *Mishkat al-Anwar* (The Niche for Lights), trans and ed. W.H.T. Gairdner (1924, Lahore: Sh. Muhammad Ashraf, 1952)

Al-Ghazali, *The Precious Pearl* (*Al-Durrah al-Fakhirah*), Jane Idleman Smith, trans and ed. (Missoula: Scholars Press, 1979)

Al-Ghazali, *Al-Qistas al-Mustaqim* (The Just Balance), trans. and ed., D.P. Brewster (Lahore: Sh. Muhammad Ashraf, 1978)

ARABIC PRIMARY SOURCES

Ibn 'Ajibah al-Hasaniyy, Ahmad Ibn Muhammad, *Iqaz al-Himam fi Sharh al-Hikam* (Cairo: Abd al-Hamid Ahmad Hanafi, No Date)

Ibn al-Jawziyy, *al-Muntazam fi Tarikh al-Muluk wa al-Umam* (Hayderabad: Da'irat al-Ma'arif al-Uthmaniyyah, 1939)

_____ *Talbis Iblis* (Beirut: Dar al-Kutub al-'Ilmiyyah, 1949)

Ibn Kathir, *Al-Bidaya wa al-Nihayah* (Beirut: Maktabat al-Ma'arif, n.d.) vol. 12

_____ *Tafsir* (Beirut: Dar al-Jil, 1988)

Ibn Khaldun, *Al-Muqaddimah*, (Beirut: Dar al-Qalam, 1984)

Ibn Khallikan, *Wafayat al-A'yan wa Anba' Abna' al-Zaman*, trans. B^ Mac Guckin De Slane: The John J. Burns Library, Boston College, Chestnut Hill, MA 02167 (Paris: Printed for the Oriental Translation Fund of Great Britain And Ireland, 1843)

Ibn al-Qaiyyim, *Ijtima' al-Juyush al-Islamiyyah*, 'Awwad 'Adbullah al-Mu'attaq, ed. (Riyad: Matabi' al-Farazdaq al-Tijariyyah, 1988)

Ibn Taymiyyah, *Al-Furqan Bayn Awliya' al-Rahman wa-Awliya' al-Shaytan* (Beirut: Al-Maktab al-Islamiyy, 1981)

_____ *Naqd al-Mantiq* (Cairo: Maktabat al-Sunnah al-Muhammadiyyah, 1951)

Al-Makiyy, Abu Talib, *Qut al-Qulub* (Cairo: Dar Sadir, 1892)

Al-Subkiyy, Taj al-Din, *Tabaqat al-Shafi'iyyah al-Kubra*, 'Abd al-Fattah Muhammad al-Hilw and Mahmud Muhammad al-Tanahiyy, eds., (Cairo: Matba'at 'Isa al-Babi al-Halabi & Co., 1968)

Al-'Uthman, 'Abd al-Karim, *Al-Dirasat al-Nafsiyyah 'ind al-Muslimin wa al-Ghazali bi Wajhin Khas*, 2nd ed. (Cairo: Maktabat Wahbah, 1981)

Al-Zubaydiyy, Murtada, *Ithaf al-Sadah al-Mutaqin bi Sharh Asrar Ihya' 'Ulum al-Din*, (Beirut: Dar Ihya' al-Turath al-'Arabiyy)

OTHER SOURCES

Abu Zahrah, Muhammad, *Tarikh al-Madhahib al-Islamiyyah* (Cairo: Dar al-Fikr al-'Arabiyy, n.d.)

Ahmed, Munir-al-din, *Muslim Education and the Scholar's Social Status up to the 5th Century Muslim Era in the Light of "Tarikh Baghdad"* Sami al-Saqqar, trans. and ed. (Riyad: Dar al-Marrikh, 1981)

Ali, Abdullah Yusuf, *Ma'ani al-Qur'an al-Karim* (Lahore: Sheikh Muhammad Ashraf, 1934)

Alon, Ilai, "*Al-Ghazali on Causality*", *Journal of the American Oriental Society* 100. 4 (1980)

Al-'Alwani, Taha Jabir, *Usul al-Fiqh al-Islami*, eds. Yusuf Talal DeLorenzo and A.S. al-Shaikh-Ali (Herndon: The International Institute of Islamic Thought, 1990)

Aristotle, "*Metaphysics*", *The Basic Works of Aristotle*, Richard McKeon, ed. (New York: Random House, 1941)

_____ *Nicomachean Ethics*, Martin Ostwald, trans. and ed. (Indianapolis: Bobbs-Merill Educational Publishing, 1983)

Al-A'sam, 'Abd al-Amir, *Faylasuf al-Ghazzaliyy* (Beirut: Dar al-Andalus, 1981)

'Abd Al-Baqi, Muhammad Fu'ad, ed., *Allu'lu' wa al-Marjan Fima Ittafaqa 'Alayhi al-Shaykhan* (No city: Dar al-Fikr, n.d.)

'Azzam, 'Abdallah, *Fi al-Jihad Adab wa-Ahkam* (No City: Matbu'at al-Jihad, 1987)

Badawi, 'Abdurrahman, *Dawr al-'Arab fi Takwin al-Fikr al-Awrubbiyy* (Al-Kuwait: Wakalat al-Matbu'at, 1979)

_____ *Mawsu'at al-Falsafah*, 2 vols. (Beirut: Al-Mu'assassah al-'Arabiyyah li al-Dirasat wa al-Nashr, 1984)

_____ *Mu'allafat al-Ghazali*, 2nd ed. (Kuwait: Wikalat al-Matbu'at, 1977)

Al-Bugha, Mustafa; Al-Khin, Mustafa; and al-Shurbajiyy, 'Ali, *Al-Fiqh al-Manhajiyy 'ala Madhhab al-Imam al-Shafi'iyy* (Damascus: Dar al-Qalam, 1989)

Descartes, *Discources on Method and the Medidations*, John Veitch, trans. (Buffalo: Prometheus Books, 1989)

Dimashqiyyah, 'Abd Al-Rahman, *Abu Hamid al-Ghazzaliyy Wat-Tasawwuf* (Riyad: Dar Tibah, 1988)

Al-Duqr, 'Abd al-Ghaniyy, *Lexicon of Arabic Grammar (Mu'jam Qawa'id Al-Lughah al-'Arabiyyah)* (Damascus: Dar al-Qalam, 1986)

Fakhry, Majid, *A History of Islamic Philosophy* (New York: Columbia University Press, 1970)

Hava, J.G., *Al-Fara'id al-Durriyyah* (Beirut: Dar al-Mashriq, 1972)

Hyman, Arthur and Walsh, James J., eds., *Philosophy in the Middle Ages* (Indianapolis: Hackett Publishing Co., 1987)

James, William, "*The Varieties of Religious Experiences*", : Ralph W. Clark, *Introduction to Philosophical Thinking* (St. Paul: West

Publishing Co., 1987)

Laoust, Henri, *La Politique De Gazali* (Paris: Librairie Orientaliste Paul Geuthmer, 1970)

Lazarus-Yafeh, Hava, *Studies in al-Ghazzali* (Jerusalem: The Magnes Press: The Hebrew University, 1975)

Leaman, Oliver, *An Introduction to Medieval Islamic Philosophy* (Cambridge: Cambridge University Press, 1985.

Lewis, Bernard, *The Political Language of Islam* (Chicago: The University of Chicago Press, 1988)

Makdisi, George, "*The Non-Ash'arite Shafi'ism of Ghazzali*," *Reveu des Etudes Islamiques* 54 (1986)

Marmura, Mirchael, "Ghazali and Demonstrative Science," *Journal of the History of Philosophy* III (1965)

Mubarak, Zaki, *Al-Akhlaq 'ind al-Ghazzaliyy* (Beirut: Al-Maktabah al-'Asriyyah, n.d.)

Al-Nadwah al-'Alamiyyah li al-Shabab Al-Islamiyy, *Al-Mawsu'ah al-Muyassarah fi al-Adyan wa al-Madhahib al-Mu'asirah* (Riyad: Matba'at Safir, 1989)

Al-Nadawiyy, Abu al-Hasan, *Rijal al-Fikr wa al-Da'wa fi al-Islam*, 7th ed. (Kuwait: Dar al-Qalam, 1985)

The New Lexicon Webster's Dictionary of the English Language (New York: Lexicon Publications, Inc., 1989)

Al-Qardawiyy, Yusuf, *Al-Imam al-Ghazzaliyy Bayn Madihih wa Naqidih* (Al-Mansurah: Dar al-Wafa', 1988)

_____*Kayfa Nata'amal Ma' al-Sunnah al-Nabawuiyyah* (Al-Mansurah: Dar al-Wafa', 1990)

Rasa'il Ikhwan al-Safa wa Khillan al-Wafa (Dar Beirut: Beirut 1983)

Rizvi, S. Rizwan Ali, *Nizam al-Mulk Tusi* (Lahore: Sh. Muhammad Ashraf, 1978)

Al-Sharbasiyy, Ahmad, *al-Ghazzaliyy* (Beirut: Dar Al-Jil, 1975)

Swarz, Merlin, "*A Seventh-century (A.H.) Sunni creed: The 'Aqidah Wasitiya of Ibn Taymiya*," *Humaniora Islamica* 1 (1973)

Sheikh, M. Saeed, *Islamic Philosophy* (London: The Octagon Press, 1982)

Al-Tahhan, Mahmud, *Taysir Mustalah al-Hadith* (Riyad: Maktabat al-Ma'arif, 1981)

Trimingham, J., *The Sufi Orders in Islam* (London: Oxford University Press, 1971)

Tuqan, Qadri Hafiz, *Al-'Ulum 'ind al-'Arab* (Beirut: Dar Iqra', 1983.

Al-Wakil, 'Abd al-Rahman, *Hadhihi Hia al-Sufiyyah* (Beirut: Dar al-Kutub al-'Ilmiyyah, 1984)

Watt, W. Montgomery, *Muslim Intellectual: A Study of al-Ghazzali* (Edinburgh: The Edinburgh University Press, 1963).

Wolfson, Harry A., "*Nicolaus of Autrecourt and Ghazali's Argument Against Causality*", *Speculum* (1969)

DR. MUSTAFA ABU-SWAY is a Senior Research Fellow at the International Institute of Islamic Thought and Civilization (ISTAC) in Kuala Lumpur. Previously, he was the head of the Department of Philosophy at the International Islamic University Malaysia (IIUM).

Dewan Bahasa dan Pustaka
Peti Surat 10803
50926 Kuala Lumpur
Fax: 03-2482726

www.ingramcontent.com/pod-product-compliance
Lightning Source LLC
LaVergne TN
LVHW021300210726
843527LV00036B/540